64

October
2010

ECONOMIC POLICY

Published in association with the European Economic Association

Blackwell Publishing Ltd for Centre for Economic Policy Research, Center for Economic Studies of the University of Munich, and Paris School of Economics, in collaboration with the Maison des Sciences Economiques.

STATEMENT OF PURPOSE

Economic Policy provides timely and authoritative analyses of the choices which confront policy-makers. The subject matter ranges from the study of how individual markets can and should work to the broadest interactions in the world economy.

Economic Policy is a joint activity of the Centre for Economic Policy Research (CEPR), the Center for Economic Studies (CES) and the Paris School of Economics (PSE). The Paris School of Economics replaces the research center, Paris-Jourdan Sciences Economiques, which is now part of the larger school. *Economic Policy* offers an independent, non-partisan, European perspective on issues of worldwide concern. It emphasizes problems of international significance, either because they affect the world economy directly or because the experience of one country contains important lessons for policy-makers elsewhere.

All the articles are specifically commissioned from leading professional economists. Their brief is to demonstrate how live policy issues can be illuminated by the insights of modern economics and by the most recent evidence. The presentation is incisive and written in plain language accessible to the wide audience which participates in the policy debate.

Prior to publication, the contents of each volume are discussed by a Panel of distinguished economists from Europe and elsewhere. The Panel rotates annually. Inclusion in each volume of a summary of the highlights of the Economic Policy Panel discussion provides the reader with alternative interpretations of the evidence and a sense of the liveliness of the current debate.

Economic Policy is owned by the Maison des Sciences Economiques, CEPR and CES. The 51st panel meeting was held in Madrid and was hosted by the Banco de España. We gratefully acknowledge this support, without implicating any of these organizations in the views expressed here, which are the sole responsibility of the authors.

ECONOMIC POLICY

PANEL

64

October 2010

CONTENTS

Editors' introduction

Volcanic ash from Iceland prevented some of the panellists from flying to Madrid and attending the April 2010 panel meeting hosted by the Banco de España. Nevertheless, the panel provided an important and lively discussion on the papers presented. Four of these papers are published in this issue. The papers cover important policy areas, ranging from currency mismatch, bank capital regulation, multinational banks and inflation risk.

Currency mismatch – the extent to which an economy's liabilities are denominated in foreign currency while its assets are denominated in domestic currency – is widespread in emerging Europe. While currency mismatch was an important aspect of the Mexico crisis in 1994 and the East Asian crisis in 1997–98, it reached unprecedented levels in Eastern Europe before the recent crisis.

CURRENCY MISMATCH

The first paper in this issue by Romain Ranciere, Aaron Tornell and Athanasios Vamvakidis points out that currency mismatch is a vehicle that exposes the economy to systemic risk, but it is also an engine of growth that has allowed new and small firms to finance profitable investment projects. The paper analyses this dual role at the macro and the micro levels. A key contribution of the paper is the construction of a new currency mismatch measure combining information on foreign currency assets and liabilities of banks. The currency mismatch measure focuses on the banking sector. If one looks exclusively into the banks' balance sheets, the notional degree of currency mismatch is often small, as banks with foreign currency liabilities also tend to lend in foreign currency. However, there is de facto currency mismatch if banks' debtors cannot hedge their exchange rate risk. Thus, in case of a large depreciation, a large share of domestic debtors could go bust, affecting the asset portfolio of the banks that lent to them and generating a risk of a systemic crisis. An appropriate measure of currency mismatch needs to account for this

Economic Policy October 2010 pp. 591–595 Printed in Great Britain

source of systemic risk. Such a measure is not available in the literature because of the lack of readily available data on the composition of banks' assets and liabilities and the extent to which borrowers in foreign currency are hedged. Using a variety of data sources on banks and borrowers, the paper computes a de facto measure of currency mismatch. Interestingly, this measure is much larger than notional currency mismatch measures that do not control for borrowers' ability to hedge.

The paper also looks at the consequence of currency mismatch. Using aggregate data, the paper finds that across emerging European economies, increases in currency mismatch are associated with higher growth in tranquil times, but also with more severe crises both across the set of 10 emerging European economies, as well as across the larger group of 29 emerging economies. On net, after taking into account the crisis period, there is a positive link between currency mismatch and growth. The estimates for the period 1998–2009 indicate that a country that increased its currency mismatch by 6.6 percentage points each year had a 4% higher GDP at the end of the period (including the crisis year) than a country that did not experience a currency mismatch increase. In the firm-level analysis, the paper finds that in emerging Europe, currency mismatch relaxes borrowing constraints, reduces interest rates and enhances growth across sets of firms that arguably are the most credit constrained (small firms in sectors producing non-tradable goods) but not across large firms. The paper uses data for a large cross-section of European economies from the Business Environment and Enterprise Performance Survey (BEEPS) of the European Bank for Reconstruction and Development. The regression analysis suggests that across financially constrained groups of firms, currency mismatch reduces the interest rate by 2 percentage points on average, and increases the average loan maturity by 10 months. Furthermore, firms with currency mismatch exhibit 2.3 percentage points faster annual growth.

The panel appreciated the innovative approach of the authors to develop the currency mismatch measure and the empirical analysis. A number of issues were raised on the differences in currency mismatch between households and firms and on extending the insights and results to countries which had experienced large depreciations.

Policy discussions on the recent financial crisis feature widespread calls to address the pro-cyclical effects of regulation. The main concern is that the new risk-sensitive bank capital regulation (Basel II) may amplify business cycle fluctuations. The 1988 Basel Accord consolidated capital requirements as the cornerstone of bank regulation. It required banks to hold a minimum overall capital equal to 8% of their risk-weighted assets. Following widespread criticism about the risk-insensitiveness of these requirements, the Basel Committee on Banking Supervision (BCBS) approved in 2004 a reform, known as Basel II, whose primary goal was to arrive at significantly more risk-sensitive capital requirements. Basel II introduced a menu of approaches for determining capital requirements.

REFORMING BASEL II

The standardized approach uses external ratings to refine the risk weights of the 1988 Accord but leaves the capital charges for loans to unrated companies essentially unchanged. The internal ratings-based approach allows banks to compute the capital charges for each exposure from their own estimate of the probability of default. As a result of this risk-sensitiveness, a widespread concern about Basel II is that it might amplify business cycle fluctuations, forcing banks to restrict their lending when the economy goes into recession. Multiple committees, institutions, central banks and supervisory authorities all over the world are currently working on designing mechanisms to abate this pro-cyclicality.

The paper by Rafael Repullo, Jesús Saurina and Carlos Trucharte discusses leading alternative procedures that have been proposed to mitigate the pro-cyclicality of the Basel II capital requirements. As a first step, the paper shows that capital requirements under Basel II move significantly along the business cycle. The analysis is based on the results of the estimation of a logistic model of the one-year-ahead probabilities of default of Spanish firms during the period 1987–2008. The empirical model provides an estimate of the probability of defaults of the loans in the entire portfolio of commercial and industrial loans of the Spanish banks over the sample period, so using the Basel II formula one can compute the corresponding aggregate capital requirements per unit of loans. The paper finds that Basel II capital requirements increase more than 50% from peak to trough, which is a very significant change compared with the flat requirements of Basel I. The paper next considers the effect of different procedures to mitigate the cyclicality of these requirements over the business cycle. After examining a variety of alternatives, the paper concludes that the best way is to smooth capital requirements with a formula that depends on the deviation of the rate of growth of GDP with respect to its long-run average. This procedure has clear advantages in terms of simplicity, transparency, low cost of implementation, and consistency with banks' risk pricing and risk management systems. The proposed adjustment maintains the risk-sensitivity of Basel II capital requirements, so banks with riskier portfolios would bear a higher capital charge, but a cyclically varying scaling factor is introduced to increase capital requirements in good times and to reduce them in bad times. Such changes should contribute to reduce the incidence and magnitude of both credit bubbles and credit crunches. The panel appreciated the paper as a timely and important policy contribution, and discussed the proposed adjustment of the Basel II in the context of the wider use of alternative policy instruments to mitigate the problem of systemic risk and cyclicality of capital requirements, and the pros and cons of fixed rules versus approaches which allow regulators room for discretion.

MULTINATIONAL BANKS

Increased participation of foreign banks in the local banking system has been one of the forms of financial integration. In several regions of the world, and in particular in Eastern Europe, foreign multinational banks have become the dominant players in the local banking system. The financial crisis has stressed the role of multinational banks which have often been accused of having caused the crisis or at least of having amplified it. The paper of Giorgio Barba Navaretti, Giacomo Calzolari, Alberto Franco Pozzolo and Micol Levi that analyses this issue is therefore very timely. They ask several questions. First, do foreign banks behave differently than domestic banks? Second, do multinational banks (MNBs) amplify or stabilize external financial shocks? What was their role in the financial crisis? The empirical analysis is carried out on a large panel of 5,500 European banks between 2000 and 2008. The data set allows comparing foreign affiliates of MNBs to standalone domestic banks and domestic banking groups. To the first question, the authors answer yes. The authors argue that MNBs behave differently, because they have an internal capital market (ICM) allowing them to support affiliates in distress with liquidity or, on the contrary, allowing them to reallocate resources away from affiliates. From this point of view, ICMs may stabilize or destabilize local banking systems. To the second question, the paper stresses the stabilizing role of MNBs due to the support that the ICM has given to foreign affiliates in distress, isolating their lending from the local availability of financial resources (measured by the rate of growth of local deposits). Indeed, even in 2007 and 2008 ICMs helped to isolate lending activities of foreign affiliates from the local availability of funding. In order to avoid endogeneity issues, the authors proceed to estimate whether the correlation between the growth rate of lending with the growth rate of deposits as the dependent variable is indeed lower for affiliates of banks, in particular within the EU15, after controlling for a number of bank and country characteristics. Hence, the paper concludes that the activities carried out by MNBs through their affiliates have not been a source of financial instability in host economies. Rather, they have enhanced the supply of resources in those local markets. The panel found the paper a very useful and careful exercise, particularly relevant for the emerging European countries. The discussion focused on the question whether the rather positive and optimistic results of the paper for the role of MNBs could be generalized in other contexts.

INFLATION RISK

The high volume of public debt issuance that is expected over the coming years has reawakened interest in the design of sovereign bonds. In 'Inflation risk and the inflation risk premium', Geert Bekaert and Xiaozheng Wang provide a timely analysis of the benefits from issuing inflation-indexed bonds. For a large panel of countries, these authors show that it is not feasible to hedge inflation risk by holding generic assets such as equities, real estate, gold or nominal bonds since the comovements between inflation and the returns on these assets have been relatively weak over the last several decades. (That said, the performance of such assets as inflation hedges is marginally superior for emerging markets than for advanced countries.) Moreover, Bekaert and Wang also estimate that the inflation risk premium is both high and time-varying, such that the provision of an inflation hedge would be highly valued.

Accordingly, the issuance of inflation-indexed bonds performs an important social role by providing a mechanism by which investors can obtain protection against inflation. The authors review the experiences of the United States, United Kingdom and France in operating markets for inflation-indexed bonds. The main risk factor is ensuring that the market for inflation-indexed bonds is sufficiently liquid (which was not the case in the early years of the US TIPS market). Provided that a liquid market can be established, the potential benefits of inflation-indexed securities are substantial. Accordingly, an expansion of such programmes may be an important component in public debt management in the coming years.

Currency mismatch

SUMMARY

Currency mismatch is a vehicle that exposes the economy to systemic risk, but it is also an engine of growth. We analyse this dual role at the macro and the micro levels. At the aggregate level, we construct a new measure of currency mismatch in the banking sector that controls for bank lending to unhedged borrowers – that is, those with no foreign currency income. Using our measure, we find that across emerging European economies, increases in currency mismatch are associated with higher growth in tranquil times, but also with more severe crises. On net, after taking into account the crisis period, we find a positive link between currency mismatch and growth. These results are also confirmed for a broader sample of emerging economies. In our firm-level analysis, we find that in emerging Europe, currency mismatch relaxes borrowing constraints, reduces interest rates and enhances growth across sets of firms that arguably are the most credit constrained – that is, small firms in non-tradables sectors – but not across large firms. An advantage of our approach is that it considers both listed and non-listed firms, and so we are able to effectively capture the effects of currency mismatch across the entire economy, not just the financially privileged stock market listed firms.

— *Romain Ranciere, Aaron Tornell and Athanasios Vamvakidis*

Economic Policy October 2010 Printed in Great Britain

Currency mismatch, systemic risk and growth in emerging Europe

Romain Ranciere, Aaron Tornell and Athanasios Vamvakidis

Paris School of Economics and International Monetary Fund; University of California Los Angeles; International Monetary Fund

1. INTRODUCTION

Currency mismatch – the extent to which an economy's liabilities are denominated in foreign currency while its assets are denominated in domestic currency – is widespread in emerging Europe. While currency mismatch was an important aspect of the Mexico crisis in 1994 and the East Asian crisis in 1997–98, it reached unprecedented levels in Eastern Europe before the recent crisis.

This paper analyses the dual role of currency mismatch, focusing on the experience of emerging Europe. On the one hand, currency mismatch has been a prime

We would like to thank Enrique Alberola, Joshua Aizenman, Erik Berglöf, Guillermo Calvo, Jin Han, Andrea Ichino, Jean Imbs, Maurizio Mazzocco, Joe Ostroy, Amine Ouazad and Romain Wacziarg as well as participants at the *Economic Policy* panel meeting for helpful comments, and the following people for sharing their data sets with us: Reza Baqir (IMF Vulnerability Exercise for Emerging Economies); Herman Kamil (foreign currency borrowing by sector in Latin America); Stephanie Prat (foreign currency foreign assets and liabilities for various emerging economies); and Christoph Rosenberg and Marcel Tirpak (direct borrowing in East Europe from abroad). The views expressed in this paper are those of the authors and do not necessarily represent those of the IMF or IMF policy.
The Managing Editor in charge of this paper was Tullio Jappelli.

Economic Policy October 2010 pp. 597–658 Printed in Great Britain

vehicle for agents to take on insolvency risk and has resulted in large exposures to systemic risk for the economy as a whole. On the other hand, it has been an engine of growth that has allowed new and small firms to finance profitable investment projects. In particular, we investigate whether currency mismatch has been associated with faster economic growth, but also more severe crises.

A key contribution of this paper is the construction of a new currency mismatch measure. Due to the lack of readily available data, there is a dearth of currency mismatch measures that capture the underlying undertaking of systemic risk. In this paper, we construct such a measure. We then present a theoretical mechanism that links economic growth with currency mismatch. In our framework, currency mismatch helps relax borrowing constraints, but also generates financial fragility, leading to more severe crises. Our other contribution is to analyse, both from a macro and micro perspectives, whether these effects are present in the data. At the macroeconomic level, we analyse the links between currency mismatch, economic growth, and the severity of the crises over the period 1998–2009 in emerging Europe and in a broader sample of emerging economies. At the micro level, we use firm-level data to investigate whether the channels through which the theoretical mechanism works are operative at the firm level, by testing whether taking on currency mismatch helps firms reduce interest costs, relax borrowing constraints and improve growth performance.

Our currency mismatch measure focuses on the banking sector. If one looks exclusively into the banks' balance sheets, the *notional* degree of currency mismatch is often small, as the banks with foreign currency liabilities also tend to lend in foreign currency. However, there is *de facto* currency mismatch if banks' debtors cannot hedge their exchange rate risk – in the form of credit default risk. Thus, in case of a large depreciation, a large share of domestic debtors could go bust, affecting the asset portfolio of the banks that lent to them and generating a risk of a systemic crisis. An appropriate measure of currency mismatch needs to account for this source of systemic risk. To our knowledge, such a measure is not available in the literature. The reason is a lack of readily available data on the composition of banks' assets and liabilities and the extent to which borrowers in foreign currency are hedged.

We construct such a de facto currency mismatch measure by combining information on foreign currency assets and liabilities of banks with BEEPS[1] firm-level data and other data sources from national authorities and the IMF confidential vulnerability exercises. We measure the fraction of foreign currency loans granted to borrowers with no foreign currency income, and exclude it from the asset side of the banks' balance sheets. We then compute our de facto currency mismatch measure by dividing the banks' foreign currency denominated net

[1] Business Environment and Enterprise Performance Survey of the European Bank for Reconstruction and Development.

unhedged liabilities by total bank assets. We construct such a measure for 10 emerging European economies for which such detailed data is available, over the period 1998–2009. We then compute a similar de facto currency mismatch measure for a set of 19 additional emerging economies, for which somewhat less detailed data are available. Interestingly, we find that this de facto measure is much larger than other currency mismatch measures that do not control for the banks' borrowers' ability to hedge.

Using our currency mismatch measure, we find that there are statistically significant links between currency mismatch and economic growth, both across the set of 10 emerging European economies, as well as across the larger group of 29 emerging economies. A greater increase in currency mismatch is associated with faster economic growth during tranquil times, but also with a more severe crisis. On net, we find a positive link between currency mismatch and growth despite the output cost of the recent crisis. Our estimates for the period 1998–2009 indicate that a country that increased its currency mismatch by 6.6 percentage points each year – equal to one standard deviation – had on net a 4% higher GDP at the end of the period (including the crisis year) than a country that did not experience a currency mismatch increase. These results are robust to a number of tests and alternative specifications.

To demonstrate the dual role of currency mismatch, we present a conceptual framework in which contract enforceability problems generate borrowing constraints, as lenders require collateral to ensure that borrowers will repay their debt. If a majority of agents believe that there are bailout guarantees against systemic crises and there is a – small – probability that the exchange rate might experience a severe depreciation, it is optimal to borrow in foreign currency, even if it entails a – small – probability of bankruptcy. Therefore, currency mismatch emerges as a best-response of agents to the policy environment. Borrowers find currency mismatch optimal because (1) the expected interest payments on euro debt are lower than those on domestic currency debt, even after correcting for expected depreciation; and (2) they can borrow more. Risk premia on euro debt do not fully reflect the extent of insolvency risk, because the government is expected to grant a bailout in the rare event of a severe financial crisis. In other words, systemic bailout guarantees generate an implicit subsidy that can be exploited only by taking on insolvency risk. This mechanism generates a positive link between economic growth and currency mismatch, as the latter helps relax borrowing constraints. However, it also implies more severe crises in countries with higher currency mismatch.

At the firm level, the above arguments imply that firms that take on currency mismatch enjoy better borrowing conditions and grow faster outside crisis times, especially in sectors that tend to be financially constrained, such as small firms in the non-tradables sector. In our empirical firm-level analysis, we investigate whether firms that take on currency mismatch enjoy such benefits, relative to similar firms with no currency mismatch. We use data for a large cross-section of European economies from the BEEPS. The regression analysis suggests that across financially constrained groups of firms, currency mismatch reduces the interest rate by 2 percentage points on average, and increases the average loan maturity by 10 months. Furthermore, firms with currency mismatch exhibit 2.3 percentage points faster annual growth. Interestingly, these effects are not present across groups of large firms, which are usually less financially constrained.

Much of the literature on the impact of currency mismatch on firms' performance uses stock market listed firms, and finds that balance sheet effects associated with currency mismatch have been a minor issue. However, the sample of listed firms is a biased sample of large privileged firms, which are not representative of the majority of firms in these countries. An advantage of our approach is that it considers both listed and non-listed firms, and so we are able to effectively capture the effects of currency mismatch across the entire economy, not just the prime listed firms.

Brown *et al.* (2009) are the first to use a representative sample of firms in Eastern Europe from the BEEPS to study foreign currency borrowing. Our work differs from theirs in two dimensions. First, we focus specifically on currency mismatch – that is, on foreign currency borrowing by firms with no foreign currency income – rather than on foreign currency borrowing. Second, we mainly assess the impact of currency mismatch on the terms of borrowing and on firm performance rather than its determinants.

The rest of the paper is structured as follows. Section 2 describes the boom and bust experienced by emerging Europe during the last decade. Section 3 presents the conceptual framework. Section 4 describes how we construct our de facto currency mismatch measure and analyses the macroeconomic effects of currency mismatch. Section 5 presents the firm-level analysis and Section 6 presents the conclusions. The appendix contains a simple model, a description of our empirical methodology and the data sources. Finally, an unpublished supplementary appendix contains figures and tables with additional empirical results.[2]

2. THE BOOM AND BUST CYCLE IN EMERGING EUROPE

Before the recent crisis, emerging Europe included some of the fastest growing emerging economies, growing at rates that in some cases were even higher than in emerging Asia, even after controlling for differences in initial per capita GDP (Table 1, first column). This growth performance was in part driven by EU-related reforms and expectations that euro adoption will follow EU membership. Indeed, most countries in the region either joined the EU or started membership negotiations,

[2] The unpublished supplementary appendix of this paper can be found at http://www.romainranciere.com/economic_policy_appendix.pdf

Table 1. Emerging Europe and other emerging economies before the crisis (2007, except when indicated otherwise)

	Real per capita GDP growth[a]	Asset share of foreign banks		(Foreign assets + foreign liabilities)/GDP		Domestic credit to private sector (% of GDP)		Current account balance/GDP	External debt/GDP	General deficit/GDP	General government debt/GDP	Share of public sector long-term external debt in total
	2000–2007	2000	2006	2000	2007	1997	2007	2007	2007	2007	2007	2007
Emerging Europe												
Albania	2.1	35.2	90.5	...	...	4.1	30.3	−9.1	17.6	−3.8	52.7	96.2
Belarus	4.9	...	...	42.7	56.1	8.3	25.1	−6.8	27.7	0.4	11.5	67.5
Bosnia & Herz.	1.5	21.6	94.0	...	...	57.0	54.7	−12.7	48.4	−0.1	30.1	62.8
Bulgaria	3.2	75.3	80.1	174.4	243.2	9.3	66.8	−25.1	99.8	3.5	19.8	27.5
Croatia	1.6	84.1	90.8	119.4	235.0	37.3	72.1	−7.6	83.4	−1.2	33.2	32.1
Czech Rep.	1.1	65.4	84.7	144.0	171.3	70.3	49.5	−3.2	42.9	−0.6	28.9	...
Estonia	5.1	97.4	99.1	142.2	298.9	24.7	94.4	−18.1	112.6	2.9	3.4	...
Hungary	1.0	67.4	82.9	151.5	340.0	24.3	61.6	−6.4	103.5	−4.9	65.8	...
Latvia	6.2	74.4	62.9	127.7	264.1	11.0	93.9	−22.6	126.9	0.7	7.8	7.9
Lithuania	4.8	54.7	91.8	82.1	159.1	11.1	61.2	−14.6	77.4	−1.0	17.0	...
Macedonia, FYR	−0.8	53.4	53.2	123.6	140.9	27.3	38.4	−7.2	49.8	0.6	23.4	59.3
Moldova	3.9	...	...	214.4	151.7	7.0	36.9	−17.0	54.6	−0.2	27.7	40.0
Poland	1.0	72.6	74.3	84.6	130.6	20.8	39.9	−4.7	54.9	−2.0	44.8	32.3
Romania	2.8	46.7	87.9	74.6	112.2	8.4	35.8	−13.9	47.1	−3.1	19.8	27.1
Serbia	2.4	0.5	78.7	...	...	24.9	33.0	−15.3	64.9	−1.9	33.3	34.6
Slovak Rep.	2.4	42.7	97.0	120.5	149.2	55.1	42.4	−5.4	52.0	−1.9	29.4	...
Slovenia	1.0	15.3	29.5	82.4	244.2	26.4	79.0	−4.2	...	0.3	23.4	...
Turkey	0.6	...	...	77.3	98.8	19.5	29.0	−5.8	38.4	−2.1	39.4	36.9
Ukraine	5.0	11.1	35.0	104.4	149.5	2.5	59.1	−3.7	57.2	−2.0	12.8	21.0
Euro area	−2.4	...	...	...	...	86.0	121.4	0.4	...	−0.7	65.7	...
Other emerging economies												
Emerging Asia	4.0	...	...	...	...	102.4	98.9	6.8	13.6	−0.2	48.2	...
Latin America	−1.7	...	...	...	...	34.7	36.3	0.4	22.8	−1.2	48.6	...
Middle East and North Africa	...	...	...	...	...	...	...	16.5	27.6	7.1	32.7	...
Sub-Saharan Africa	−1.7	...	...	...	...	58.1	70.7	−3.0	25.4	0.7	33.5	...

[a]Residuals from a growth regression that controls for initial GDP per capita.

or at a minimum applied for membership during the last decade. Slovenia and the Slovak Republic have also introduced the euro as their currency.[3]

As part of the EU-driven reforms and the liberalization of these economies, capital controls and credit market regulations were dismantled in most countries. The opening up of the economy combined with privatization in the financial sector led to a boom in foreign bank ownership throughout emerging Europe. The share of foreign banks in total bank assets in 2006 ranged from 29% in Slovenia to 99% in Estonia, with an average of 77% and a median of 84% (Table 1, second and third columns). Financial openness, measured as foreign assets plus foreign liabilities over GDP, increased substantially between 2000 and 2007 (Table 1, fourth and fifth columns). Structural reforms, the opening of the capital account, financial liberalization and the domination of foreign banks with easy access to financing from their parent banks were the main ingredients of the economic boom in emerging Europe during the pre-crisis period. Borrowing costs fell sharply throughout the region during the pre-crisis period, particularly in foreign currency. Furthermore, private credit between 1997 and 2007 expanded in emerging Europe faster than in other emerging economies (Table 1, sixth and seventh columns).

The boom led to the build-up of large external imbalances before the crisis, with high current account deficits and external debt levels (Table 1, eighth and ninth columns). Associated with the lending boom, real exchange rates appreciated in most countries in the region, regardless of exchange rate regime.

Emerging Europe's boom was driven by the private sector, not by government spending. The private sector saving-investment balances clearly dominated the current account balances. Private sector investment increased by 3.1 percentage points of GDP on average in the region between 2004 and 2007. In contrast, public sector investment increased by only 1 percentage point of GDP. Private sector savings fell by an average of 2.1 percentage points of GDP, while public savings actually increased, by an average of 1.8 percentage points of GDP during the same period. Most emerging European economies had small general government deficits and some had surpluses before the crisis. Moreover, the fiscal balances improved in almost all the economies in the region in the years leading to the crisis. General government debt levels were small throughout emerging Europe, with the exception of Hungary. Also, compared with other emerging economies, the government deficit and debt levels in emerging Europe before the recent crisis do not stand out, while the share of public sector external debt to total external debt – excluding short-term debt for which sectoral data are not available – was relatively low and declined even further before the crisis in most countries of the region (Table 1, last three columns).

[3] The road to the EU includes a large number of broad economic, legal, and institutional reforms to comply with the EU *acquis*, including the opening of the capital account.

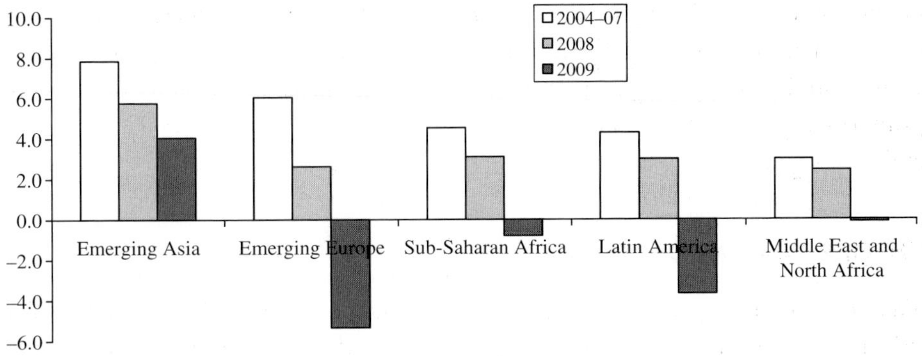

Figure 1. Real per capita GDP growth in emerging economies, 2004–2009

Source: IMF WEO database.

External imbalances were smaller in economies that started with a more developed financial sector and were more advanced in terms of institutional reforms. For example, current account deficits and external debt levels were substantially smaller in the Czech Republic, Poland, Slovenia, and the Slovak Republic. In the last two countries, lending interest rates converged to euro area levels as these countries introduced the euro – eliminating previous differentials between borrowing in domestic and in foreign currency. Also, these economies had relatively higher per capita GDP levels than most other economies in the region.[4]

Emerging Europe was hit by the crisis considerably more than other emerging economies. Real GDP growth turned sharply negative in 2009 and was substantially below what has been observed in other emerging economies (Figure 1). Borrowing costs increased sharply in all economies in the region, although from historically low levels.

Although there was no explicit systemic bailout guarantee in emerging Europe before the recent crisis, multilateral and bilateral external financing during the crisis effectively provided such guarantee through various programmes including the Vienna Initiative. Eight countries in the region introduced IMF programmes, which in addition to IMF financing in most cases included funds from the EU, the World Bank and bilateral sources (mostly from advanced European economies with bank sector exposures to emerging Europe). Moreover, the IMF programmes included specific assumptions on foreign bank rollover rates, which were often negotiated and agreed between the respective banks and the authorities of the host advanced economies. Although such financing does not necessarily prove that there was an

[4] There is a recent literature on external imbalances in emerging Europe. Vamvakidis (2009) discusses the vulnerabilities of emerging Europe before the recent crisis, most of which resulted from high levels of external debt. Rosenberg and Tirpak (2009) investigate the determinants of foreign currency borrowing by the private sector. They find that it is explained mainly by the extent to which domestic banks finance credit expansion from abroad, the level of deposit dollarization, and the interest rate differential. Finally, Árvai *et al.* (2009) examine the financial interlinkages within Europe and potential contagion channels.

implicit systemic bailout guarantee, it has been large enough to effectively bail out both lenders and borrowers in emerging Europe. In many cases the bailout was granted indirectly via the support of exchange rate pegs, as the collapse of the pegs, primarily in the Baltics, could have led to large losses due to balance sheet effects and cross-border spillovers.

3. THEORETICAL MECHANISM

This section discusses why taking on currency mismatch and the implied insolvency risk might be optimal from the perspective of both lenders and borrowers. It then analyses the macroeconomic implications of such decisions in terms of higher economic growth, but also systemic risk. Appendix A presents a model that formalizes the mechanism.[5]

Currency mismatch arises when domestically oriented firms and households denominate their debt in foreign currency – for example euros – while the cash flows that will service that debt are denominated in domestic currency. Consider a set-up in which agents can denominate their debt in either domestic or foreign currency. To generate borrowing constraints we assume that there are contract enforceability problems in credit markets. Lack of enforceability implies that borrowers cannot commit to repay their debt and might have incentives to divert funds. Lenders then impose borrowing constraints to ensure that they will be repaid.

In such an environment, domestically oriented borrowers have no incentives to take on currency mismatch, as they will have to internalize the insolvency risk via higher interest rates and lower leverage. This environment, however, is not a complete description of the real world: we also need to consider the existence of bailout guarantees against systemic crises. It is a stylized fact that if a critical mass of borrowers is on the brink of bankruptcy, governments typically implement policies to ensure that creditors get repaid – at least in part – and avoid a systemic economic meltdown. In other words, governments insure creditors against systemic crises. These bailouts may come in the form of handing out cheques, an easing of monetary policy, or the maintenance of an exchange rate peg.[6] However, if an isolated borrower defaults, the lender is not bailed out. It is therefore necessary that a critical mass of borrowers be at the brink of default.

In the presence of guarantees, a domestically oriented firm will find it optimal to take on currency mismatch if two conditions hold: (1) it expects that a critical mass of borrowers also take on currency mismatch; and (2) there is a – small – probability of a severe real exchange rate depreciation, so that the government will indeed

[5] This mechanism is based on Schneider and Tornell (2004) and Ranciere and Tornell (2009). It relates to the sudden stops literature that analyses the dynamics of different macro variables during a financial crisis (e.g. Calvo *et al.*, 2008). An important difference is that we focus not only on crises, but also on the dual role of foreign currency debt, during normal times and during crisis.

[6] Indeed, bailouts in emerging Europe during the recent crisis often took the form of supporting the pegs.

grant a bailout. From the lenders' perspective, the bailout guarantee means that they will be repaid both under no depreciation and under depreciation. In the first case, the borrowers will repay, as their debt contract is incentive compatible. In the second case, the government will repay lenders via a bailout. The key implication is that the interest rate that the lenders charge does not include a premium for the insolvency risk that currency mismatch entails. It follows that from a borrower's perspective, the expected interest costs are smaller for debt denominated in foreign currency than for debt denominated in domestic currency: it is actuarially cheaper to borrow in euros than in domestic currency.

The lower expected interest payments generate an additional advantage of currency mismatch: it relaxes the borrowing constraint. This is because the reduction in the expected debt service makes it less attractive for borrowers to divert funds instead of repaying debt. That is, currency mismatch relaxes the incentive compatibility constraint imposed by lenders in order to ensure that they will be repaid. It follows that if the likelihood of a sharp depreciation is small, a borrower finds it profitable to take on debt that will be repaid in euros rather than debt that will be repaid in domestic currency, given that a critical mass of other borrowers are doing the same (see Box 1).

Box 1. Determinants and effects of currency mismatch

Microeconomic mechanism: There exist two credit market frictions in the economy:

- contract enforceability problems → borrowing constraints
- systemic bailout guarantees → incentives to take on risk

These frictions imply that borrowers face the following trade-off in their debt denomination decision:

- domestic currency debt → high interest rate and low leverage
- foreign currency debt → low interest rate and high leverage

To see why, consider competitive risk-neutral lenders with an opportunity cost of capital of $1 + r$ in terms of euros, and consider a loan of 1 euro:

(i) if the loan is to be repaid in domestic currency, the promised repayment is $1 + \rho^{\text{dom}} = (1 + r)/E(p_{t+1})$ with $1/E(p_{t+1})$ the real exchange rate

(ii) if the loan is to be repaid in euros – there is currency mismatch – and there is a bailout guarantee in case of a severe depreciation that will bankrupt borrowers, the promised repayment is $1 + \rho^{\text{cn}} = (1 + r)$

The equality $1 + \rho^{\text{dom}} = (1 + r)$ follows because lenders will be repaid for sure either by the borrower or the bailout.

If a severe depreciation occurs with probability $1 - u$, the expected interest costs are respectively $[1 + \rho^{dom}]E(p_{t+1}) = 1 + r$ and $[1 + r]\, u$. Thus, from the borrower's perspective, the expected repayment is lower under currency mismatch since $[1 + r]\, u < 1 + r$.

Because the expected repayment is lower under currency mismatch, the borrower's incentives to repay are higher. This ameliorates contract enforceability problems and relaxes borrowing constraints.

Macroeconomic effects

- Severe borrowing constraints → bottlenecks that impede faster growth
- Currency mismatch → relaxes borrowing constraints
  → increases investment
  → increases economic growth in no-crisis times

However, currency mismatch also → generates systemic risk
→ increases likelihood of a financial crisis

This discussion implies that a violation of uncovered interest rate parity is a key driver of currency mismatch. Table 2 suggests that indeed this violation was present in emerging Europe before the recent crisis. Consensus exchange rate forecast data indicate that during 2004–2007, lending interest rates in foreign currency adjusted for expected depreciation were lower than interest rates in domestic currency by an average of 2.5 percentage points – Hungary was the only exception.

Turning to the macroeconomic implications, there is a safe equilibrium where no agent expects a bailout and, therefore, no domestically oriented borrower denominates debt in euros. In such equilibrium, a severe depreciation will not lead to generalized bankruptcies due to balance sheet effects. As a result, no borrower has incentives to take on currency mismatch and there will be neither a financial crisis, nor political pressures to grant a bailout in case of an isolated default.

However, if a majority of agents believe that there are systemic bailout guarantees, there is also a risky equilibrium, where a critical mass of domestically oriented borrowers have incentives to denominate their debt in foreign currency as: (1) they can borrow more funds; and (2) the expected interest costs are lower. Lenders do not 'charge' borrowers for the insolvency risk they take, as they know that the taxpayer will repay the debt in case of a systemic crisis. In other words, systemic bailout guarantees generate an implicit subsidy that can be cashed in only by taking on insolvency risk.

If many constrained agents borrow in foreign currency, borrowing constraints are relaxed. Such increase in leverage permits higher aggregate investment and consumption, which in turn leads to faster economic growth during no-crisis times, provided constrained agents have profitable investment opportunities. However,

Table 2. Violation of uncovered interest rate parity in Emerging Europe, 2004–2007

	Lending rates in domestic currency	Lending rates in foreign currency	Expected appreciation	Violation of uncovered interest rate parity
Romania	13.4	7.7	0.34	6.1
Ukraine	16.7	11.3	−0.53	4.8
Croatia	10.5	6.6	0.16	4.0
Slovak Rep.	8.2	4.4	−0.45	3.4
Bulgaria	9.3	6.4	−0.03	2.8
Latvia	6.6	4.8	−0.09	1.7
Poland	6.6	4.2	−1.00	1.4
Lithuania	5.2	4.1	0.01	1.1
Estonia	5.5	5.5	−0.02	0.0
Hungary	8.3	10.1	0.98	−0.8

Note: The last column is equal to: lending interest rate in domestic currency − lending interest rate in foreign currency + expected exchange rate appreciation (end of year, one-year rates, in percent).

Sources: Lending interest rates in domestic currency are from the IMF's IFS. Lending interest rates in foreign currency are from the IMF's IFS (Croatia, Lithuania, Poland and Ukraine), Haver Analytics (Bulgaria, Estonia, Hungary and Latvia) and Central Bank websites (Romania and Slovak Republic). Data on expected exchange rate appreciation are from Consensus Forecast, Inc.

currency mismatch also leads to systemic risk. This is because a large real depreciation could lead to generalized bankruptcies, especially of domestically oriented borrowers with euro-debt in their books. Hence, currency mismatch leads to faster growth, but also increases the likelihood of a financial crisis.

Will average economic growth in an economy with currency mismatch be higher than in a safe economy, even after taking into account occasional financial crises? The answer hinges on the frequency and severity of crises during the sample period. This is an empirical issue, which we address in the next section.

4. AGGREGATE CURRENCY MISMATCH: MEASUREMENT AND MACROECONOMIC CONSEQUENCES

This section introduces a new currency mismatch measure that captures the presence of systemic risk by explicitly taking into account the extent to which borrowers hedge their foreign currency liabilities. This measure is then used to analyse the macroeconomic consequences of currency mismatch.

4.1. Measuring aggregate currency mismatch

Here, the currency mismatch measure is computed over the period 1998–2009, for 10 countries in emerging Europe for which there is detailed data. In the next subsection, the sample is extended to include non-European emerging economies, increasing the sample to a total of 29 emerging economies.

There are different ways in which one can measure the degree of currency mismatch.[7] A straightforward way is to compare the net national debt or debt service requirements to the net exports of a country. Another, also straightforward, way is to look at the ratio of foreign currency denominated liabilities to foreign currency denominated assets of the banking sector. These measures have the virtue of being simple and using readily available data. However, they might miss instances in which systemic risk is developing.

While the first measure captures external aggregate imbalances, it is not designed to capture sectoral imbalances that could generate systemic risk. For instance, while an economy might have a low foreign currency debt relative to its net exports, that debt might be concentrated in borrowers with no foreign currency income. Moreover, the presence of a vibrant export sector does not imply that a government would be able to tax exporters during a crisis in order to bail out debtors with foreign currency exposures.

The second measure, by looking exclusively at bank balance sheets, will often find that the *notional* degree of currency mismatch is small, as banks with foreign currency liabilities also tend to lend in foreign currency – often because of prudential requirements. However, if domestic bank debtors cannot effectively hedge their exchange rate risk, banks are indirectly exposed to exchange rate risk, through credit risk. Thus, there is a *de facto* systemic risk, which is not reflected in a notional currency mismatch measure that considers only banks' balance sheets.

The recent experience of the emerging European economies illustrates the deficiencies of the available currency mismatch measures. During the pre-crisis boom, banks in emerging Europe borrowed in foreign currencies to extend loans denominated in foreign currencies both to the corporate sector and to households. Indeed, the share of foreign currency lending to total lending reached well above 50% in most emerging European economies in 2007, which was substantially higher than in other emerging economies (see Figure 2). However, if a substantial share of this credit was extended to sectors with no foreign currency revenues and financed consumption and investment in non-tradable goods, the de facto insolvency risk taken on by banks would be substantial and would have contributed to aggregate systemic risk.

A currency mismatch measure that appropriately captures the evolution of systemic risk should therefore control for indirect channels by which foreign currency debt can generate insolvencies across different classes of bank's debtors. In other words, such an index should control for the sources of foreign currency income for different classes of foreign currency borrowers.

This is one of the key contributions of this paper. We construct a de facto currency mismatch index that covers the period 1998–2009. This index is computed

[7] For a discussion of the literature and measures of currency mismatch see Eichengreen *et al.* (2007) and Goldstein and Turner (2004).

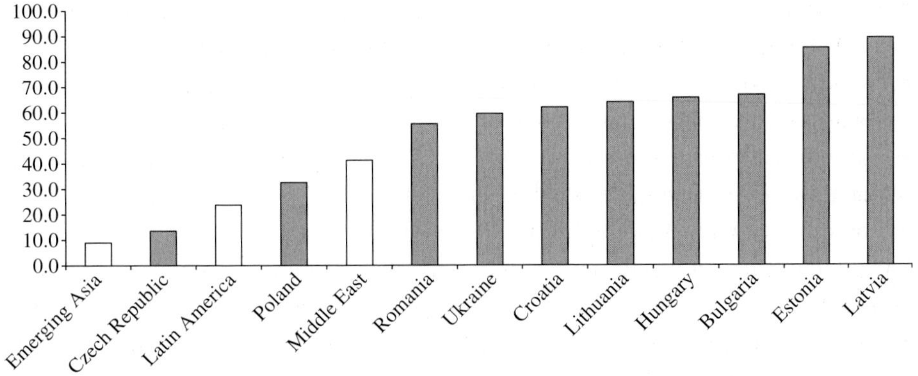

Figure 2. Bank loans in foreign currency in percent of total bank loans, emerging Europe, 2007

Source: IMF, Database of Vulnerability Exercise for Emerging Economies.

as the ratio of foreign currency denominated net *unhedged* liabilities to total bank assets, where the former is determined by the share of banks' net foreign currency liabilities that is lent to unhedged borrowers (see Box 2 and Appendix B for details).

Box 2. A new measure of currency mismatch

Currency mismatch in the banking sector is usually measured as the difference between foreign currency assets and liabilities. However, to the extent that some of the foreign currency assets are claims towards unhedged borrowers, banks are exposed to exchange rate risks indirectly, through credit default risk. Bank balance sheet data do not capture such an indirect exchange rate risk, as their foreign currency assets and liabilities are often matched. Our measure of currency mismatch captures this indirect exchange risk by excluding foreign currency loans to unhedged borrowers from foreign currency assets. The formula of the new currency mismatch measure in the banking sector is the following:

Foreign currency denominated net unhedged liabilities / total bank assets = {[*foreign currency foreign liabilities* + *foreign currency domestic liabilities*] − [*foreign currency foreign assets* + *foreign currency domestic assets*] + [*foreign currency lending to unhedged households* + *foreign currency lending to unhedged nonfinancial firms*]} / [*total bank assets*]

The components of the numerator in the above formula include:

- Foreign currency foreign liabilities: foreign currency claims of non-residents towards the domestic banking sector (i.e. loans of foreign banks, including parent foreign banks to their subsidiaries, and foreign currency deposits of non-residents).

- Foreign currency domestic liabilities: foreign currency claims of residents towards the domestic banking sector (i.e. foreign currency deposits of residents).
- Foreign currency foreign assets: foreign currency claims of the banking sector towards non-residents (i.e. deposits, or loans in foreign currencies).
- Foreign currency domestic assets: foreign currency claims of the banking sector towards residents (i.e. foreign currency loans).
- Foreign currency lending to unhedged households: the part of the banks' foreign currency domestic assets that is foreign currency lending to unhedged households.
- Foreign currency lending to unhedged non-financial firms: the part of the banks' foreign currency domestic assets that is foreign currency lending to unhedged firms.

The adjustment includes foreign currency lending to unhedged households and non-financial firms. As such lending is subject to exchange rate risk through balance sheet effects in households and non-financial firms, a sharp exchange rate depreciation would turn a large share of such loans to non-performing loans. Therefore, a currency mismatch of a bank's borrower will lead to a currency mismatch for the bank if the borrower cannot repay the loan during a crisis. Therefore, foreign currency loans to unhedged borrowers should be subtracted from the asset side of the banking sector in order to calculate a currency mismatch measure that captures more accurately the extent of systemic risk.

This measure of currency mismatch assumes that foreign currency lending to non-financial corporates and to households that have no foreign currency income is subject to exchange rate risk. In contrast, it assumes that exporters are able to hedge all exchange rate risk. However, it should be noted that even loans to borrowers with foreign currency income may not be serviced during a crisis if their foreign income declines, for example, due to a drop in exports as foreign demand drops sharply.[8]

The construction of such a measure requires refined data about bank balance sheets that permits tracking the evolution of credit to different sectors, including non-financial firms and households, and measuring the extent to which the debtors are hedged for exchange rate risk. Such data is not readily available, which might explain the lack of such de facto currency mismatch measures in the literature.

We construct the currency mismatch measure by using data from a large number of sources, some of which are confidential IMF data (see Appendix B for details).

[8] Indeed, the IMF's World Economic Outlook (WEO) estimates that emerging Europe's exports of goods and services fell by 11% in volume, or 21% in nominal US dollars, in 2009.

Data on foreign currency domestic and foreign asset and liabilities by sector and data on total bank assets are from Haver Analytics and from the internal and confidential IMF Vulnerability Exercise for Emerging Economies. The share of foreign currency lending to corporates with no foreign currency income is from a number of sources, including various EBRD and World Bank firm survey data, country authority data, and various country studies.

We have data for the extent to which firms hedge their foreign currency exposure, but not for the extent to which households do. Thus, we can assume that either households hedge foreign exchange risk to the same extent as firms do, or they do not hedge at all. For emerging Europe, we compute our currency mismatch measure under both alternatives, because we have data on foreign currency loans to households and to firms separately. However, for the other 19 emerging economies we only have data on foreign currency loans to the whole private sector, without separating households and firms. Thus, for these 19 countries we can only compute our measure under the assumption that households' hedging is the same as that of firms. As the fourth and last columns in Table 3 show, for the 10 emerging European countries the currency mismatch measures under these two assumptions are quite similar (the correlation between the two is near to one). Therefore, to be consistent throughout the paper, our regressions use the measure under which households and firms hedge to the same extent.

Figure 3 shows the de facto currency mismatch in all emerging European economies with available data during 1998–2009, ranked based on the change in currency mismatch during this period.[9] The sample includes 10 countries that account for 86% of East Europe's GDP, excluding Russia. The estimates show that currency mismatches increased throughout emerging Europe during the boom years before the recent crisis, particularly in Bulgaria, Latvia, Estonia and Lithuania. On average, currency mismatches as a share of bank assets increased by 16 percentage points during the last 10 years in the region. Before the crisis, the currency mismatch measure reached the highest level in Romania, Estonia, Croatia, Latvia and Lithuania. The only economies without currency mismatches before the crisis (a negative measure in 2007) included the Czech Republic and, less so, Ukraine.[10]

To assess the importance of controlling for foreign currency lending to unhedged borrowers, Figure 4 shows an unadjusted notional currency mismatch (foreign currency denominated net liabilities without adjusting for foreign currency lending to unhedged borrowers) next to the de facto adjusted measure. The comparison shows that while most countries do not exhibit currency mismatch according to the unadjusted measure, they exhibit very large mismatches according to the measure

[9] See below for estimates for non-European emerging economies.

[10] Although Ukraine was overheating before the global financial crisis and eventually had a severe crisis and an IMF programme, its external imbalances did not reach levels as high as in most of the rest of emerging Europe (see Table 1).

Table 3. Currency mismatches in emerging Europe in percent of bank sector assets: adjusting for unhedged borrowing, 2004–2007

	Unadjusted	Adjusted for unhedged foreign currency borrowing from domestic banks: By households	By firms	Fully adjusted	Including unhedged foreign currency loans from abroad	Assuming totally unhedged households
2004						
Bulgaria	−28.7	−26.7	−3.9	−1.9	2.0	−1.2
Croatia	28.5	28.6	32.2	32.3	35.8	32.4
Czech Rep.	−30.7	−30.7	−28.8	−28.8	−26.8	−28.7
Estonia	−33.1	−18.4	−13.1	1.5	4.9	11.5
Hungary	−2.1	−0.9	4.9	6.1	8.4	7.1
Latvia	−31.0	−21.6	−19.1	−9.6	−9.0	−8.0
Lithuania	−13.4	−9.7	−0.8	3.0	4.6	6.5
Poland	−7.3	−2.3	−4.3	0.7	2.3	3.2
Romania	12.1	18.0	24.9	30.8	35.0	32.1
Ukraine	−43.2	−38.0	−26.3	−21.1	...	−19.5
2007						
Bulgaria	−31.9	−27.0	−4.0	0.9	6.9	2.6
Croatia	21.7	21.8	24.6	24.7	31.6	24.7
Czech Rep.	−24.5	−24.4	−22.4	−22.4	−20.0	−22.4
Estonia	−25.9	3.5	4.3	33.7	39.3	53.6
Hungary	−5.8	0.6	1.6	8.0	11.2	13.5
Latvia	−26.3	−5.7	−5.4	15.1	17.4	18.5
Lithuania	−5.1	2.7	6.3	14.1	17.0	21.4
Poland	−9.1	−4.9	−3.8	0.4	2.6	2.5
Romania	10.9	22.8	23.5	35.4	39.5	38.1
Ukraine	−34.2	−20.9	−19.7	−6.3	...	−2.0

Note: The numerator is expressed as liabilities minus assets and, therefore, an increase in the above percentages reflects an increase in currency mismatch.

Source: Authors' calculations (see Appendix B).

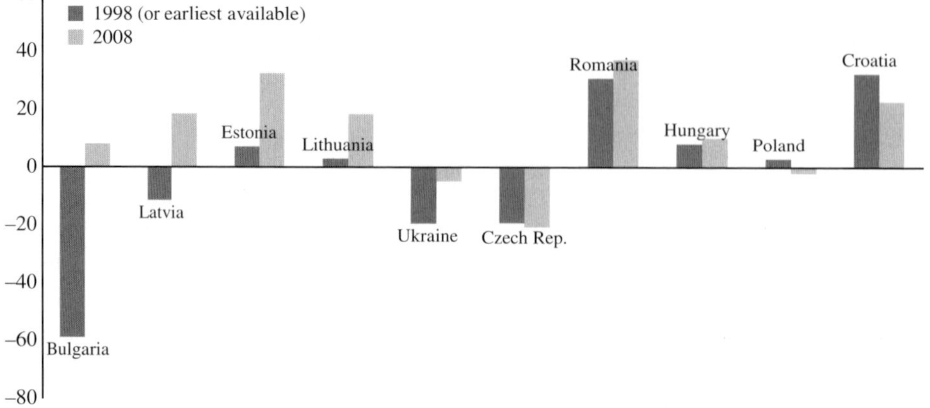

Figure 3. Currency mismatch in emerging Europe, 1998–2008

Source: Authors' calculations.

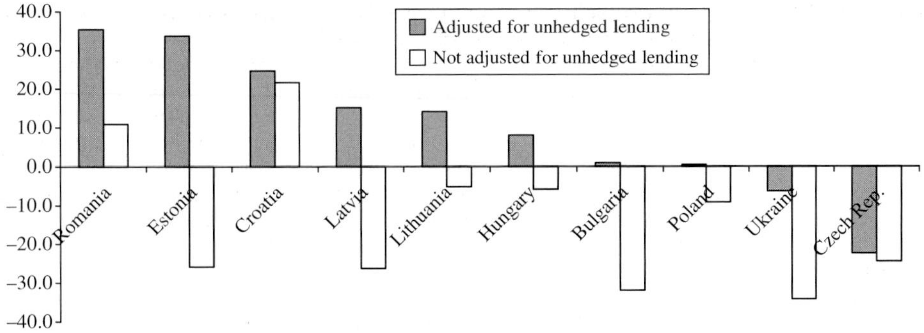

Figure 4. Currency mismatches in emerging Europe, with and without adjustment for unhedged lending, 2007

Source: Authors' calculations.

that adjusts for unhedged foreign currency lending. The difference is on average equal to 23 percentage points, and is particularly sharp in Estonia, Latvia and Bulgaria.

Did unhedged lending go mostly to households or to the corporate sector? Table 3 shows the calculated currency mismatches for 2004 and 2007, without adjusting for unhedged foreign currency borrowing (first column), adjusting only for unhedged borrowing by households (second column), adjusting only for unhedged borrowing by firms (third column), and fully adjusting for unhedged borrowing (fourth column). A comparison of unadjusted and fully adjusted for unhedged foreign currency borrowing currency mismatches in 2004 and in 2007 shows that currency mismatches increased in most countries during this period, in most cases substantially. A comparison of the second and third columns, which compares the extent to which the adjustment for unhedged foreign currency borrowing is due to household versus firms, shows that most of the unhedged borrowing during the pre-crisis period was done by firms. However, unhedged foreign currency borrowing by household increased substantially by 2007 – which in some cases may reflect the mortgage-financed housing boom in some of the countries in the region.

In many countries, firms took on additional insolvency risk via *direct* foreign currency borrowing from abroad, particularly in response to central bank measures to limit currency mismatch in the domestic banking sector.[11] Although we do not include such direct borrowing in our baseline currency mismatch measure, the fifth column in Table 3 contains currency mismatch estimates that include direct foreign currency borrowing from abroad.[12] The estimates suggest that such borrowing increased currency mismatch in all countries in the sample before the crisis.

[11] Direct borrowing from abroad by corporates was often accompanied by a repayment guarantee by the domestic foreign owned bank to the parent bank abroad. Therefore, the exchange rate risk was still assumed by the domestic banking sector, while the loan was repaid to the parent bank.

[12] Based on data in Rosenberg and Tirpak (2009); see Appendix B for details.

Table 4. Currency mismatch measures in emerging Europe, 2004–2007

	Net external debt/ exports			External debt service/ exports			Foreign currency denominated net unhedged liabilities/ total bank assets		
	2004	2007	Change	2004	2007	Change	2004	2007	Change
Bulgaria	2.8	4.5	1.7	0.3	0.6	0.2	−1.9	0.9	2.8
Croatia	3.5	5.0	1.5	0.4	0.6	0.3	32.3	24.7	−7.6
Czech Rep.	1.2	1.0	−0.2	...	...	...	−28.8	−22.4	6.4
Estonia	4.1	5.0	0.9	0.4	0.6	0.2	1.5	33.7	32.2
Hungary	5.4	4.4	−1.0	0.3	0.2	0.0	6.1	8.0	1.9
Latvia	3.4	10.0	6.6	0.2	0.4	0.1	−9.6	15.1	24.7
Lithuania	3.7	4.0	0.3	0.4	0.8	0.3	3.0	14.1	11.1
Poland	3.2	4.5	1.3	0.4	0.3	−0.1	0.7	0.4	−0.3
Romania	4.7	9.0	4.3	0.1	0.5	0.4	30.8	35.4	4.6
Ukraine	2.0	3.8	1.7	0.3	0.3	0.0	−21.1	−6.3	14.8
Correlation with new measure	0.7	0.7	0.3	−0.2	0.5	0.0	...	...	...
Rank Correlation with new measure	0.8	0.8	0.2	0.0	0.4	0.1	...	...	...

Note: Standard currency mismatch measures in the literature divide net external debt or external debt service with exports or net exports. As most emerging European economies had negative net exports before the crisis, the denominator in the table is total exports. An increase in all measures reflects higher currency mismatch.

Table 4 compares the new currency mismatch measure with two standard measures in the literature. The first is net external debt to exports of goods and services – net debt is defined as total external debt minus foreign assets of the central bank and the banking sector. The second is external debt service to exports of goods and services. These comparisons suggest that our measure of currency mismatch provides new information. Although the share of net external debt to exports seems to be highly correlated with our measure, the correlation of the changes is very small. The share of external debt service to exports is even less correlated with our measures, both in terms of levels and changes.[13]

4.2. The boom-bust cycle and currency mismatch in emerging Europe

This section analyses the macroeconomic effects of currency mismatch. As Figure 5 shows, during the boom years, a higher increase in currency mismatch was associated with faster real GDP growth (Figure 5.1) and faster credit growth (Figures 5.2 and 5.3). As the theoretical framework suggests, the increasing credit-to-GDP ratio

[13] Like this paper, a recent literature has looked at sector level balance sheet data (e.g., Rosenberg *et al.*, 2005 and Prat, 2007). Prat (2007) computes the banks' currency mismatch as the share of their foreign currency liabilities not covered by their foreign currency loans. From the perspective of capturing systemic risk, a shortcoming of the latter approach is that it does not adjust for foreign currency loans made to unhedged borrowers. Our contribution is to make this adjustment by subtracting from the bank's foreign currency assets those loans made to agents with no foreign currency income.

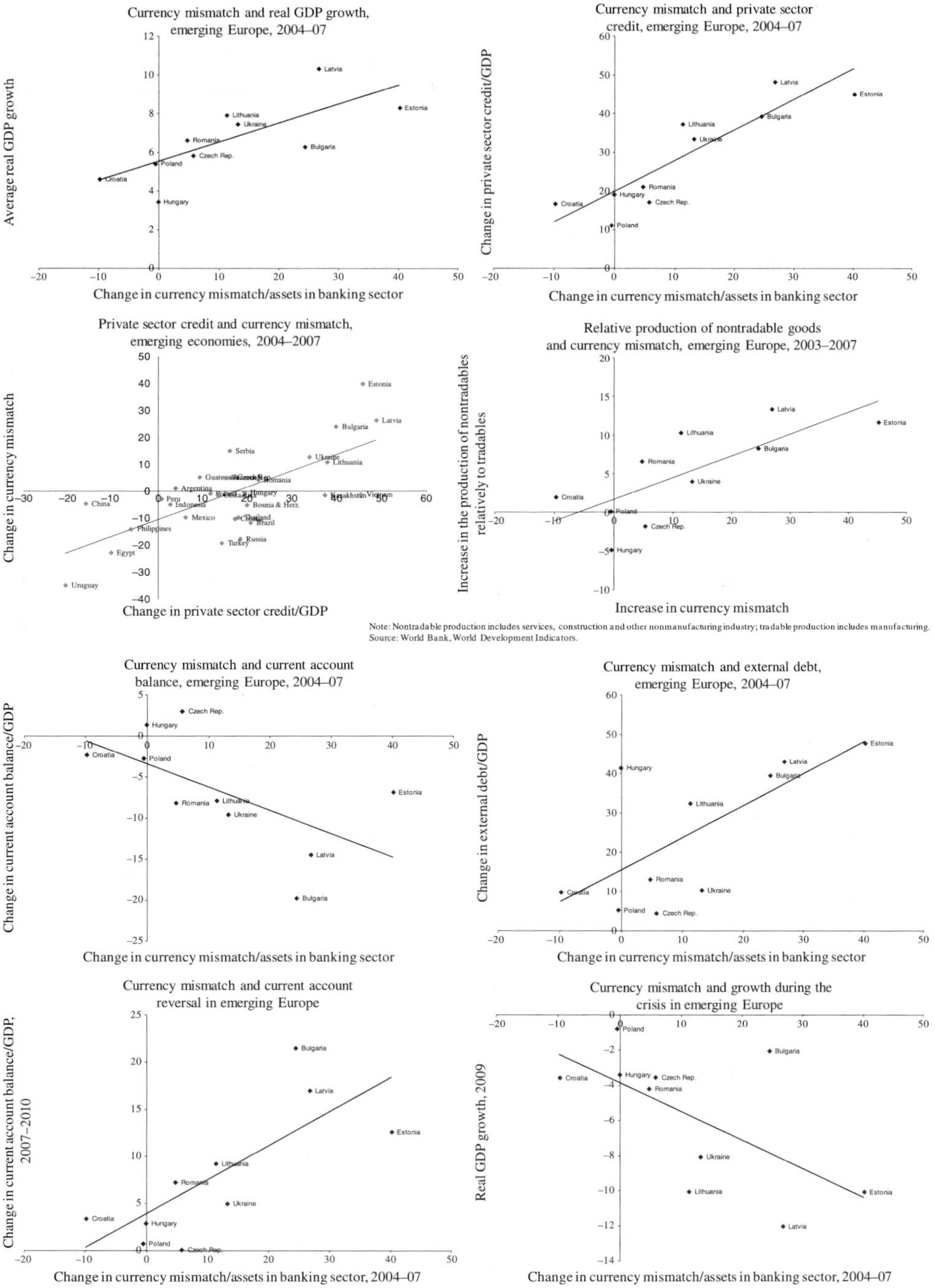

Figure 5. Currency mismatch and the recent boom and bust cycle in emerging Europe

can be explained by the faster growth of the non-tradables sector relative to the tradable sector, with the former benefiting proportionally more from the relaxation of borrowing constraints. The sharp increase in the current account deficit and the accumulation of external debt were a byproduct of the increasing non-tradables-to-tradables output ratio. Indeed, Figure 5.4 shows that, during the boom years, the production of non-tradables relative to tradables in emerging Europe was highly correlated with the increase in currency mismatch. At the same time, Figure 5.5 and Figure 5.6 show that high currency mismatch was correlated with higher current account deficits and higher levels of external debt.

During the crisis, these patterns reversed. As Figure 5.7 shows, the greater the increase in currency mismatch during the boom, the sharper the current account reversal and, as Figure 5.8 shows, the steeper the fall in GDP during the crisis (no data is available yet for the non-tradables-to-tradables output ratio during the crisis).

Next we use panel regressions to explore the link between currency mismatch and emerging Europe's recent boom and bust cycle. We regress annual real GDP growth on the current and lagged changes in currency mismatch, a crisis dummy variable that takes the value of 1 in 2009 (the year when growth turned negative in East Europe), interaction terms of the crisis dummy with the current and lagged changes of currency mismatch, the change in the ratio of external debt to GDP and a time trend. The regression is estimated for the 10 countries in emerging Europe in our sample, over the period 1998–2009.[14]

We use both a pooled OLS estimator and a fixed effects estimator. While the fixed effect estimator has the advantage of controlling for country-specific unobserved heterogeneity, it restricts the estimation to the within-country dimension. This is potentially problematic for the estimation of the growth impact of financial fragility since there is only one crisis in the sample. This is why we also present results using the pooled OLS estimator.[15] Table 5 shows the results of the estimation. The first two columns present the pooled estimates, while the fifth and sixth columns present estimates with fixed effects.

Although the results should be treated with caution given the relatively small sample, they suggest that changes in currency mismatch were positively correlated with growth in the pre-crisis period, but negatively correlated with growth during the recent crisis. The change in currency mismatch enters positively and statistically significant (although at the 10% level in the specification with fixed effects). The lagged currency mismatch is not statistically significant in these specifications (it is significant when the current value is not included, see Appendix B). The crisis dummy variable is negative and statistically significant in all specifications. With the exception of the specification with fixed effects, the interaction term of the lagged change in currency mismatch with the crisis dummy variable is negative and statistically significant. The latter suggests that countries in emerging Europe that

[14] The results are robust if per capita real GDP, or PPP-adjusted per capita real GDP is used instead.

[15] Regressions using random effects yield findings that are similar to the pooled estimation. The results are available upon request, but not reported because of the small cross-sectional size of our panel.

Table 5. Currency mismatch and growth in emerging economies, 1998–2009

	Pooled panel				Fixed effects			
	Emerging Europe		Emerging economies		Emerging Europe		Emerging economies	
Change in currency mismatch	0.11**	0.12**	0.07**	0.07**	0.12*	0.11*	0.09**	0.09**
	(0.05)	(0.05)	(0.03)	(0.03)	(0.06)	(0.06)	(0.04)	(0.04)
Lagged change in currency mismatch	0.06	0.06	0.04	0.04	0.05	0.04	0.05	0.04
	(0.05)	(0.04)	(0.04)	(0.04)	(0.07)	(0.06)	(0.04)	(0.04)
Crisis dummy	−12.93***	−13.42***	−13.42***	−14.09***	−12.97***	−14.01***	−13.02***	−13.80***
	(0.60)	(1.64)	(0.56)	(1.69)	(2.42)	(2.63)	(0.78)	(1.71)
Interaction term: (change in currency	−0.10**	−0.22	−0.06**	−0.02	0.01	−0.14	0.04	0.09
mismatch) × (crisis dummy)	(0.05)	(0.18)	(0.03)	(0.09)	(0.39)	(0.40)	(0.06)	(0.21)
Interaction term: (lagged change in	−0.84***	−0.84***	−0.83***	−0.92***	−0.69	−0.68	−0.71***	−0.77***
currency mismatch) × (crisis dummy)	(0.05)	(0.13)	(0.04)	(0.07)	(0.87)	(0.96)	(0.11)	(0.10)
Time trend		−0.16		0.23		−0.09		0.19
		(0.27)		(0.30)		(0.23)		(0.33)
Change in external debt/GDP		0.05		−0.05		0.07		−0.05
		(0.11)		(0.06)		(0.08)		(0.10)
Adjusted R^2	0.68	0.68	0.53	0.53	0.65	0.65	0.5	0.50
Number of countries	10	10	29	29	10	10	29	29

Note: The dependent variable is real GDP growth (from the IMF World Economic Outlook database). Currency mismatch is measured as explained in the text and Appendix A. The crisis dummy takes the value of 1 in 2009, which is the year when growth turned negative throughout emerging Europe. The sample for emerging Europe includes 10 economies: Bulgaria, Croatia, Czech Rep., Estonia, Hungary, Latvia, Lithuania, Poland, Romania, and Ukraine. The broader sample for emerging markets includes in addition: Argentina, Brazil, Bosnia and Herzegovina, China, Costa Rica, Egypt, Guatemala, Indonesia, Kazakhstan, Mexico, Peru, Philippines, Russia, Serbia, Thailand, Turkey, Uruguay, Venezuela, and Vietnam. The period is 1998–2009. Heteroscedasticity-consistent standard errors in parentheses.

*, **, and *** indicate statistical significance at the 10, 5 and 1% level, respectively.

increased their currency mismatch before the crisis were affected by the crisis more. The insignificant estimate of the interaction term with the current value of currency mismatch could be explained by the fact that some countries were forced to reduce their currency mismatch during the crisis.

These results hold even when we control for the change in the external debt-to-GDP ratio, which does not turn out to be statistically significant. This suggests that it was not the increase in external debt that drove fast growth in emerging Europe before the crisis and the collapse of growth during the crisis, but the increase in currency mismatch. Therefore, an emerging European economy that increased its external debt without increasing its currency mismatch in relative terms did not experience the same boom-bust cycle that took place in the rest of the region during the last decade.

The economic significance of the estimates is sizeable. According to the second regression in Table 5, if currency mismatch increases in a country by 6.6 percentage points (equal to one standard deviation), growth increases by 0.8 percentage points per year, leading to higher GDP by 8.7% during the pre-crisis period (1998–2008), relative to a country where currency mismatch remains unchanged.[16] In the meantime, the point estimate of the interaction term of the crisis dummy with the lagged currency mismatch indicates that a country that increased its currency mismatch by 6.6 percentage points the year before the crisis experienced a 4.7 percentage point more severe drop in GDP during the crisis, compared with a country that did not increase its currency mismatch.[17] Considering the entire boom-bust episode altogether, a country that was increasing its currency mismatch by 6.6 percentage points each year would have had on net a 4% higher GDP at the end of the period (including the crisis year) than a country that did not experience a currency mismatch increase.[18]

The results of Table 5 are robust to a battery of additional tests that are presented in Table B1 in Appendix B. The results hold when the regression includes the change in the ratio of non-tradable production to GDP and, to partly address causality concerns, the lagged change of currency mismatch without including its current change. The results also hold when the measure of currency mismatch assumes that households are not able to hedge currency risk at all, or when currency mismatch is divided by GDP instead of total bank assets.

[16] This is the cumulative sum of the estimate (equal to 0.12) times one standard deviation of the change in the currency mismatch (equal to 6.6) during the period 1998–2007.

[17] This is equal to: $(6.6 \times 0.12) - (6.6 \times 0.84)$.

[18] Taking the case of Estonia as an example, the estimates suggest that its GDP in 2009 was higher by 3.9 percentage points, compared with what it would have been if Estonia had not increased its currency mismatch during the last decade. In contrast, in Brazil and Mexico, where currency mismatch increased only marginally during this period, GDP was higher by only 0.1 and 0.3 percentage points respectively, compared with what it would have been without any currency mismatch increase.

4.3. Currency mismatch and the recent boom and bust cycle in emerging economies

This section expands the country sample to include non-European emerging economies, as well as additional European emerging economies, for which data are available in less detail than in the initial 10 emerging European economies sample. Here we repeat the panel growth regression of the previous subsection for an expanded sample of 29 emerging economies, for the period 1998–2009. We also take advantage of the larger sample in order to estimate a cross-sectional growth regression, using averages over the period 2000–2009 and controlling for additional growth determinants.

It is challenging to compute the currency mismatch for non-European emerging economies because of the lack of detailed data on domestic banks' foreign currency loans to residents and foreign currency deposits of residents. In addition, data on foreign currency loans are not available separately for firms and households. The exceptional magnitude of foreign currency borrowing across sectors before the recent crisis has fostered a data collection effort in Eastern Europe that seems unparalleled in the rest of the emerging world, despite the role of currency mismatch in the financial crises of the 1990s. Nevertheless, this section uses a number of sources and simplifying assumptions to expand the de facto currency mismatch measure to 19 additional countries (see Appendix B for more details):

- Data on foreign currency loans to residents and foreign currency deposits of residents are from the internal and confidential IMF Vulnerability Exercise for Emerging Economies, which is based on data provided by country authorities. Some gaps in the data on foreign currency deposits of residents are complemented by using data in Arteta (2003, 2005) and Haver Analytics.
- Data on banks' foreign assets and liabilities are from a data set constructed by Prat (2007) for Argentina, Brazil, China, Indonesia, Mexico, Peru, Philippines, Russia, Thailand, Turkey and Uruguay. Data from the IMF's International Financial Statistics (IFS) are used for Bosnia and Herzegovina, Costa Rica, Egypt, Guatemala, Kazakhstan, Serbia, Venezuela and Vietnam. Unfortunately, the IFS data on bank foreign assets and liabilities do not specify currency denomination. Thus, for these eight countries we have assumed that all the banks' foreign assets and liabilities are denominated in foreign currency. As discussed below, this assumption does not turn out to make a big difference.
- Data for the share of unhedged foreign currency borrowing comes from various sources. For Latin America, the share is based on firm survey data in Kamil (2004, 2010). For other regions, data come from various World Bank Enterprise Surveys, setting the share of unhedged foreign currency borrowing equal to the share of non-exporting firms with foreign currency loans to the total number of firms with foreign currency loans – assuming that foreign currency loans in the tradable sector are fully hedged. As the previous subsection explains, due to lack

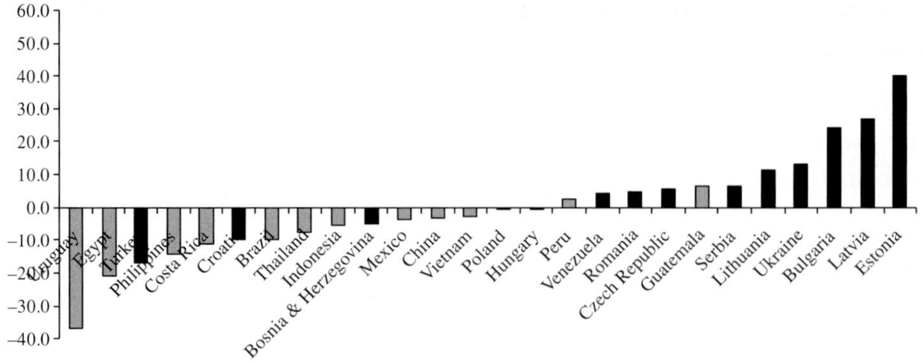

Figure 6. Increase in currency mismatch in emerging economies before the crisis (2004–2007)

Source: Authors' calculations.

of separate data on foreign currency loans to firms and households, the share of unhedged borrowing is assumed to be the same for households and firms.

In order to assess whether the currency mismatch measure using IFS data on bank foreign assets and liabilities captures currency mismatch in a similar way as the measure based on more detailed data, we compare the currency mismatch generated by them with the baseline currency mismatch measure for the 10 emerging European economies of the previous section. The simple correlation of the changes in the two currency mismatch measures is 0.85, suggesting that using IFS data is a reasonable approximation.[19]

In the extended set of 29 countries, emerging Europe stands out as the region with the sharpest increase in currency mismatch. As Figure 6 shows, the six economies with the largest increase in currency mismatch are in this region: Estonia, Latvia, Bulgaria, Ukraine, Lithuania and Serbia.[20]

The results in Table 5 (columns 3 and 4 for a pooled panel and 7 and 8 for a panel with fixed effects) confirm the links between currency mismatch and growth during the recent boom and bust cycle in emerging economies. The change in currency mismatch enters positively and is statistically significant at the 5% level in all specifications. This suggests that emerging economies that were increasing their currency mismatch during the pre-crisis period were growing faster. However, these economies were hit harder by the recent crisis, as suggested by the negative and statistically significant estimate of the interaction term of the lagged change in currency mismatch with the crisis dummy. The interaction term of the current value of currency mismatch with the crisis dummy is not always significant, as some

[19] The results for emerging Europe are robust if we use the currency mismatch measure with IFS net foreign assets data instead of data from Haver Analytics.

[20] This figure uses the IFS data for NFA for the additional 19 emerging economies.

countries were forced to reduce their currency mismatch during the crisis. These results hold even when we control for the change in the external debt-to-GDP ratio.

The estimates in the last regression in Table 5 suggest that a country that was increasing its currency mismatch by 5.7 percentage points each year in the sample period (equal to one standard deviation for this sample), would have higher GDP by up to 1.8% at the end of the period than a country that kept its currency mismatch the same, including during the crisis.

These results are confirmed by a cross-country growth regression that regresses average per capita PPP-adjusted GDP growth during 2000–2009 on standard determinants of growth as well as the change in currency mismatch.[21] Table 6 shows that the change in the currency mismatch measure enters positively and statistically significant at the 5% level in all specifications. The first regression suggests that controlling only for initial per capita GDP, countries that increased their currency mismatch the most during this decade grew faster. The second and third regressions show that this result holds even after controlling for the standard growth determinants in the literature. The fourth regression suggests that increasing currency mismatch was positively linked to growth even outside east Europe. Finally, the last regression shows that the growth effect of currency mismatch persists even after controlling for the change in the external debt-to-GDP ratio – which does not enter significantly.

These effects of currency mismatch are economically significant. The estimates suggest that a country that increased its currency mismatch by 17.8 percentage points during this period (equal to one standard deviation) would have higher annual GDP per capita growth by about 0.4% (or higher by 4 percentage points by the end of the sample period) than a country with unchanged currency mismatch. This number includes the growth collapse during the recent crisis. It remains to confirm whether this result will still hold after data on the recovery period is available.

5. CURRENCY MISMATCH AND FIRM PERFORMANCE

The theoretical section explains why currency mismatch should be viewed as a mechanism that relaxes credit constraints, especially those of agents with no access to international capital markets, and that such relaxation might lead to faster growth, but might also generate financial fragility. The previous section investigates whether these aggregate effects of currency mismatch are present in the data. This

[21] These controls include the log of the initial per capita PPP-adjusted GDP, the age dependency ratio, the ratio of investment-to-GDP, the ratio of trade-to-GDP, the inflation rate, the growth rate of the terms of trade, and a dummy variable for Europe. The period starts in 2000, because of missing values for the currency mismatch measure in earlier years. For 2009, we include projections from the IMF's WEO database. The change in the currency mismatch is for the period 2000–2008 (the results are robust if we limit the whole sample to the period 2000–2008).

Table 6. Currency mismatch and long-run growth in emerging economies, 2000–2009

Change in currency mismatch	0.03**	0.02**	0.02**	0.02**	0.02**
	(0.01)	(0.01)	(0.01)	(0.01)	(0.01)
Initial per capita GDP	−1.10	−1.04***	−1.11**	−1.21**	−1.68***
	(0.68)	(0.37)	(0.38)	(0.47)	(0.41)
Age dependency ratio		−0.10***	−0.09***	−0.09***	−0.12***
		(0.02)	(0.02)	(0.03)	(0.03)
Investment/GDP		0.18***	0.19***	0.19***	0.13**
		(0.04)	(0.04)	(0.05)	(0.05)
Trade/GDP		−0.01	−0.01	−0.01	−0.01
		(0.006)	(0.006)	(0.007)	(0.007)
Inflation rate		0.03	0.00	−0.01	0.02
		(0.03)	(0.03)	(0.05)	(0.05)
Growth of terms of trade			0.10	0.12	0.08
			(0.09)	(0.09)	(0.09)
Europe dummy				0.32	−0.23
				(0.85)	(0.95)
Change in external debt/GDP					0.02
					(0.01)
Adjusted R^2	0.1	0.68	0.68	0.67	0.71
Observations	29	29	29	29	29

Note: Cross-country regressions, for the period 2000–2009 (projections from the IMF's WEO database for 2009). The dependent variable is average real GDP per capita PPP-adjusted growth. Currency mismatch is measured as explained in the text and the appendix. All other data are from the IMF World Economic Outlook database (October 2009), except of the trade share, external debt and the age dependency rate, which are from the World Bank's World Development Indicators. The sample includes 29 emerging economies: Argentina, Brazil, Bulgaria, Bosnia and Herzegovina, China, Costa Rica, Croatia, Czech Rep., Egypt, Estonia, Guatemala, Hungary, Indonesia, Kazakhstan, Latvia, Lithuania, Mexico, Peru, Philippines, Poland, Romania, Russia, Serbia, Thailand, Turkey, Ukraine, Uruguay and Venezuela, and Vietnam (Argentina, drops from the sample because we do not have data for recent years). Heteroscedasticity-consistent standard errors in parentheses.

*, **, and *** indicate statistical significance at the 10, 5 and 1% level, respectively.

section investigates whether the theoretical mechanism is operative at the microeconomic level. Namely, the section investigates whether currency mismatch relaxes borrowing constraints and increases growth across sets of firms that arguably are the most credit constrained – that is, small firms in non-tradables sectors – but not across large firms.

In our model, currency mismatch increases growth because domestically oriented firms in financially constrained sectors that take on currency mismatch: (1) face lower interest rates; and (2) grow faster than similar firms with no currency mismatch. Here, we examine whether during tranquil times firms with a currency mismatch face lower borrowing costs and grow faster than firms with similar characteristics, but without a currency mismatch.

For the firm-level regressions to be consistent with the model, it is necessary that firms with similar characteristics choose different levels of currency mismatch. This dichotomy emerges in the risky equilibrium of our model because in such equilibrium there can exist a small subset of borrowers that choose not to take on currency mismatch. This is because while a majority of borrowers expect a bailout in case of crisis, this minority set does not expect a bailout. As long as this subset is small enough, a risky equilibrium exists because a bailout will indeed be granted during a crisis – as a critical mass of borrowers will default. It follows that in a risky equilibrium there can be two firms with the same observable characteristics, but with different bailout expectations. One firm will take on currency mismatch and enjoy lower interest rates than the other firm that does not take on currency mismatch, and so will be able to grow faster during no-crisis times. The firm-level regressions in this section assess whether this difference in interest rates and growth is present in the data, after controlling for a large number of observable firm characteristics.

The sample includes about 10,000 firms in Central and Eastern Europe and in former Soviet republics, surveyed by the EBRD in 2005 and 2008 through the BEEPS.[22] An advantage of this survey over existing stock-market based data sets is that it is representative of all sectors in the economy and covers stock-market listed as well as non-listed firms.[23] A drawback, however, could be that the information on sales and terms of borrowing have been collected through questionnaires and interviews, rather than observed in audited balance sheets and financial statements.[24]

We proceed in three steps. First, we form subsets of firms with similar characteristics and identify firms for which currency mismatch is clearly observable. Second, we analyse the link between currency mismatch and the terms of borrowing. And third, we measure the effect of currency mismatch on firm growth, while controlling for a large number of factors that could also determine the decision to borrow in foreign currency and firm performance. We use two empirical approaches: a simple linear regression framework and a propensity score matching technique that explicitly accounts for the possible endogeneity of currency denomination.

Most of the results are based on the 2005 BEEPS. However, we also take advantage of the 2008 survey to estimate a panel regression and look at the impact of currency mismatch in 2004–2005 on the growth performance of firms during 2005–2008.[25]

5.1. Sets of firms with currency mismatch

We classify a firm as having currency mismatch if it has debt denominated in foreign currency that is not backed by foreign revenues. In order to make meaningful inferences, we analyse the effects of currency mismatch across sets of firms with

[22] Table B2, panel 2 (in Appendix B) presents the descriptive statistics for the variables used in the regression analysis of this section.

[23] Much of the literature on the impact of currency mismatch in Latin America and East Asia (e.g. Allayanis *et al.*, 2003; Bleakey and Cowan, 2006, 2009) uses samples of firms listed in the stock market and concludes that balance sheet effects associated with currency mismatch was a relatively minor issue. An exception is Kamil (2010) who uses a sample of listed and non-listed firms in Latin America and finds that pegged regimes are associated with a higher degree of currency mismatch. This later finding suggests that pegged regimes, by providing an implicit guarantee, encourages risk-taking, as our theoretical mechanism implies.

[24] Note our dataset benefits from some recent cleaning of the 2005 sales data performed by the World Bank, when the 2002–2008 panel version of the BEEPS data was put together.

[25] We do not use the 2002 EBRD survey, because the question about foreign currency debt was different (see below).

similar characteristics, and test whether the effect of currency mismatch is stronger in certain subsets of firms. To this end, we consider only firms with debt on their books, and partition this set into different subsets that capture the sector, size and access to external finance.

With respect to the sector, we consider two sets of firms with currency mismatch: firms with sales that come only from non-tradables sectors and firms that do not export.[26] In the second set, the lack of foreign currency revenues is determined by the lack of exports, which could be correlated with firm-specific characteristics that are related to performance and access to financial markets.[27] Because of this, we take the set of non-tradables firms to be our preferred set. Furthermore, since firms in non-tradables sectors can have some exports – e.g., tourism – we also consider a third more restricted set of non-tradables firms with zero exports. Within each of these three sets of firms, we consider two subsets. The first set includes firms with debt denominated in foreign currency, which form the 'treated group'. The second set includes firms with debt denominated in domestic currency, which form the 'control group'.

Regarding size, we partition the set of firms according to whether they are small – have less than 100 employees – or they are large – have more than 100 employees. The small firms are the most likely to be credit constrained and dependent on bank financing.

Regarding access to external finance, we partition the set into those firms that are either listed in the stock market or are state-owned, and those firms that are privately held.[28] Listed firms have direct access to financing through equity markets. State-owned or quasi-public firms could also have access to special sources and terms of borrowing.

The 2005 survey includes 10,421 firms in 28 countries,[29] 3,910 of which have at least one loan on their book: 2,955 firms have their last loan denominated in domestic currency and 955 firms in foreign currency. Out of this sample, 1,772 firms are in the non-tradables sector, 2,739 are small firms, 2,545 do not export and 3,325 firms are privately held and not listed.

The 2005 EBRD survey reports only the currency denomination of the last loan for firms that have at least one loan on their books. We therefore assume that the denomination of the last loan reflects the denomination of the debt stock. Although this could be considered to be a strong assumption, the survey information on the last loan may be more reliable than information on the debt stock, with the latter

[26] The list of non-tradables sectors is presented in Table A1 in the unpublished appendix. The largest non-tradables sectors by number of firms are wholesale retail and repair, and construction.

[27] This is the selection into exports effect (see Melitz, 2003).

[28] There are very few non-tradables firms with less than 100 employees that are listed.

[29] Albania, Armenia, Azerbaijan, Belarus, Bosnia & Herzegovina, Bulgaria, Croatia, Czech Rep., Estonia, Macedonia FYR, Georgia, Hungary, Kazakhstan, Kyrgyz, Latvia, Lithuania, Moldova, Montenegro, Poland, Romania, Russia, Serbia, Slovakia, Slovenia, Tajikistan, Turkey, Ukraine and Uzbekistan.

possibly based on the memory of those answering the survey rather than on actual data.[30] One could also consider the results as evidence from a cross-section on the determinants of the latest borrowing terms – interest rate and maturity – based on actual (last) loans, rather than 'average information' on borrowing conditions during recent years. For similar reasons, for example, the Survey of Small Business Finances (SSBF) performed by the US Federal Reserve also asks only the information on the last loan. However, one potential pitfall when we analyse the link between currency mismatch and growth in sales between two periods is that the last loan might have been contracted after the initial period. For this reason, we perform a robustness test computing growth in sales between 2005 and 2008, and using the last loan reported in the 2005 survey.

5.2. Empirical methodology

We identify the theoretical mechanism by analysing the differential effect of currency mismatch across different sets of firms. In particular, we consider the set of small non-tradables firms, a set in which, arguably, currency mismatch relaxes borrowing constraints the most. Challenges in identifying the impact of currency mismatch on the borrowing conditions and performance of firms include dealing with possible endogeneity and omitted variable biases and with the non-randomness of the choice of currency denomination. In particular, one would need to control for variables that jointly determine the choice of currency denomination and the terms of borrowing, or firm performance. Our identifying assumption is that after controlling for observable characteristics, there is an unobservable random component that affects the choice of currency mismatch and is uncorrelated with future growth performance. In our model, this unobservable component corresponds to differences in bailout expectations.

We start our empirical exercise by running two sets of linear regressions. In the first set, we regress the interest rate and the maturity of the loan on an indicator of currency mismatch and a set of firm-specific and loan-specific variables. In the second set, we run standard firm-level growth regressions with two alternative sets of control variables. In addition, we include a large array of fixed effects. We control for country-specific fixed effects, industry-specific fixed effects and, in the most stringent configuration, for country-industry fixed effects. The latter fixed effects control for the demand for goods and services in a specific industry and in a specific country. This is especially relevant for non-tradables firms whose demand is essentially domestic.

In order to address some of the shortcomings of the linear regression framework and to test for a causal relationship between currency mismatch and terms of

[30] Indeed, the answer to this question in the 2005 survey seems more reliable than the more general question asked in the 2002 survey, which was about the share of foreign currency borrowing in the stock of debt.

borrowing or firms' performance, we implement a *propensity score matching procedure* (PSM). This procedure is designed to explicitly match firms that are similar in their likelihood of having a currency mismatch. The basic idea of propensity score matching is based on a simulation of a randomized experiment, in which we pair 'treated' firms with 'control' firms with similar characteristics that could affect the likelihood of having a currency mismatch and the outcome of currency mismatch. We then compare the means, across the treated and the control group, of the outcome variables of interest: interest rate, maturity, growth in sales, and growth in employment.

One desirable feature of a matching framework is that the observations used to estimate the causal effect are selected *without* reference to the outcome, as in a controlled experiment. One important assumption, however, is that, conditional on the variables used to perform the matching, the expected value of the variable of interest, in the absence of currency mismatch, would be the same for the treated and the control firms that have been paired together. If this assumption holds, we should expect to see the control firms as identical twins of the treated firms, if the latter *had not received treatment*. Thus, the difference between the treated and control firms would be an appropriate estimate of the effect of currency mismatch – the treatment effect.[31]

The basic econometric results supporting matching through a propensity score – defined as the probability of treatment conditional on the observables – are derived in Rosenbaum and Rubin (1983) and discussed in detail in the appendix of Levchenko *et al.* (2009).

5.3. Linear regression results

5.3.1. Terms of borrowing. Under our theoretical mechanism, currency mismatch enables firms to borrow at a lower interest rate by allowing their lenders to exploit the implicit subsidy in systemic bailout guarantees. In the 2005 survey, firms report the currency denomination of their last loan, as well as its other characteristics. We regress the interest rate on the last loan on the currency denomination of that loan and two sets of controls: first, firm-specific controls, such as sales and years of operations; and second, loan-specific characteristics related to the collateralization of the loan. As discussed above, each specification is estimated for a different array of fixed effects: (1) country-specific fixed effects; (2) country-specific and industry-specific fixed effects; and (3) country-industry-specific fixed effects.

Table 7 reports the results for the set of small non-tradables firms. The estimates suggest that interest rates on foreign currency loans are between 2 and 2.5% lower

[31] The PSM methodology has two major advantages over OLS: (1) The PSM allows estimation of the average impact of currency mismatch without arbitrary assumptions about functional forms and thus can account for both non-linear and interaction effects; (2) By imposing a matching – that is, certain degree of similarity between treated and control observation – the PSM methodology is likely to produce estimates that are less biased and robust to misspecification of the regression function than estimates based on full unmatched samples.

Table 7. Loan interest rate and currency mismatch

Dependent variable	Interest rate on last loan reported in 2005 BEEPS Survey					
Sample	Small firms in non-tradables sectors					
Estimation	OLS					
Currency mismatch dummy	−2.50***	−2.46***	−2.31***	−2.28***	−2.23***	−2.04***
	(0.37)	(0.37)	(0.41)	(0.4)	(0.4)	(0.44)
Log of sales (2004)	−0.29***	−0.33***	−0.37***	−0.24*	−0.27**	−0.29**
	(0.11)	(0.11)	(0.12)	(0.13)	(0.13)	(0.14)
Log of years in operation	−0.76***	−0.76***	−0.63**	−0.68**	−0.69**	−0.47
	(0.27)	(0.28)	(0.3)	(0.29)	(0.3)	(0.34)
Collateral dummy for:						
Land or building				0.46	0.48	0.56
				(0.36)	(0.37)	(0.41)
Equipment				0.011	−0.02	0.16
				(0.49)	(0.5)	(0.52)
Accounts receivable				1.17*	1.22*	1.55*
				(0.69)	(0.71)	(0.86)
Personal assets				−0.51	−0.5	−0.5
				(0.65)	(0.66)	(0.59)
Other collateral				0.42	0.46	0.16
				(0.6)	(0.61)	(0.62)
Number of firms	986	986	986	821	821	821
Adjusted R^2	0.614	0.613	0.624	0.609	0.608	0.628
Country fixed effects	Yes	Yes	No	Yes	Yes	No
Industry fixed effects	No	Yes	No	No	Yes	No
Country-industry fixed effects	No	No	Yes	No	No	Yes

Notes: The currency mismatch dummy is equal to 1 if last loan is denominated in foreign currency and 0 if last loan is denominated in domestic currency. Small firms are firms with less than 100 employees. The list of non-tradables sector is presented in Table A1 in the unpublished appendix. Heteroscedasticity robust standard errors are reported.

* Significant at 10%; ** significant at 5%; *** significant at 1%.

than the ones on domestic currency loans. This effect is significant at the 1% level and holds in all the specifications. The control variables have the expected sign, with larger and older firms paying a lower interest rate. Additional controls capturing the effect of collateral reduce the estimated difference between foreign and domestic currency interest rates by only 0.3 percentage points.[32,33]

A possibility is that the difference in interest rate between domestic and foreign currency loans reflects the expected rate of currency depreciation. In order to control for this effect, we use data on one-year ahead currency forecasts for 14 countries in Emerging Europe from Consensus Forecast, Inc. to compute domestic interest rates that are adjusted for expected currency depreciation. We then re-estimate firm-level regressions on the effect of foreign currency borrowing on

[32] Adding the maturity of the loan to the regression does not change the results. The effect of the maturity variable is close to zero and insignificant. Results are available upon request.

[33] The results in Table A2 in the unpublished appendix for the smaller set of small non-tradables privately held non-listed firms with zero exports are very similar. This is also the case for the set of non-exporting small firms in Table A3 in the appendix.

Table 8. Loan interest rate and currency mismatch; robustness: the role of exchange rate depreciation

Dependent variable	Adjusted interest rate on last loan reported in 2005 BEEPS Survey					
Sample	Small firms in non-tradables sectors					
Estimation	OLS					
Currency mismatch dummy	−3.49***	−3.47***	−3.40***	−3.12***	−3.09***	−2.76***
	(0.49)	(0.5)	(0.54)	(0.55)	(0.55)	(0.57)
Log of sales (2004)	−0.24*	−0.29**	−0.30**	−0.22	−0.27*	−0.23
	(0.12)	(0.12)	(0.13)	(0.16)	(0.15)	(0.16)
Log of years in operation	−0.94***	−0.92***	−0.91**	−0.75**	−0.72*	−0.70*
	(0.34)	(0.34)	(0.36)	(0.38)	(0.38)	(0.4)
Collateral dummy for:						
Land or building				0.028	0.012	−0.074
				(0.43)	(0.43)	(0.46)
Equipment				−0.29	−0.33	−0.39
				(0.58)	(0.59)	(0.6)
Accounts receivable				0.57	0.6	1.06
				(0.7)	(0.73)	(1.02)
Personal assets				−0.63	−0.67	−0.69
				(0.9)	(0.91)	(0.78)
Other collateral				0.33	0.42	0.13
				(0.7)	(0.72)	(0.7)
Number of firms	661	660	660	539	538	538
Adjusted R^2	0.636	0.636	0.646	0.629	0.63	0.654
Country fixed effects	Yes	Yes	No	Yes	Yes	No
Industry fixed effects	No	Yes	No	No	Yes	No
Country-industry fixed effects	No	No	Yes	No	No	Yes

Notes: The currency mismatch dummy is equal to 1 if last loan is denominated in foreign currency and 0 if last loan is denominated in domestic currency. Small firms are firms with less than 100 employees. The list of non-tradables sector is presented in Table A1 in the unpublished appendix. Heteroscedasticity robust standard errors are reported. The domestic currency interest rates have been adjusted for exchange rate depreciation using one-year ahead forecasts from Consensus Forecast Inc.

* Significant at 10%; ** significant at 5%; *** significant at 1%.

interest rate. The results are presented in Table 8. Our baseline effect – foreign currency borrowing makes foreign borrowing cheaper – is robust to this adjustment. The effect is actually slightly larger. The reason is that in 2005, market participants were on average forecasting an appreciation of many currencies in emerging Europe.

The BEEPS survey does not provide information on the size of the loan and therefore we cannot test whether currency mismatch is associated with larger loans, as our theoretical framework would predict. However, we can use the maturity of the last loan as a proxy for the 'commitment' made by the lender. We thus test whether loans associated with currency mismatch exhibit a longer maturity. We use the same specification as for the interest rate and repeat the exercise on the same three sets of firms.

The estimates confirm the role of currency mismatch in relaxing borrowing conditions. Table 9 shows that foreign currency loans to non-tradables firms have a

Table 9. Loan maturity and currency mismatch

Dependent variable	Maturity in months on last loan reported in 2005 BEEPS survey					
Sample	Small firms in non-tradables sectors					
Estimation	OLS					
Currency mismatch dummy	10.2***	10.4***	8.84***	8.28***	8.41***	6.88*
	(2.9)	(2.89)	(3.17)	(3.1)	(3.06)	(3.52)
Log of sales (2004)	−0.038	0.42	0.3	0.00087	0.44	0.65
	(0.9)	(0.9)	(1.03)	(1.05)	(1.06)	(1.28)
Log of years in operation	−2.76	−2.68	−2.56	−3.25	−2.97	−3.06
	(1.9)	(1.93)	(2.07)	(2.34)	(2.36)	(2.71)
Collateral dummy for:						
Land or building				1.21	2.11	0.32
				(3.25)	(3.33)	(3.62)
Equipment				7.55**	7.69**	5.09
				(3.62)	(3.67)	(4.21)
Accounts receivable				10.7**	10.7**	9.10*
				(4.59)	(4.68)	(5.28)
Personal assets				5.68*	5.70*	4.21
				(3.13)	(3.09)	(3.33)
Other collateral				9.07**	7.87**	6.53
				(3.95)	(3.89)	(4.53)
Number of firms	1000	998	998	831	829	829
Adjusted R^2	0.109	0.123	0.124	0.108	0.124	0.109
Country fixed effects	Yes	Yes	No	Yes	Yes	No
Industry fixed effects	No	Yes	No	No	Yes	No
Country-industry fixed effects	No	No	Yes	No	No	Yes

Notes: The currency mismatch dummy is equal to 1 if last loan is denominated in foreign currency and 0 if last loan is denominated in domestic currency. Small firms are firms with less than 100 employees. The list of non-tradables sector is presented in Table A1 in the unpublished appendix. Heteroscedasticity robust standard errors are reported.

* Significant at 10%; ** significant at 5%; *** significant at 1%.

maturity of 7 to 10 months longer than loans in domestic currency. This difference is statistically significant at the 1% level.[34]

The results presented above indicate that currency mismatch is associated with better terms of borrowing as predicted by our theoretical mechanism. The interest rate regressions are a direct test of our model. The result that risk-taking through currency mismatch is associated with lower interest rate implies that currency mismatch is associated with some form of implicit subsidy. The loan maturity regression is less of a direct test of our model and therefore alternative interpretations of the results are possible. For example, banks could be extending longer maturity loans in foreign currency because they are also funded in foreign currency at longer maturity.

[34] Similar effects are shown in Table A4 in the unpublished appendix for the set of small non-tradables privately held non-listed firms with zero exports. For the set of small non-exporting firms, the difference in maturity is 10 to 12 months, as shown in Table A5 in the appendix.

5.3.2. Growth in sales. Our theoretical framework implies that in tranquil times, firms with a currency mismatch outperform firms without a currency mismatch. The 2005 BEEPS allows us to test this hypothesis, as it provides the cross-sectional information on the currency denomination of the last loan, as well as time series information on three-year growth performance between 2001 and 2004. We estimate the following standard firm growth regression:

$$\ln y_{i,t} - \ln y_{i,t-3} = \ln y_{i,t-3} + \alpha CM_i + \beta X_{i,t} + \delta + \varepsilon_{i,t},$$

where $\ln y_{i,t}$ is the firm's sales, CM is a dummy variable equal to 1 if the firm's last loan is denominated in foreign currency, X is a set of firm-specific control variables, δ is a set of fixed effects and $\varepsilon_{i,t}$ is the residual error term. Three combinations of fixed-effects are introduced: country-specific fixed effects, country- and industry-specific fixed effects, and country-industry fixed effects. Two sets of controls are considered. The simple control set includes firm's years of operations and initial sales. The comprehensive control set includes initial productivity, the share of foreign inputs in total production inputs and two measures of the quality of the workforce: the share of skilled workers and the share of workers with a university degree.[35]

Table 10 presents the results for the sample of small non-tradables firms. The first three regressions are performed with the simple control set for the three combinations of fixed effects. The next three regressions include the comprehensive set of control variables. In all regressions, the currency mismatch indicator is positive and statistically significant at either the 1 or 5% level. On average, firms with a currency mismatch outperform firms without a currency mismatch by 6.6 to 8.8 percentage points, which are 2.2 to 2.9 percentage points per year. Similar estimates are obtained for the smaller set of small, non-listed and privately held non-tradables firms, with no exports.[36]

While results for the set of small non-exporting firms broadly confirm the above findings, the growth effect of currency mismatch is reduced by around half and is only significant in 3 out of 6 regressions.[37] This result could be driven by non-exporting firms in the manufacturing sector. The lack of exports in a manufacturing sector firm could be associated with a lower growth potential. Arguably such firms benefit less from investing and taking on risk through currency mismatch.

5.3.3. Large firms. Large firms are less likely than small firms to be credit constrained. Thus, under our theoretical mechanism, taking on currency mismatch should have less pronounced effects in large non-tradables firms than in small non-tradables firms. The estimates in Table 11 clearly show that this is the case. In the

[35] The share of foreign input is likely to be a determinant of foreign currency loans.

[36] See Table A6 in the unpublished appendix.

[37] See Table A7 in the unpublished appendix.

Table 10. Growth in sales and currency mismatch

Dependent variable	Growth in sales between 2001 and 2004					
Sample	Small firms in non-tradables sectors					
Estimation	OLS					
Currency mismatch dummy	0.087***	0.081**	0.088**	0.070**	0.066**	0.070**
	(0.032)	(0.032)	(0.035)	(0.033)	(0.033)	(0.035)
Initial log of sales (2001)	−0.041***	−0.041***	−0.045***	−0.019*	−0.021*	−0.025**
	(0.0099)	(0.01)	(0.011)	(0.011)	(0.012)	(0.012)
Log of years in operation	−0.026	−0.025	−0.018	−0.047*	−0.045*	−0.031
	(0.025)	(0.025)	(0.027)	(0.026)	(0.026)	(0.028)
Initial labour productivity				−0.062***	−0.057***	−0.056***
Log(Sales/Employment) in 2001				(0.017)	(0.018)	(0.02)
Share of foreign input in production				0.0011***	0.0011***	0.0012***
				(0.00038)	(0.00041)	(0.00043)
Share of employees with a university degree				0.0013***	0.0013**	0.0012**
				(0.00047)	(0.0005)	(0.00054)
Share of skilled workers				0.024	0.019	−0.0083
				(0.047)	(0.048)	(0.051)
Number of firms	1010	1008	1008	955	953	953
Adjusted R^2	0.049	0.051	0.06	0.073	0.072	0.081
Country fixed effects	Yes	Yes	No	Yes	Yes	No
Industry fixed effects	No	Yes	No	No	Yes	No
Country-industry fixed effects	No	No	Yes	No	No	Yes

Notes: Growth in sales is defined as log difference in sales between 2004 and 2001. The currency mismatch dummy is equal to 1 if last loan is denominated in foreign currency and 0 if last loan is denominated in domestic currency. Small firms are firms with less than 100 employees. The list of non-tradables sectors is presented in Table A1 in the unpublished appendix. Heteroscedasticity robust standard errors are reported.

* Significant at 10%; ** significant at 5%; *** significant at 1%.

Table 11. Interest rate, growth in sales and currency mismatch; estimation on a sample of large firms

Panel A: Interest rate

Dependent variable	Interest rate on last loan reported in 2005 BEEPS Survey		
Sample	Large firms in non-tradables sector		
Estimation	OLS		
Currency mismatch dummy	0.47	0.5	1.49
	(1.31)	(1.32)	(1.68)
Log of sales (2004)	−0.41	−0.67**	−0.47
	(0.32)	(0.31)	(0.34)
Log of years in operation	−0.057	−0.14	0.19
	(0.47)	(0.5)	(0.62)
Number of firms	228	228	228
Adjusted R^2	0.54	0.543	0.605
Country fixed effects	Yes	Yes	No
Industry fixed effectd	No	Yes	No
Country-industry fixed effects	No	No	Yes

Panel B: Growth in sales

Dependant variable	Growth in sales between 2001 and 2004		
Sample	Large firms in non-tradables sector		
Estimation	OLS		
Currency mismatch dummy	−0.02	−0.022	−0.015
	(0.043)	(0.049)	(0.061)
Initial log of sales (2001)	−0.084***	−0.088***	−0.10***
	(0.023)	(0.023)	(0.036)
Log of years in operation	−0.11***	−0.11***	−0.14***
	(0.031)	(0.032)	(0.044)
Number of firms	233	233	233
Adjusted R^2	0.196	0.189	0.126
Country fixed effects	Yes	Yes	No
Industry fixed effects	No	Yes	No
Country-industry fixed effects	No	No	Yes

Notes: The currency mismatch dummy is equal to 1 if last loan is denominated in foreign currency and 0 if last loan is denominated in domestic currency. Growth in sales is defined as the log difference in sales between 2004 and 2001. Large firms are firms with more than 100 employees. The list of non-tradables sector is presented in Table A1 in the unpublished appendix. Heteroscedasticity robust standard errors are reported.

* Significant at 10%; ** significant at 5%; *** significant at 1%.

set of large non-tradables firms, currency mismatch does not have a statistically significant impact on the interest rate paid by firms or their growth performance.

This finding is consistent with the literature on firm size and credit constraints. Guiso *et al.* (2004) find that financial development helps small firms more than large firms in Italy. Beck *et al.* (2005) using survey data find that the negative impact of reported obstacles on firm growth is stronger for small firms than large firms. Beck *et al.* (2008) using cross-industry, cross-country data, find that financial development exerts a disproportionately positive effect on small firms.

5.3.4. Robustness tests. *Uneven sampling.* A potential issue is the uneven sampling of firms with respect to the population of firms across different countries. We propose here a test of robustness of our results to uneven sampling that follows Wooldridge (2001, ch. 17).

Since we do not have information of firm demographics for many of the countries in the sample, we characterize over and under sampling in terms of the share of the labour force surveyed. First, we compute for each country the total number of employees in the firms surveyed. Second, we compute the ratio of the surveyed labour force to the total labour force in each country using World Development Indicator data for 2005. Third, we re-estimate our baseline regressions for interest rates and sales using a weighted least square estimator (WLS), using as weights the inverse of the ratio of surveyed to total labour force. The results confirm the findings of OLS regressions.[38]

Reverse causality. Because we regress past growth in sales on the maturity on the last loan, our growth results are subject to potential reverse causality running from growth performance to currency denomination of loans. To address this issue, we combine in a single panel the 2005 and the 2008 surveys, retaining only firms that have been surveyed in both surveys. An advantage of this approach is that we can assess the growth performance of firms that had a currency mismatch in 2004 over the subsequent period 2004–2007. As currency mismatch is predetermined in this case, this robustness test controls for potential reverse causality. A drawback is that by combining the two panels, the number of firms is reduced from 998 to 241 in the case of small non-tradables firms. Moreover, the inclusion of firms in both surveys may not be random. Note also that having initial currency mismatch does not fully solve for endogeneity, as unobserved information on future growth potential can affect current borrowing choices.

We estimate specifications for the set of small non-tradable firms (including country-specific fixed effects or country-specific fixed effects and industry-specific fixed effects), and the set of small, non-listed, privately held non-tradables firms. In all specifications, firms with a currency mismatch at the beginning of the period experience a much stronger growth performance in the subsequent period, confirming the above results. This effect is significant at the 1% level and it is three times larger than the above estimates.[39]

[38] See Table A9 in the unpublished appendix.

[39] See Table A10 in the unpublished appendix.

5.4. Propensity score matching results

The linear regression framework deals with selection issues by including control variables and fixed effects. Therefore the results might not be robust in the presence of non-linear and interaction effects. In contrast, propensity score matching by explicitly matching firms that are similar in their likelihood of having a currency mismatch does not impose any functional form.

The propensity matching procedure follows three steps. In the first step, we use a logit model to estimate the probabilities of a currency mismatch, which we call the propensity scores, for the sample of small non-tradables firms. The logit is based on firms' characteristics and fixed effects.[40] Next, following Dehejia and Wahba (2002), we group observations into intervals with similar propensity scores – referred to as propensity score strata – and test whether the means of each right-hand side variable do not differ across treated and non-treated units within each stratum.[41] In the third step, we construct the relevant control group for each treated firm using a proximity measure based on propensity scores and compare the mean of the outcome variables of interest for the treated and the control group.[42] For the proximity measure, we use the kernel matching estimator proposed by Heckman *et al.* (1998).

The results are presented in Table 12 and indicate for each outcome – growth in sales, employment, interest rate and maturity – the difference in means for the treated group and the control group. Two control groups are considered: (1) a 'naïve' control group that includes all firms without currency mismatch and thus does not deal with selection issues, and (2) the matching-based control group. When the matching-based control group is used, the difference in means of outcome between the treated and control group measures the average treatment effect on the treated group.

For the growth in sales, the mean differences are similar for both control groups. The matching estimator reports a 7.9 percentage points difference between treated and control firms, which is 2.6 percentage points per year. This estimate is strikingly similar to the estimates obtained in the linear regressions. For the growth in employment, accounting for selection reduces the difference between control and treated groups from 14 to 10 percentage points. However, the difference remains statistically significant at the 10% level. For the interest rate, matching similar leads to a higher difference in interest rates between treated and control firms (2.7 versus 1.8%). For the maturity, the average treatment of treated firms is 10 months and is statistically significant at the 1% level.

[40] To make the results comparable with the results from the linear regression, we use the same set of control variables in the logit specification: years of operations, past sales and country-fixed effects. The specification is consistent with the findings of Brown *et al.* (2009), who stress the importance of country-specific factors in explaining foreign currency borrowing. Similar results are obtained with country-industry fixed effect.

[41] This is a test of the *balancing hypothesis*, which needs to be verified for the Rosenbaum and Rubin (1983) theorem to be valid.

[42] The resulting effect is called the average treatment on treated.

Table 12. Propensity score matching estimation results

Outcome variable	Mean treated group	Mean unmatched control group	Mean matched control group	Difference treated – unmatched	Difference treated – matched: average treatment on treated
Mean growth in sales (2001–2004)	0.167	0.101	0.087	0.066** (0.031)	0.079** (0.038)
Mean growth in employment (2001–2004)	0.239	0.091	0.133	0.147*** (0.0493)	0.105* (0.057)
Interest rate on lost loan (2005)	12.7	14.69	15.51	−1.99*** (0.584)	−2.81*** (0.681)
Maturity of last loan (2005)	39.88	29.78	29.76	10.09*** (2.56)	10.12*** (3.49)

	Treated units	Control unit	Total
Number of observations with common PSM support	200	687	887

Notes: The PSM estimation is based on propensity scores estimated from a logit regression of currency mismatch on sales and years of operations and country-specific effects. The matching procedure used the kernel estimator of Heckman *et al.* (1998). The sample includes the small firms (less than 100 employees) in non-tradable sectors. Standard errors are in parentheses next to the corresponding coefficients.

* Significant at 10%; ** significant at 5%; *** significant at 1%.

In order to understand the role played by the matching procedure and the correction for the selection effect, we can compare the PSM results to the results obtained by using an unmatched control group. In this case, the effect on sales is slightly lower (+6.6 percentage points versus +7.0 percentage points) as well as the effect on interest rate (−1.99 percentage points versus −2.81 percentage points).

In sum, the results obtained with the PSM method point in the same direction as the regression results. Under both methods, taking on currency mismatch reduces the interest costs of firms and improves their growth performance.

6. CONCLUSIONS AND POLICY IMPLICATIONS

This paper has explored the dual role of currency mismatch. On the one hand, taking on currency risk relaxes borrowing constraints and could have a positive impact on growth. On the other hand, it could be a source of systemic risk, as it makes large parts of the economy prone to a crisis in case of a real depreciation. At the aggregate level, we found that increases in currency mismatch are associated with faster economic growth, even after we control for the recent crisis and its growth costs. At the firm level, we found that currency mismatch helps constrained firms that otherwise would not have been able to fund profitable projects – small firms and the non-tradables sector.

This evidence, however, does not justify either excessive risk taking or a lack of financial regulation. Large increases in currency mismatch in relatively financially developed countries – such as Poland or the Czech Republic – will not necessarily lead to faster growth. Furthermore, lending booms that simply finance consumption or overinvestment are not desirable. Indeed, we find groups of firms for which undertaking currency mismatch is not associated with faster growth – large firms in the non-tradables sector – or for which the growth effect is considerably smaller and in some cases insignificant – non-exporting firms in the manufacturing sector. Therefore, currency mismatch should be considered as a second-best, allowing financially constrained sectors to borrow and finance potentially profitable projects. The first-best is better enforceability of contracts that help deepen financial markets.

Systemic bailout guarantees, which are a key assumption of the theoretical framework in the paper, are often implicit. In the face of generalized defaults, governments face enormous pressure for a bailout regardless of whether a too-big-to-fail firm goes bust or a critical mass of small borrowers does so. This endogeneity has been revealed by the fact that all crisis-hit countries in emerging Europe granted bailouts despite differences in their policy regimes. Bailouts took several forms and were financed with the help of IMF and EU loans, foreign governments' support as well as private sector involvement through the 'Vienna initiative'. Very much like in the spirit of our model, this initiative was launched when it appeared that the depth of the crisis would depend on coordination – or lack of thereof – between lenders. The Vienna initiative avoided the halt of new lending and the fire-sale of assets that would have followed had banks pulled out of a country in panic (Berglöf, 2009). Foreign mother banks agreed to roll over the exposure of their subsidiaries in emerging Europe, as the IMF made loans and the EBRD made bank equity injections de facto contingent on agreements to rollover bank debt. In addition, the countries of the mother banks' allowed them to use some of the national bailout money to recapitalize their subsidiaries in Eastern Europe. In some countries, such as Latvia, the bailout took the form of supporting an otherwise unsustainable currency peg. The use of international reserves to defend the currency is analogous to a bailout, as it allows creditors to exit the country without suffering the effect of currency depreciation.

The bailout, however, has not prevented a credit crunch. While domestic firms' balance sheets were not directly hit by a large nominal depreciation and generalized bankruptcies did not take place, the expectation of future real appreciation ceased to exist. As the theoretical section of this paper explains, a lending boom equilibrium with an appreciating real exchange rate is supported by – implicit or explicit – systemic bailout guarantees. After the crisis, the likelihood of a new bailout in case of a future crisis fell considerably, and so borrowing constraints became tighter. A downward feedback-loop mechanism started: less credit leads to less demand for non-tradables, like real estate, which in turn puts downward pressure on non-tradables prices, which reduces collateral values, which further reduces credit, and so on. The Vienna Initiative has successfully avoided a sharp real depreciation and generalized bankruptcies. However, one should not expect that it will stop the credit crunch, the associated real depreciation and the decline of the non-tradables sector relative to the tradables sector that typically occurs during a crisis.

Although the experience of emerging Europe has some parallels with the dollarization of Argentina in 1990s, there are fundamental differences. Dollarization regimes were introduced in Latin America to impose fiscal discipline by limiting the ability of governments to influence the monetary base. As we now know, these policies generally failed to generate fiscal discipline in those countries. Although some emerging European economies did have currency boards or fixed regimes, some others had floating regimes. Moreover, in both cases, fiscal deficits remained under control before the crisis, while some economies even had surpluses.

A lesson from emerging Europe is that to avoid excessive crisis costs, governments should have enough reserves – or have lined up external lines of credit – to cover the potential rollover requirements of the financial system that would realize if a crisis were to materialize. These lines of credit permit fiscally sound governments to smooth the effects of rare financial crises by allowing them to access financing and repaying by taxing during good times.

Using our *de facto* measure we have found that currency mismatches tend to be much larger than other measures that do not control for indirect mismatches in the banks' balance sheets. It follows that in assessing systemic risk, policy-makers should monitor not only mismatches in banks' balance sheets, but should also look for indirect imbalances via the ability of banks' borrowers to repay debts.

Even if some degree of macro-prudential regulation to limit foreign currency borrowing might appear desirable to avoid excessive risk-taking, its implementation is far from straightforward. In the presence of incentives to take on excessive risk, agents will eventually find ways around regulations. Indeed, prudential regulations in emerging Europe before the crisis required banks to match their foreign currency assets and liabilities and were formally satisfied by banks, as they were borrowing and lending in foreign currency. However, many of the recipients of such bank loans were not hedged. When regulators in some countries identified this indirect exposure of banks to exchange rate risks, they imposed stricter prudential regulations, reserve requirements, and direct restrictions on foreign currency borrowing by banks – for example, in Croatia and in Romania – and, in some cases, on the amount of foreign currency loans or total credit that banks could extend – for example, in Bulgaria and in Croatia. Interestingly, banks often responded to such restrictions by helping their customers receive direct loans abroad – often with a letter of guarantee. From a systemic perspective, it made no difference whether the foreign currency loan came directly from abroad or was intermediated through domestic banks. As this paper has argued, the driving force was the underlying incentives for such currency mismatch, such as bailout guarantees.

Finally, an inconvenient paradox of financial regulation is that it could reach the wrong target, harming the more financially constrained agents in the economy – those benefiting the most from risk-taking – without disciplining the agents that are the source of excessive risk-taking.[43] Following the recent crisis, governments around the world are considering new financial regulations to address systemic risks. At the same time, credit for new firms with investment opportunities that could help spur economic growth remains limited. Therefore, a key challenge for new regulations is to avoid strangling healthy risk-taking by bank-dependent firms.

Discussion

Volker Nocke

University of Mannheim, CESifo and CEPR

This is an interesting and topical paper. It contains at least two potentially important contributions. First, it provides a new index of aggregate currency mismatch that takes into account the currency mismatch of creditors in the non-financial sector. Second, it reports very interesting correlations of currency mismatch and growth, both at the firm level and the country level. In the non-tradables sector, firms that take on foreign currency loans seem to grow faster than firms that do not. Similarly, countries with a greater level of aggregate currency mismatch seem to grow faster than countries with a smaller level of aggregate currency mismatch, even when taking into account the induced increase in the likelihood of a severe crisis.

As regards the first contribution, the new index has its limitations and problems, as every index has. For instance, the index does not take into account the riskiness of a foreign currency loan at the firm level. A firm may take on an unhedged foreign currency loan but the extent to which this loan is risky depends on the firm's characteristics (such as its income stream and asset level), all of which are not observed by the authors. Nevertheless, the index seems to be a clear improvement over what is out there in the literature. As such it should be of great interest to policy-makers and researchers.

As to the second contribution, I find the reported correlations very intriguing. But, to my mind, there remain at least two open issues. First, while the proposed theoretical mechanism seems very plausible, it does not convincingly account for firm-level differences. Second, it seems unclear to me whether there is indeed a causal link between currency mismatch and growth and, if so, whether it is in the asserted direction.

[43] See Forbes (2007) for a demonstration of this point in the case of Chile.

Let me begin with the first issue. The theoretical model assumes that all firms are homogeneous and thus remains silent as to why some firms take on foreign-currency loans (and invest more) while others do not (and invest less). Now, the authors suggest that if firms had different expectations about the probability of a bailout in case of a crisis, then otherwise identical firms would choose different levels of currency mismatch. I do not find this argument very persuasive, for two reasons. From a theory point of view, the argument is unsatisfactory as it leaves unexplained why different firms should have different expectations. In any case, it is not a 'deep' explanation. But more importantly, it seems to me that the argument is inconsistent with the model. What matters for the market interest rates are not the expectations of firms (creditors) but the expectations of banks (lenders). If some banks expect a bailout in the event of a crisis, then competition between them forces them to offer low interest rates for foreign currency loans, and firms will find these loans very attractive even if they do not expect a bailout. According to the model, lenders benefit only indirectly – through lower interest rates – when governments grant bailout guarantees to lenders: for a given interest rate and a given crisis probability, the pay-off of a firm is independent of any bailout payment.

Let me now turn to the second, closely related issue. At the firm level, all that is shown is a positive correlation between currency mismatch and firm growth. Very little is observed about individual firms, and the empirical strategy does not account for unobserved firm-level heterogeneity. Moreover, as discussed above, the underlying theoretical framework does not allow for observed nor unobserved firm heterogeneity. As a microeconomic theorist, I am therefore not sure how to interpret the empirical results. At the country level, the model explains differences in growth performance and currency mismatch by different countries being in different equilibria. Is this really all that is going on? I would like to see more evidence that differences in currency mismatch do indeed drive the differences in growth rates rather than some other factors.

To conclude, this is an impressive piece of work that should be of great interest to policy-makers and researchers. I can see many exciting avenues for future research, both at the theory and empirical level.

Enrique Alberola and Pedro del Rio

Banco de España[44]

The paper by Ranciere, Tornell and Vamvakidis is an important contribution to the literature of financial stability as it constructs a novel and improved index of currency mismatches. The new index takes into account not only the direct

[44] With the technical support of Alvaro Claudio. The opinions of the authors are not necessarily those of their institution.

exposure of banks to exchange rate risk (via their net open positions) but also the indirect channel through the exposure of households and firms that are not hedged against exchange rate risks.

This is the key contribution of the paper, as it helps capture the whole spectrum of systemic exchange rate risks for a country, of particular importance in emerging Europe. It is also original in the literature due to the lack of readily available data. To highlight the relevance of the indirect exposure of banks to exchange rate risks – through the exposure of unhedged borrowers – it is sufficient to note that the average measure of currency mismatch in emerging Europe increases by 23 percentage points (and by 40–60 percentage points in Latvia and Estonia).

In general terms, the construction of the index of currency mismatch is adequate and it helps capture the total vulnerability of countries to exchange rate risk. However, it can be said that it is still built over some optimistic assumptions: for instance, it is assumed that exporting firms are completely hedged because they receive their revenues in foreign currencies, but it obviates that exporting firms' revenues fall during recessions, making it less likely that they can afford to repay their debts. As a matter of fact, during the global financial crisis, the problem of these countries did not come through exchange rate depreciations, but through economic recession and financial crunch, refuting that assumption. Another disputable assumption is that the share of households in one economy that is hedged is similar to the share of hedged firms in that economy, when it is quite likely that it will be substantially lower. These problems are difficult to overcome due to the lack of available data, but they open new avenues of research by using, for instance, survey measures. In any case, the authors rightly make an effort to check the robustness of the results by considering alternative assumptions (for instance, they suppose that households are not hedged at all).

The risks from currency mismatches are manifold. From a financial stability perspective, while direct market exchange rate risk faced by banks can be controlled through hedging or regulation, banks would still face the indirect exchange rate risk through currency mismatches on their borrowers' balance sheets. A significant depreciation of the local currency would translate into a deterioration of the debt-servicing capacity of unhedged borrowers. In the case that a large part of the private sector was negatively affected, it could pose a systemic financial stability risk for the country if the exchange rate shock was sufficiently large or if it was compounded by an increase in interest rates on foreign currency loans. Additionally, as a consequence of a significant deterioration of the quality of foreign currency loan portfolios, banks may be significantly exposed to earnings risk, through a significant decrease in interest income, and to funding risk, as they have to rollover existing funding over the duration of the loan portfolio while funds available for repayment of its own liabilities are decreased by loan arrears.

From a macroeconomic point of view, there is a risk that foreign currency lending may lead to excessive credit growth during boom periods, for instance if a potential appreciation of the domestic currency creates an additional wealth effect, increasing the demand for new foreign currency loans. This stimulates aggregate demand and may lead to the overheating of the economy, external imbalances, private sector excessive indebtedness, and vulnerability to external financing. Subsequently, when the cycle busts it leads to larger credit squeezes.

But also as a consequence of a high level of foreign currency denominated loans, the room for monetary policy manoeuvre and the effectiveness of monetary policy to affect domestic economy can be limited. For example, loans in foreign currency weaken monetary transmission mechanisms. Perhaps more importantly, central banks have to take into account potential adverse financial stability implications of a reduction in policy rates, as they put downward pressure on the exchange rate and negatively affect balance sheets. Additionally, a high proportion of foreign currency loans may perpetuate fixed exchange rate regimes, which could be inappropriate for the needs of the country concerned, and it also affects other policies requiring, for instance, a tighter fiscal stance.

Finally, problems with currency mismatches are not restricted to the host countries. Home countries of parent banks can also suffer the financial stability consequences of deteriorating loan portfolios of the subsidiaries. And these and other countries' taxpayers, together with international financial institutions, have to bear also the costs of possible bailouts of banking sectors.

The conceptual framework of the paper, built on the theoretical model of Schneider and Tornell (2004) and Ranciere and Tornell (2009) challenges this 'conventional wisdom', showing that it can be optimal for lenders and borrowers to take on currency mismatch risk if there are two imperfections in financial markets: (1) contract enforceability problems which generate borrowing constraints; and (2) systemic guarantees to bail out lenders which makes currency mismatch attractive. This is a nice and reasonable model which operates via a simple and quite plausible mechanism, although there could also be other alternative channels, for example through currency bets based on expectations of exchange rate appreciation or of the stability of exchange rate pegs (credibility effects, euro adoption expectations). Indeed, in practice the reality in emerging Europe operated in a slightly different way, as there was not an internal bailout but a resort to external support (EU and IMF) with a mechanism to overcome coordination failures (the Vienna Initiative). Probably, this type of rescue was difficult to imagine, beforehand, but it conveys the spirit of the model indeed.

What is more questionable is that this environment is always conducive to higher economic growth. While it is clear that currency mismatches can relax borrowing constraints of firms and enhance investment growth (confirmed by the empirical evidence at the firm level), in order to generate positive (and sustainable!) effects on growth, investment must be productive. This is shown in a key sentence of the paper: '…will lead to faster economic growth…provided constrained agents have profitable investment opportunities'. Otherwise, these funds could end up being channelled to non-productive projects and even fuelling financial or real asset bubbles, with negative and protracted effects on growth not in the short run but in the medium and long run. Arguably, the wide availability of credit and the behaviour of some housing markets in Eastern Europe suggests that, to some extent, this was the case.

The empirical part of the paper offers evidence that, at the macroeconomic level, increases in currency mismatch are associated with higher growth in quiet times, but with a greater severity of crises. On net, after taking into account the crisis period, a positive link with GDP growth is found. The microeconomic evidence, at firm level analysis, also endorses this point. This conclusion is important because it supports the idea that currency mismatches are overall conducive to higher growth. For this reason, it would be convenient to consider in the empirical analysis the dramatic fall in output in emerging Europe, particularly in those countries with high currency mismatches.

A key aspect is to what extent currency mismatches have been the driving force behind boom-bust cycles in these countries: one could argue that they have contributed to a more general credit boom which affected countries with and without significant currency mismatches (see, for example, the case of Ukraine, with negative currency mismatches, but with a very large credit boom). In this sense, the paper offers a rather benign view of credit developments in these countries (as positive financial deepening), while in some cases they could rather be seen as foster imbalances (credit and housing booms, excessive reliance on external financing, overheating).

A more fundamental problem of the empirical analysis is the truncation of the sample period. In order to compute the correct size of adjustment as a result of the crisis, one needs to consider the whole adjustment period, not just 2009, as well as, ideally, potential growth rates in the medium term (which would convey the legacy of currency mismatches). To stress the point, we perform a simple exercise. If we replicate Figure 1, considering three different time periods (2004–2007 and 2008–11, with forecasts from Consensus) and splitting emerging Europe into two groups of countries – those with sizeable increases in currency mismatches and those with no or low increases – we find that the first group is the only one suffering a forecasted fall in output in the aftermath of the crises. They also display the lowest growth rate for the whole 2004–11 period, albeit marginally (see Figures 7 and 8). In order to make the point more clearly, we can make a cross-section regression of growth on mismatches, using a short sample (2004–2007) and the long forward-looking sample (2004–2011); now the positive relation vanishes. Of course, this exercise lacks rigour, since it is based on growth forecasts, which are necessarily uncertain, but it is anyway useful to make the point.

Finally, regarding the policy implications of the paper, the messages should be much more cautious. As we are all now well aware – and the authors rightly stress – there is a delicate balance between on the one hand promoting credit growth and

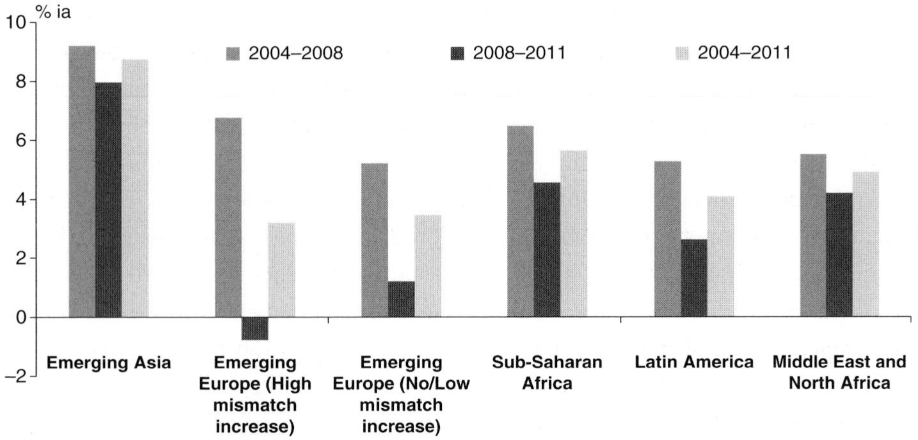

Figure 7. Real GDP grown in emerging economies, 2004–11

Notes: High mismatch increase: Romania, Estonia, Latvia, Lithuania and Bulgaria. No/low mismatch increase: Croatia, Czech Republic, Hungary, Poland and Ukraine.
Source: WEO. Emerging Europe data 2010–11: Consensus.

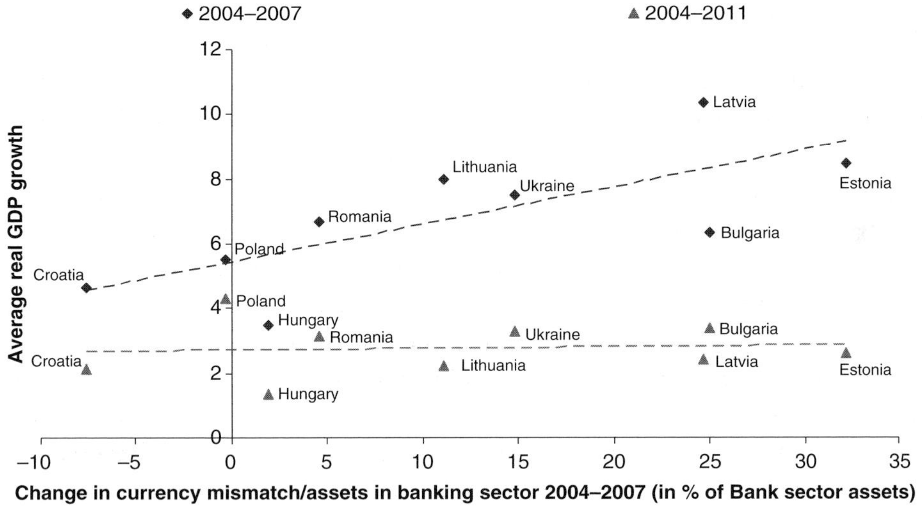

Figure 8. Currency mismatch and real GDP growth, emerging Europe

relaxing borrowing constraints and taking on too much systemic risk on the other hand. In this sense, while a too lax regulation is clearly undesirable, a too tight regulation could hinder credit growth, especially if there is a lack of local currency long-term funding. Thus, authorities should target an optimal level of foreign currency lending while also developing long-term local currency funding markets. In any case, the allocation of credit is of key importance as, in the end, what drives higher and sustainable growth are more productive investments (while in emerging Europe, an important share went to finance consumption and residential real estate).

In sum, the paper makes important contributions to the literature with the construction of a smart currency mismatch index and a theoretical model which shows the optimality of taking foreign currency loans in certain circumstances. However, its empirical results at the aggregate level still have to face the reality test, that is, the severity of adjustment in the aftermath of the crisis, which seems to be larger in high mismatch European countries. Additionally, there are other aspects of foreign currency loans that have not been considered in the paper: for instance, outsourcing the financial system may hinder domestic financial development (local markets and funding in local currency). The recent Latin American experience promoting local funding has delivered both deepened local markets and resilience to the crisis. In the EU there has been a reluctance to impose limits on foreign indebtedness and the single European financial market was at odds with barriers to external capital flows. Maybe the crisis will lead in the future to a possible shift in attitudes (via macroprudential policies), with Latin America as an important precedent.

Panel discussion

Opening the panel discussion, Refet Gürkaynak pointed out that there are many similarities between the currency mismatch literature and the more developed asset price bubble literature and suggested the authors should highlight this link in their paper. Cédric Tille recommended that the authors extend their empirical analysis to investigate differences in currency mismatch between households and firms. He believed their model mainly pertained to the hedging activity of firms and he doubted if the beneficial effects of currency mismatch would, for example, extend to unhedged households with foreign currency denominated mortgages.

Referring to the currency crisis in Latin America, Fabrizio Perri highlighted how foreign currency borrowing was considered to be a significant failure due to large depreciations and its subsequent effects. He believed it was necessary to expand the dataset to include countries which had experienced large depreciations in order to provide stronger support for the paper's empirical findings on currency mismatch. Giacomo Calzolari asked if the authors considered what effect the presence of foreign banks had on the extent of currency mismatch in a country. Georges de Ménil requested further clarification on the authors' views on the importance of local capital market development for a firm's foreign borrowing behaviour and how this related to the potential inhibiting effects of EU entry on new entrants' local capital markets. Referring to the US financial system, he considered it unnecessary for each country in the EU to have fully developed financial markets.

In response to comments made by discussants and panellists, Athanasios Vamvakidis emphasized that their theoretical model describes the conditions under which currency mismatch can lead to higher growth and a key insight was that a very high level of currency response can lead to crisis. Furthermore, he highlighted that their findings hold up against a large battery of robustness checks including the normalizing of variables by GDP, the use of different data sources and samples, controlling for the share of non-tradable goods, initial GDP and investment in their model.

In reply to the discussion by Enrique Alberola and Pedro del Rio, Roman Ranciere questioned the validity of the use of crisis and post crisis GDP forecasts by the discussants to evaluate the effects of pre-crisis changes in currency mismatches. Forecasts exhibit by nature large measurement errors. They generally assume persistence, which in the aftermath of a crisis would imply that countries that were hit harder are forecasted to have lower subsequent growth. Therefore adding forecast information to the baseline regression presented in the paper can be seriously misleading.

In reply to Cédric Tille's comments, Ranciere provided further explanation on how much of the unhedged currency corrections came from households and firms. He mentioned that by mid-2007 there was a large foreign financing of consumption booms, which was in contrast to the experience up to 2005 where the majority of foreign lending was to non-trading firms. He accepted it was important to understand how the spillover effects of foreign lending to unhedged agents impacts on the rest of the economy. Research with Aaron Tornell suggests the amount of non-tradable goods used in the tradable sectors is a key parameter in assessing the spillover effects of currency mismatch on the rest of the economy.

APPENDIX A: MODEL OF CURRENCY MISMATCH AND RELAXATION OF BORROWING CONDITIONS

Here, we formalize the intuitive argument we described in the text and show how certain credit market imperfections can generate incentives for currency mismatch, which in turn allow for higher investment and growth, but also generate systemic risk. Consider an economy with two sectors: a tradables (T) and a non-tradables (N) sector. The T-good will serve as the numeraire and we will denote by p_t the price of the N-good in terms of the T-good – i.e., the inverse of the real exchange rate.

We focus on the interaction between lenders and N-sector borrowers in an environment with contract enforceability problems and bailout guarantees.[45] The typical N-firm has internal funds w_t and borrows B_t. It then spends its investable funds in inputs that will produce N-goods next period via a linear production technology: $y_{t+1} = \theta I_t$. That is, the firm's budget constraint is

$$p_t I_t \leq w_t + B_t. \tag{A1}$$

To allow for the possibility of currency mismatch we assume that N-firms can issue two types of one-period bonds: N-bonds that have an interest rate ρ_t^N and whose

[45] The model is based on Schneider and Tornell (2004) and on Ranciere and Tornell (2009).

promised repayment is indexed to the price of $\mathcal{N}$-goods, $p_{t+1}(1+\rho_t^N)b_t^N$, and $\mathcal{T}$-bonds that have an interest rate ρ_t and whose promised repayment is not indexed, $(1 + \rho_t)b_t$. We can interpret $\mathcal{T}(\mathcal{N})$-debt as foreign (domestic) currency denominated debt. To simplify the menu of financing contracts, we assume that firms either are fully unhedged or are fully hedged.

In order to understand the role of currency mismatch in relaxing financing constraints and in generating systemic risk, it is necessary to have a setup where (1) borrowing constraints arise endogenously and (2) there are incentives to take on insolvency risk. If borrowing constraints were simply postulated as primitives in the model, we could not explain how it is that currency mismatch relaxes financing constraints and helps growth. In order to generate borrowing constraints we assume that by incurring a non-pecuniary cost $h[w_t + B_t]$, a borrower can engineer a scam that will allow her to divert the revenues to herself and not repay any debt in the next period, provided the firm has positive notional profits.

In the absence of (2), a systemic financial crisis could never occur unless one assumed a large economy-wide exogenous shock. There must be a reason that leads agents to take on insolvency risk, but that does not eliminate borrowing constraints. Here, the reason is that the government grants bailout guarantees if there is a systemic crisis, but not otherwise. We introduce 'systemic bailout guarantees' by assuming that in case a majority of $\mathcal{N}$-firms defaults, the government pays lenders of non-diverting firms the promised debt repayment amount. However, in case of an isolated default the government does not bail out lenders.

To close the model let tomorrow's real exchange rate take on two values. With probability u it takes an appreciated value $(\bar{p}_{t+1})$, while with probability $1 - u$ it takes a depreciated value $(\underline{p}_{t+1})$. Furthermore, we assume that there is enough real exchange rate variability

$$\frac{\theta \bar{p}_{t+1}}{p_t} \geq 1 + r > h > \frac{\theta \underline{p}_{t+1}}{p_t} \tag{A2}$$

The first inequality ensures that expected returns are high enough to make the production of $\mathcal{N}$-goods profitable. The third inequality ensures that in a crisis the depreciation will be large enough so as to bankrupt all $\mathcal{N}$-firms with currency mismatch. Finally, the second inequality is necessary for borrowing constraints to arise in equilibrium.

During period t, given his internal funds w, the owner of a representative $\mathcal{N}$-firm borrows from lenders. She then decides whether to implement a diversion scheme. At $t + 1$ pay-offs are as follows. If there is no diversion and no default, lenders receive their promised repayment L_{t+1} – either $(1 + \rho_t)b_t$ or $p_{t+1}(1+\rho_t^N)b_t^N$ – and the owner gets the profits π_{t+1}. If there is no diversion, but the firm defaults, lenders get L_{t+1} if a bailout is granted and zero otherwise, while the owner gets zero. Finally, if there is diversion, lenders get nothing and the owner gets all the revenues $p_{t+1}q_{t+1}$.

It follows that lenders fund only plans that do not lead to diversion. Since they are risk neutral and perfectly competitive, lenders set the interest rates so that they break even, and lend up to an amount so that developers do not divert.

Consider first the case of no currency mismatch. In this case the firm issues only N-bonds and in this way hedges its exposure to insolvency risk generated by real exchange rate fluctuations: profits will be $\pi_{t+1} = p_{t+1}[q_{t+a} - (1 + \rho_t^N)b_t^N$. Since lenders are risk neutral and the opportunity cost of capital is $1 + r$, the interest rate that they charge is

$$1 + \rho_t^n = \frac{1 + r}{u\bar{p}_{t+1} + (1 - u)\underline{p}_{t+1}} \tag{A3}$$

Furthermore, to avoid diversion by the firm, lenders impose the following borrowing constraint:

$$(1 + r)b_t^n \leq h(w_t + b_t^n) \tag{A4}$$

Since investment yields an expected return that is higher than the opportunity cost of capital (by (A2)), the firm borrows up to an amount that makes the credit constraint binding. Thus, substituting (A3) in budget constraint (A1), we have that credit and investment are:

$$b_t^n = [m^s - 1]w_t \quad I_t^n = m^s \frac{w_t}{p_t}, \quad \text{where } m^s = \frac{1}{1 - \frac{1}{1+r}h}. \tag{A5}$$

Notice that a necessary condition for borrowing constraints to arise is $h < 1 + r$. If h, the index of contract enforceability, were greater than the cost of capital, it would always be cheaper to repay debt rather than to divert. Thus, lenders will not impose a ceiling on the amount they are willing to lend and agents will not be financially constrained.

Next, consider the case where there is currency mismatch. In this case the firm chooses T-debt, and so it risks insolvency in the depreciation state because debt repayments will not be indexed to the price of the goods it sells: $\pi(\underline{p}_{t+1}) = \underline{p}_{t+1}q_{t+1} - (1 + \rho_t)b_t < 0$. Such currency mismatch might be optimal because the borrowing terms are more attractive.

Since lenders constrain credit to ensure that borrowers will repay in the no-crisis state, it follows that in the no-crisis state debt is repaid in full and there is no bailout. Meanwhile, in the crisis state there is bankruptcy and each lender receives a bailout equal to what he was promised. Thus, the interest rate on T-debt is

$$1 + \rho_t = 1 + r \tag{A6}$$

Notice that because of the bailout guarantee, the interest rate charged by lenders does not internalize the risk that the firm will go bust.

Lenders will lend up to an amount that equates the debt repayment that the firm is expected to make $u[1+r]b_t$ to the diversion cost $h[w_t+b_t]$. Therefore, substituting $u[1+r]b_t = h[w_t+b_t]$ in budget constraint (A1), we have that credit and investment are

$$b_t = [m^r - 1]w_t \quad I_t = m^r \frac{w_t}{p_t}, \quad \text{with } m^r = \frac{1}{1 - \frac{1}{u}\frac{1}{1+r}h} \tag{A7}$$

We can now see that, in the presence of systemic bailout guarantees, taking on currency mismatch has two effects. First, it reduces the expected interest cost from $1+r$ to $[1+r]u$, as revealed by a comparison of (A3) and (A6). Second, this reduction in expected debt repayments relaxes the borrowing constraint, which increases credit and investment from $I_t^N = m^s \frac{w_t}{p_t}$ to $I_t^T = m^r \frac{w_t}{p_t}$ (by (A5) and (A7)). This increase in leverage is possible because systemic guarantees mean that in a crisis lenders expect to be bailed out.

The fact that T-debt is cheaper than N-debt does not imply that borrowers will always be willing to issue T-debt. One can verify algebraically that in order for a borrower to choose currency mismatch it is necessary that: (1) he expects a bailout if a crisis occurs next period – that is, he believes a majority of borrowers chooses currency mismatch; (2) the probability of crisis next period $1-u$ is small; and (3) there is enough real exchange rate variability (i.e., (A2) holds). It then follows that a risky equilibrium exists if a majority of borrowers expects a bailout in case of systemic crisis.

Proposition: If a majority of borrowers believes that systemic bailout guarantees are present and there is a small likelihood of a severe real exchange rate depreciation – i.e., condition (A2) holds and the crisis probability $1-u$ is small – then there is a risky equilibrium in which a majority of borrowers take on currency mismatch. In this equilibrium:

(1) Borrowers that take on currency mismatch have lower interest rate costs, as the government implicitly covers the depreciation premium.
(2) Currency mismatch relaxes borrowing constraints as lower expected debt repayments reduce the agency problems.
(3) Currency mismatch leads to more investment and growth in no-crisis times.
(4) However, firms that take on currency mismatch are vulnerable to bankruptcy in case of a severe depreciation.

In our micro-level empirical analysis we test the implications of this proposition. In a risky equilibrium there can be two firms with identical observable characteristics, but with different bailout expectations. As a result a firm that expects a bailout will take on currency mismatch while a firm that does not expect a bailout will not. Since both firms have the same observable characteristics, we can thus attribute the differences in interest rate costs and growth rates to the adoption of currency mismatch.

For the macroeconomic analysis of currency mismatch consider a risky economy – with currency mismatch – and a safe economy. The proposition above implies that the risky economy will have a higher average growth rate than the safe economy. However, the risky economy will experience – rare – crises. We use this implication of the model.

We have taken the price path as exogenous. The next step is to embed the borrowing and lending equations in a dynamic general equilibrium framework and confirm that equilibrium prices satisfy (A2). Such analysis is carried out by Schneider and Tornell (2004) and Ranciere and Tornell (2009).

APPENDIX B: CALCULATION OF CURRENCY MISMATCH AND DATA SOURCES

Definition

The measure of currency mismatch in the paper is the gap between foreign currency assets and liabilities, both with respect to residents and non-residents (domestic and foreign net assets in foreign currencies), adjusted for an estimate of foreign currency lending that is not hedged, and divided by total bank assets. The formula of the calculation is the following:

foreign currency denominated net liabilities = {*foreign currency foreign liabilities*
+ *foreign currency domestic liabilities* − *foreign currency foreign assets*
− *foreign currency domestic assets* + *foreign currency lending to unhedged households*
+ *foreign currency lending to unhedged nonfinancial firms*}/{*total bank assets*}

In more detail:

- Foreign currency foreign liabilities include all foreign currency claims of non-residents towards the domestic banking sector, such as loans of foreign banks, including parent foreign banks to their domestic subsidiaries, and foreign currency deposits of non-residents. Bank loans from abroad reached high levels during the recent boom in emerging Europe. Foreign currency deposits of non-residents were also substantial in some countries.
- Foreign currency domestic liabilities include all foreign currency claims of residents towards the domestic banking sector, such as foreign currency deposits of residents. The latter have been historically very large in emerging Europe.[46]

[46] According to anecdotal evidence, during East Europe's liberalization in the early 1990s, large amounts of foreign currency that were 'held in mattresses', primarily Deutsche marks, were deposited in banks. They were later converted into euros. Initially, they served as a hedge against inflation, given memories of price instability during liberalization. Even though inflation stabilized at low levels in the current decade, most of these deposits remained, in some cases in anticipation of euro adoption.

- Foreign currency foreign assets include all foreign currency claims of the banking sector towards non-residents, such as deposits, or loans in foreign currencies.
- Foreign currency domestic assets include all foreign currency claims of the banking sector towards residents, such as foreign currency loans, which grew very rapidly during the recent boom in emerging Europe.
- Foreign currency lending to households is part of the banks' foreign currency domestic assets. However, many households have no foreign currency income and, therefore, are not hedged when they borrow in foreign currency. Therefore, the calculation of the banks' currency mismatch subtracts foreign currency lending to such households from the banks' foreign currency assets, because such lending is assumed to be subject to exchange rate risk, directly for the households, and indirectly, through credit risk, for the banks. Private sector foreign currency deposits, including of households, are large in emerging Europe and do provide a hedge. However, it is reasonable to expect that households with large foreign currency deposits do not need to also borrow in foreign currency. As data on the share of households that are not hedged are not available, we have assumed that this share is equal to the share of firms without foreign currency income (where the households are employed). As a robustness test, we also consider the case in which households cannot hedge at all.
- Foreign currency lending to non-financial firms is also part of the banks' foreign currency domestic assets. However, some of this lending goes to firms that do not have foreign currency income and are, therefore, not hedged, resulting in credit risk for the banks and, indirectly, exchange rate risk. To adjust for the latter, we subtract foreign currency loans to non-financial firms that have no foreign currency income from the banks' foreign currency domestic assets (we assume that financial firms have foreign currency income).
- Finally, we divide by total bank assets, to adjust for the size of the banking sector in each country. We also test the robustness of the results when we divide our measure by GDP.

Data sources

Data on foreign currency domestic and foreign asset and liabilities by sector and data on total bank assets are from Haver Analytics. Data are available for 10 countries: Bulgaria, Croatia, Czech Republic, Estonia, Hungary, Latvia, Lithuania, Poland, Romania and Ukraine. These economies produce 86% of East Europe's GDP, excluding Russia. Based on data availability, we measure currency mismatches for the period 1998–2009, although in most cases we focus on the boom and bust period during 2004–2007. Data on direct foreign currency from abroad, which are also discussed in the text and are added in the measure of currency mismatch as a robustness test, are from Rosenberg and Tirpak (2009).

We use a number of sources for the share of foreign currency lending to firms with no foreign currency income. Up to 2003, this share is based on EBRD survey data for 2002 and equals the share of non-exporting companies with foreign currency loans to total companies with foreign currency loans. For the subsequent years, we use EBRD survey data for 2005 for the Czech Republic, Estonia, Hungary, Lithuania and Poland.[47] For Bulgaria and Romania, the share of unhedged foreign currency lending is given by the share of corporate foreign currency lending to tradable sectors, as estimated in Sorsa *et al.* (2007). For Croatia, it is based on Central Bank survey data for the share of foreign currencies loans to unhedged clients (this includes both households and corporates; see Hilaire and Ilyina, 2007). And for Latvia, it is estimated based on data provided by the central bank for the share of tradables in corporate foreign currency loans. The results remain robust if we use only EBRD data, or if we use only data from the sources described above for Bulgaria, Romania, Croatia and Latvia, and assume that the other countries have similar shares of unhedged foreign currency lending (taking the average, or the minimum).

A number of alternative sources were combined to expand the currency mismatch data set to additional emerging economies. Data on foreign currency loans to residents and foreign currency deposits of residents are from the confidential IMF Vulnerability Exercise for Emerging Economies, based on data provided by country authorities. Some gaps in the data on foreign currency deposits of residents are complemented by using data in Haver Analytics and in Arteta (2003, 2005).

We use various sources for the share of unhedged foreign currency borrowing in the corporate sector. The share of unhedged foreign currency borrowing for Latin America is based on firm survey data in Kamil (2004, 2010) and is assumed to be equal to the share of non-exporting companies with foreign currency loans to total companies with foreign currency loans. The share for other economies is from the World Bank's Enterprise Survey (https://www.enterprisesurveys.org/Portal/Login.aspx?ReturnUrl=%2fPortal%2felibrary.aspx%3flibid%3d14&libid=14) and is also assumed to be equal to the share of non-exporting companies with foreign currency loans to total companies with foreign currency loans. We have assumed that a company with a share of foreign currency loans in total loans higher than 30% could be subject to exchange rate risk. If a company sells more than 70% of its products domestically then it is labelled as a non-exporter (the results are robust to alternative thresholds). The estimates using the World Bank data are for various years during the period that we are considering, for most cases during 2002–2004, but we use the earliest or the latest observation for the years before, or after, respectively.

[47] The EBRD survey data (BEEPS Firm Level Data) for 2002 refer to the stock of debt. However, the data for 2005 refer to the last loan only. We have assumed that the latter applies to the stock of debt as well, which is an approximation. The results are robust if we do not make this assumption and use other proxies instead, as the appendix discusses.

For bank foreign assets and liabilities in foreign currency, we use data constructed by Prat (2007) for Argentina, Brazil, China, Indonesia, Mexico, Peru, Philippines, Russia, Thailand, Turkey and Uruguay. And we use IMF IFS data for Bosnia and Herzegovina, Costa Rica, Egypt, Guatemala, Kazakhstan, Serbia, Venezuela and Vietnam. The latter, however, does not specify the currency denomination of the banks' foreign assets and liabilities. We have therefore assumed that all the banks' foreign assets and liabilities for these countries are denominated in foreign currency. The data for the long-run growth regressions are from the IMF World Economic Outlook database, except of the trade share and the age dependency ratio, which are from the World Bank's World Development Indicators.

Table B1. Currency mismatch and growth in emerging Europe, 1998–2009, robustness tests

	Assuming households do not hedge				Currency mismatch divided by GDP				Controlling for the increase in non-tradables (1998–2007)			
	Pooled panel		Fixed effects		Pooled panel		Fixed effects		Pooled panel		Fixed effects	
Change in currency mismatch	0.11**		0.11*		0.23***		0.23*		0.08**		0.08*	
	(0.04)		(0.07)		(0.07)		(0.14)		(0.04)		(0.05)	
Lagged change in currency mismatch	0.05	0.09	0.05	0.07	0.13	0.20***	0.15	0.17**	0.04	0.07***	0.04	0.05**
	(0.04)	(0.04)	(0.05)	(0.05)	(0.08)	(0.05)	(0.10)	(0.09)	(0.04)	(0.02)	(0.03)	(0.02)
Crisis dummy	−12.01***	−12.48***	−12.09***	−12.32***	−11.76***	−12.92***	−11.39***	−12.68***				
	(0.58)	(0.62)	(0.73)	(0.76)	(0.59)	(0.65)	(0.71)	(0.79)				
Interaction term: (change in currency mismatch) × (crisis dummy)	−0.27***		−0.17**		−0.77***		−0.89***					
	(0.04)		(0.07)		(0.07)		(0.16)					
Interaction term: (lagged change in currency mismatch) × (crisis dummy)	−0.99***	−0.90***	−0.88***	−0.94***	−1.97***	−1.50***	−2.07***	−1.65***				
	(0.04)	(0.04)	(0.10)	(0.07)	(0.08)	(0.05)	(0.26)	(0.15)				
Change in non-tradables/GDP									1.43***	1.47***	0.97***	1.00***
									(0.41)	(0.46)	(0.27)	(0.22)
Interaction term: (change in currency mismatch) × (change in non-tradables/GDP)									−0.02		0.00	
									(0.05)		(0.02)	
Interaction term: (lagged change in currency mismatch) × (change in non-tradables/GDP)									0.13***	0.12***	−0.01	−0.00
									(0.04)	(0.02)	(0.03)	(0.02)
Adjusted R^2	0.70	0.69	0.66	0.66	0.74	0.71	0.73	0.69	0.32	0.29	0.67	0.67
Number of countries	10	10	10	10	10	10	10	10	10	10	10	10

Note: The dependent variable is real GDP growth (from the IMF World Economic Outlook database). Currency mismatch in the last four regressions is measured as explained in the text and the appendix. In the first four regressions, the currency mismatch measure assumes that households do not hedge exchange rate risk at all. In the next four regressions, currency mismatch is divided by GDP instead of total bank assets. The crisis dummy takes the value of 1 in 2009, which is the year when growth turned negative throughout emerging Europe. The sample includes 10 emerging European economies: Bulgaria, Croatia, Czech Rep., Estonia, Hungary, Latvia, Lithuania, Poland, Romania, and Ukraine. The period is 1998–2009, except for the last four regressions, in which the period is 1998–2007, because data for the production of non-tradables is not available for more recent years – therefore, these specifications do not include the crisis dummy. Statistical significance is somewhat lower in some specifications with fixed effects, because of the small sample. Heteroscedasticity-consistent standard errors in parentheses.

*, **, and *** indicate statistical significance at the 10, 5 and 1% level, respectively.

Table B2. Descriptive statistics

Panel 1. Descriptive statistics for country panel growth regressions, averages 1998–2009

Country	Currency mismatch	Annual change in currency mismatch	External debt/ GDP	Change in external debt/GDP	PPP per capita $ GDP	Real GDP growth
Argentina	27.2	4.1	78.8	−5.9	10678	2.7
Bosnia & Herzegovina	15.9	−1.0	43.8	33.8	5584	4.8
Brazil	−1.4	0.4	27.3	−15.4	8358	2.7
Bulgaria	−27.2	5.6	80.5	2.3	8564	4.2
China	5.3	−0.7	12.2	−5.5	3791	9.5
Costa Rica	13.9	−1.1	30.3	4.9	8413	4.7
Croatia	30.7	−0.8	66.9	46.0	14009	2.8
Czech Republic	−24.4	−0.5	39.4	0.8	18964	2.9
Egypt	−3.7	−2.9	29.1	−16.3	4636	5.3
Estonia	11.3	2.2	80.3	87.0	14453	4.6
Guatemala	−16.5	1.1	31.9	11.9	4199	3.5
Hungary	9.1	0.7	78.1	75.2	15255	2.9
Indonesia	8.8	−0.1	65.2	−124.6	3039	3.2
Kazakhstan	−13.4	−0.3	76.6	55.0	7659	6.9
Latvia	6.7	4.2	90.2	94.0	11525	4.6
Lithuania	10.2	1.5	52.4	41.7	12530	4.2
Mexico	−2.2	0.8	24.1	−13.1	11886	2.3
Peru	−8.9	−0.8	42.6	−21.8	6299	4.4
Philippines	19.4	0.9	65.1	−38.7	2778	4.0
Poland	0.7	−0.5	46.4	31.5	12966	4.0
Romania	33.9	0.8	38.2	38.2	8661	3.2
Russia	9.5	2.9	46.4	−33.6	10753	4.6
Serbia	−2.8	4.1	76.8	8.0	7730	3.0
Thailand	−4.2	1.3	45.4	−65.6	6284	2.8
Turkey	11.1	−2.2	43.4	9.9	10012	3.0
Ukraine	−12.8	4.5	53.2	68.0	4973	3.8
Uruguay	53.0	−1.2	71.9	−1.4	9531	2.0
Venezuela	−5.8	0.3	32.5	−26.2	9806	2.9
Vietnam	13.8	2.2	37.8	−15.4	1980	6.9

Source: See Appendix B.

Panel 2. Descriptive statistics firm-level data

Variable	Sample: Firms with a loan in 2005 survey	
	Mean	Std. Dev.
Interest rate on last loan	0.14	0.07
Maturity of last loan (months)	31.09	29.92
Growth in sales (annualized)	0.04	0.12
Growth in employment (annualized)	0.05	0.19
Years of operation	17.07	19.37
Collateral dummy: building/land	0.74	0.44
Collateral dummy: equipment	0.90	0.29
Collateral dummy: accounts receivable	0.97	0.18
Collateral dummy: assets	0.93	0.26

Table B2. (Continued)

Panel 2. Descriptive statistics firm-level data

Variable	Sample: Firms with a loan in 2005 survey	
	Mean	Std. Dev.
Collateral dummy: other	0.95	0.22
Share foreign input in production	0.35	0.38
Share employees with university degree	0.25	0.26
Share skilled employees	0.51	0.29
Dummy last loan in foreign currency	0.25	0.43

Source: BEEPS Survey 2005, EBRD/World Bank.

REFERENCES

Allayannis, G., G. Brown and L. F. Klapper (2003). 'Capital structure and financial risk: evidence from foreign debt use in East Asia', *Journal of Finance*, 58(6), 2667–710.

Arteta, C. O. (2003), 'Are financial dollarized countries more prone to costly crises?' International Finance Discussion Paper 763, Board of Governors of the Federal Reserve System.

—— (2005). 'Exchange rate regimes and financial dollarization: does flexibility reduce currency mismatches in bank intermediation?' *B.E. Journal of Macroeconomics: Topics in Macroeconomics*, 5(1), 1–28.

Árvai, Z., K. Driessen and I. Ötker-Robe (2009), 'Regional financial interlinkages and financial contagion within Europe', IMF Working Paper 09/6.

Beck, T., A. Demirguc-Kunt and V. Maksimovic (2005). 'Financial and legal constraints to firm growth: does firm size matter?' *Journal of Finance*, 60, 137–77.

Beck, T., A. Demirguc-Kunt, L. Laeven and R. Levine (2008). 'Finance, firm size, and growth', *Journal of Money, Credit and Banking*, 40(7), 1371–405.

Berglöf, E. (2009), 'Declare victory and fight on', VOX-EU.

Bleakley, H. and K. Cowan (2006). 'Corporate dollar debt and depreciations: much ado about nothing', *Review of Economics and Statistics*, 90(4), 612–26.

—— (2009), 'Mishmash on mismatch? balance-sheet effects and emerging-markets crises', mimeo, University of Chicago.

Brown, M., S. Ongena and P. Yesin (2009), 'Foreign currency borrowing by small firms', mimeo, Swiss National Bank.

Calvo, G., A. Izquierdo and L.-F. Mejía (2008), 'Systemic sudden stops: the relevance of balance-sheet effects and financial integration', NBER Working Papers 14026.

Dehejia, R. and W. Sadek (2002). 'Propensity score matching methods for nonexperimental causal studies', *Review of Economics and Statistics*, 84, 151–61.

Eichengreen, B., R. Hausmann and U. Panizza (2007). 'Currency mismatches, debt intolerance, and the original sin: why they are not the same and why it matters', in S. Edwards (ed.), *Capital Controls and Capital Flows in Emerging Economies: Policies, Practices and Consequences*, NBER, University of Chicago Press, Chicago.

Forbes, K. (2007). 'One cost of the Chilean capital controls: increased financial constraints for smaller traded firms', *Journal of International Economics*, 71, 294–323.

Goldstein, M. and P. Turner (2004), 'Controlling currency mismatches in emerging markets', Institute of International Economics, Washington.

Guiso, L., P. Sapienza and L. Zingales (2004). 'Does local financial development matter?' *Quarterly Journal of Economics*, 119, 929–69.

Heckman, J., H. Ichimura, J. Smith and P. Todd (1998). 'Characterizing selection bias using experimental data', *Econometrica*, 66(5), 1017–98.

Hilaire, A. and A. Ilyina (2007), 'External debt and balance-sheet vulnerabilities in Croatia', in *Republic of Croatia: Selected Issues*, International Monetary Fund, Washington.

Kamil, H. (2004), 'A new database on the currency composition and maturity structure of firms' balance sheets in Latin America, 1990–2002: definition of variables, methodology of construction and data sources', Inter-American Development Bank Database, http://www.iadb.org/res/pub_desc.cfm?pub_id=DBA-001.

—— (2010), 'How do exchange rate regimes affect firms' incentives to hedge currency risk in emerging markets?', International Monetary Fund, Washington DC, unpublished.

Levchenko, A., R. Ranciere and M. Thoenig (2009). 'Growth and risk at the industry level: the real effects of financial liberalization', *Journal of Development Economics*, 89(2), 210–22.

Melitz, M. J. (2003). 'The impact of trade on intra-industry reallocations and aggregate industry productivity', *Econometrica*, 71(6), 1695–725.

Prat, S. (2007). 'The relevance of currency mismatch indicators: an analysis through determinants of emerging market spreads', *Economie Internationale*, 111(3).

Ranciere, R. and A. Tornell (2009), 'Systemic risk and the US Financial Crisis', mimeo.

Rosenbaum, P. R. and D. B. Rubin (1983). 'The central role of the propensity score in observational studies for causal effects', *Biometrika*, 70, 41–55.

Rosenberg, C., I. Halikias, B. House, C. Keller, J. Nystedt, A. Pitt and B. Setser (2005), 'Debt-related vulnerabilities and financial crises: an application of the balance sheet approach to emerging market countries', IMF Occasional Paper 240.

Rosenberg, C. and M. Tirpak (2009). 'Determinants of foreign currency borrowing in the new member states of the EU', *Journal of Economics and Finance*, 59(3), 216–28.

Schneider, M. and A. Tornell (2004). 'Balance sheet effects, bailout guarantees and financial crises', *Review of Economic Studies*, 71, 883–913.

Sorsa, P., B. Berend Bakker, C. Duenwald, A.M. Maechler and A. Tiffin (2007), 'Vulnerabilities in Emerging Southeastern Europe: how much cause for concern?' IMF Working Paper 07/236.

Vamvakidis, A. (2009). 'Convergence in emerging Europe: sustainability and vulnerabilities', *Eastern European Economics*, 47(3), 5–27.

Wooldridge, J. (2001), *Econometric Analysis of Cross Section and Panel Data*, MIT Press, Cambridge, MA.

Reforming Basel II

SUMMARY

Policy discussions on the recent financial crisis feature widespread calls to address the pro-cyclical effects of regulation. The main concern is that the new risk-sensitive bank capital regulation (Basel II) may amplify business cycle fluctuations. This paper compares the leading alternative procedures that have been proposed to mitigate this problem. We estimate a model of the probabilities of default (PDs) of Spanish firms during the period 1987–2008, and use the estimated PDs to compute the corresponding series of Basel II capital requirements per unit of loans. These requirements move significantly along the business cycle, ranging from 7.6% (in 2006) to 11.9% (in 1993). The comparison of the different procedures is based on the criterion of minimizing the root mean square deviations of each adjusted series with respect to the Hodrick–Prescott trend of the original series. The results show that the best procedures are either to smooth the input of the Basel II formula by using through-the-cycle PDs or to smooth the output with a multiplier based on GDP growth. Our discussion concludes that the latter is better in terms of simplicity, transparency, and consistency with banks' risk pricing and risk management systems. For the portfolio of Spanish commercial and industrial loans and a 45% loss given default (LGD), the multiplier would amount to a 6.5% surcharge for each standard deviation in GDP growth. The surcharge would be significantly higher with cyclically varying LGDs.

— *Rafael Repullo, Jesús Saurina and Carlos Trucharte*

Economic Policy October 2010 Printed in Great Britain

Mitigating the pro-cyclicality of Basel II

Rafael Repullo, Jesús Saurina and Carlos Trucharte

CEMFI and CEPR; Banco de España; Banco de España

1. INTRODUCTION

The 1988 Basel Accord consolidated capital requirements as the cornerstone of bank regulation. It required banks to hold a minimum overall capital equal to 8% of their risk-weighted assets. As all consumer and business loans were included in the full weight category, 8% became the universal capital charge for household and corporate lending, while for mortgages the capital requirement was 4%.

Following widespread criticism about the risk-insensitiveness of these requirements (Jackson, 1999), the Basel Committee on Banking Supervision (BCBS) approved in 2004 a reform, known as Basel II, whose primary goal was 'to arrive at significantly more risk-sensitive capital requirements' (BCBS, 2006, para. 5). Basel II introduced a menu of approaches for determining capital

The views expressed in this paper are those of the authors and should not be attributed to the Banco de España or the Eurosystem. We thank the comments of Juan Ayuso, Antonella Foglia, Leonardo Gambacorta, Charles Goodhart, Michael Gordy, Jordi Gual, Diana Hancock, Patricia Jackson, Javier Mencía, and Geoffrey Miller, Augustin Landier, Morten Ravn (the discussant), and three anonymous referees, as well as those of audiences at Banca d'Italia, Banco de España, Banque de France, the Federal Reserve Bank of Boston, the CEPR 2009 Conference on Financial Regulation and Macroeconomic Stability, the Bocconi 2009 Finlawmetrics Conference, and the Economic Policy Panel. Financial support from the Spanish Ministry of Science and Innovation (Grant No.EC2008–00801) is gratefully acknowledged.
The Managing Editor in charge of this paper was Tullio Jappelli.

Economic Policy October 2010 pp. 659–702 Printed in Great Britain

requirements. The *standardized approach* uses external ratings to refine the risk weights of the 1988 Accord (henceforth, Basel I), but leaves the capital charges for loans to unrated companies essentially unchanged. The *internal ratings-based* (IRB) approach allows banks to compute the capital charges for each exposure from their own estimate of the probability of default (PD) and, in the advanced IRB approach, the loss given default (LGD) and the exposure at default (EAD); see Box 1.

Box 1. Key features of the Basel II framework

In June 2004 the Basel Committee on Banking Supervision released the revised capital adequacy framework, commonly referred to as Basel II, with the aim of a better alignment of capital requirements to banking risks.[1] In other words, the idea was to improve on the relatively risk-insensitive framework of Basel I, by requiring higher capital charges to riskier borrowers.

Basel II adopts a three-pillar structure: Pillar 1 requires banks to maintain a minimum amount of capital for credit, market and operational risks. It sets out the quantitative and qualitative requirements and algebraic formulae to calculate capital for the different types of asset classes identified. Pillar 2, devoted to the supervisory review process, is intended to ensure that banks possess adequate capital for the full range of risks they run. In doing this, banks should develop their own risk management techniques to contribute to the overall assessment of their capital levels under the monitoring of the supervisory authorities. Pillar 3 aims to bolster market discipline to complement the other two pillars by setting out disclosure requirements applicable to banks in areas such as required capital, risk exposures, and risk assessment procedures.

Focusing on Pillar 1, and in particular on credit risk, Basel II provides a menu of approaches to calculate the minimum capital requirement according to the sophistication of a bank's activities and its internal risk management capabilities. The three approaches are:

- the standardized approach;
- the foundation internal ratings-based approach;
- the advanced internal ratings-based approach.

The standardized approach is based on external credit assessments, when they are available, and if they are not, exposures require the same capital charge as in Basel I (8%). The main principle behind the internal ratings-based (IRB) approaches is that banks assign exposures to different asset

[1] In June 2006 the Basel Committee released a final comprehensive version that included the 2004 Capital Accord, the elements of the 1988 Capital Accord that were not revised during the Basel II process, and the 1996 Amendment incorporating market risks.

classes and, within them, banks assign different internal rating grades according to their credit quality (creditworthiness).[2] In particular, banks estimate, for each borrower or homogenous groups of them, a series of credit risk drivers that determine the corresponding capital charges. These drivers are:

- the one-year ahead probability of default (PD);
- the loss given default (LGD);
- the exposure at default (EAD);[3]
- the maturity (M) of the exposure.

In the advanced approach banks are required to compute all four drivers, whereas in the foundation approach they are only required to estimate the PD and rely on supervisory estimates for the others. These parameters are then plugged into a formula that gives the capital requirement corresponding to each exposure.

The Basel II formula is derived from the requirement that capital must cover losses in a particular credit risk model with a confidence level of 99.9% (see Gordy, 2003, for details). For example, in the case of corporate exposures the capital requirement k per unit of exposure is:

$$k = LGD \times \left[N\left(\frac{N^{-1}(PD) + \sqrt{\rho} N^{-1}(0.999)}{\sqrt{1-\rho}} \right) - PD \right] \times \frac{1 + (M - 2.5)b}{1 - 1.5b} \times 1.06 \tag{B1}$$

where $N(\cdot)$ is the standard normal cumulative distribution function,

$$\rho = 0.12\left(\frac{1 - e^{-50PD}}{1 - e^{-50}} \right) + 0.24\left(1 - \frac{1 - e^{-50PD}}{1 - e^{-50}} \right) \tag{B2}$$

and

$$b = [0.11852 - 0.05478 \times \ln(PD)]^2 \tag{B3}$$

Thus the capital requirement is the LGD multiplied by three terms. The first one, within square brackets, is the 99.9% percentile of the distribution of the losses of a large portfolio of loans with a probability of default PD minus the expected losses (that are supposed to be covered with loan loss provisions). The second term is a maturity adjustment that is increasing in the maturity M of the loan, and equal to 1 for $M = 1$ year. The term ρ in the formula is a parameter intended to capture the extent of correlation in defaults in the loan portfolio. It is decreasing in PD, so riskier loans are supposed to be less correlated –

[2] Broadly speaking asset classes are divided into two main categories: corporate and retail exposures. Retail exposures are in turn divided into residential mortgages exposures, qualifying revolving exposures, and other retail exposures. Securitizations are treated separately.

[3] For on-balance sheet items this parameter will be the amount of the exposure. For off-balance sheet items, credit conversion factors are used to obtain credit equivalent amounts.

in terms of the credit risk model they have higher idiosyncratic risk. The third term is a scaling factor that increases the capital requirement by 6%. This factor was computed using quantitative impact studies data to broadly maintain the aggregate level of the capital requirements.

Figure B1 plots the relationship between the capital requirement k and the PD, for LGD = 45% and M = 1. The function is increasing (for the relevant range) and concave in PD, so increases in the probability of default translate into less than proportional increases in the capital requirement.

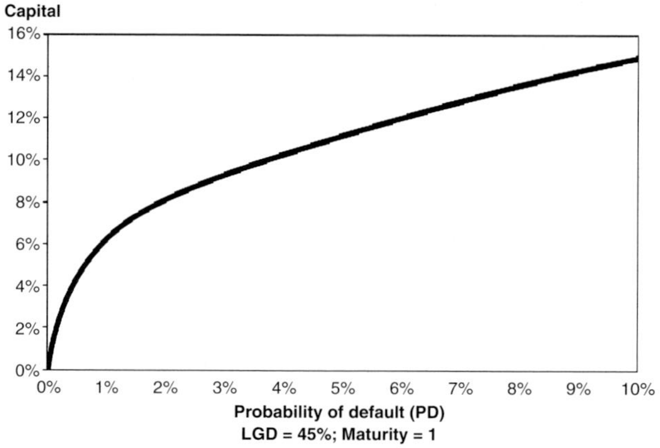

Figure B1. The Basel II capital charge curve for corporate exposures

Note: This figure shows the Basel II capital requirement for corporate exposures as a function of the PD assuming an LGD of 45%, and a maturity $M = 1$ year.

Source: Authors' calculations.

As a result of this risk-sensitiveness, a widespread concern about Basel II is that it might amplify business cycle fluctuations, forcing banks to restrict their lending when the economy goes into recession. Even in the old Basel I regime of essentially flat capital requirements, bank capital regulation had the potential to be pro-cyclical because bank profits may turn negative during recessions, impairing banks' lending capacity (Borio *et al.*, 2001; Gambacorta and Mistrulli, 2004).[4] Under the IRB approach of Basel II, capital requirements are an increasing function of the PD, LGD and EAD parameters estimated for each borrower, and these inputs are likely to rise in downturns. For example, using the formula in Box 1 one finds that an increase in the PD from 1% to 3% (something in line with the US experience[5]) increases the capital requirement for corporate exposures from 6.21% to 9.32%.[6] Clearly, a jump of 50% in required capital would not be easy to accommodate in the middle of a recession.

[4] In fact, there is a debate in the literature on whether the implementation of the Basel I capital requirements in the United States might have brought about a credit crunch in the early 1990s; see Bernanke and Lown (1991), Berger and Udell (1994), Hancock and Wilcox (1994), Hancock, Laing and Wilcox (1995), and Peek and Rosengren (1995a, b).

[5] See the discussion in Appendix B in Repullo and Suarez (2009).

[6] Assuming a constant LGD of 45% and a maturity, M, of 1 year.

So concerns about Basel II are stronger than those regarding Basel I because the worsening of borrowers' creditworthiness in recessions will significantly increase the requirement of capital for banks and might lead to a severe contraction in the supply of credit.[7] At the same time, there is the complementary concern that the lower capital requirements in expansions may contribute to the emergence of credit and asset price bubbles.[8]

The recent financial crisis, with its boom and bust lending cycle, has brought to the forefront the need to address the potential pro-cyclical effects of risk-sensitive bank capital regulation. The idea is to devise procedures that correct the bias towards exacerbating the inherent cyclicality of lending, and consequently distorting investment decisions, either by restricting access for some agents to bank finance or, in the opposite direction, by fuelling credit booms.

Multiple committees, institutions, central banks and supervisory authorities all over the world are working on mechanisms to abate this pro-cyclicality. To name a few, the G-20 at the summit held in Washington (G-20, 2008) requested Finance Ministers to formulate specific recommendations, among others, on mitigating pro-cyclicality in regulatory policy. The Basel Committee (BCBS, 2008) in its comprehensive strategy to address the lessons of the banking crisis also highlights the need to dampen the pro-cyclicality in the financial system. The European Union (EU, press release July 2009) created a working group to address pro-cyclicality issues by analysing potential policy responses to reduce their impact. Furthermore, the G-20 at the Pittsburgh summit (G-20, 2009) called on Finance Ministers and Central Bank Governors to reach agreement on an international framework of reform in four critical areas, the first one being 'building high-quality capital and mitigating pro-cyclicality'. The Financial Stability Board (FSB) issued in April 2009 a series of reports covering different areas of interests in response to the current crisis, recommending that the Basel Committee should monitor the impact of the Basel II framework and make appropriate adjustments to dampen the excessive cyclicality of the minimum capital requirements; see FSB (2009). The EU Economic and Financial Committee working group on pro-cyclicality (2009) finds that there is a host of potential elements that can contribute to reducing the pro-cyclical effects on the financial system, including counter-cyclical capital requirements.

Both Treasury Secretary Geithner (2009) and Chairman Bernanke (2009) advocate that capital regulation should be revisited to ensure that it does not induce excessive pro-cyclicality. In the same vein, Adair Turner (2009) proposes the need for regulatory approaches to capital regulation to avoid unnecessary pro-cyclicality in capital adequacy requirements.

[7] These concerns would be exacerbated by mark-to-market accounting, which increases the cyclical movements in banks' capital, and consequently has the potential to amplify the pro-cyclical effects of bank capital regulation.

[8] See Panetta and Angelini (2009) for an extensive discussion of the literature on pro-cyclicality in the financial sector.

One can conclude that there is widespread agreement that something must be done. The devil is, of course, in the details. How should the pro-cyclicality problem be tackled without throwing out the risk-sensitiveness of the new capital regulation regime? This is what this paper is about.

We present, analyse, and discuss the leading alternative procedures that have been proposed to mitigate the pro-cyclicality of the Basel II capital requirements. As a first step, we show that capital requirements under Basel II move significantly along the business cycle. The analysis is based on the results of the estimation of a logistic model of the one-year-ahead PDs of Spanish firms during the period 1987–2008. The database includes all commercial and industrial loans granted in Spain during this period, and comes from the Credit Register of the Bank of Spain. The dependent variable is a binary variable that takes value one when a firm defaults in the course of a year on its outstanding loans at the end of the previous year, and zero otherwise. The explanatory variables comprise characteristics of the firm (industry, location, age, credit line utilization, and previous delinquencies and loan defaults), characteristics of its loans (size, collateral and maturity), characteristics of the banks from which the firm borrows (distribution of exposures among lenders and changes in the main provider of finance), and macroeconomic controls (the rate of growth of the GDP, the rate of growth of bank credit, and the return of the stock market).

The empirical model provides an estimate of the *point-in-time* (PIT) PDs of the loans in the entire portfolio of commercial and industrial loans of the Spanish banks over the sample period, so using the Basel II formula we can compute the corresponding aggregate capital requirements per unit of loans. We find that Basel II capital requirements increase more than 50% from peak to trough, which is a very significant change compared with the flat requirements of Basel I.

We next consider the effect of different procedures to mitigate the cyclicality of these requirements over the business cycle. According to Gordy and Howells (2006) there are two basic alternatives: one can smooth the input of the Basel II formula, by using some sort of *through-the-cycle* (TTC) adjustment of the PDs, or smooth the output by using some adjustment of the Basel II capital requirements computed from the PIT PDs.[9] We analyse both approaches. Following the work of Saurina and Trucharte (2007) on mortgage portfolios, we first construct TTC estimates of the PDs by setting the value of the macroeconomic controls at their average level over the sample period, and then compute the corresponding Basel II capital requirements. Second, we analyse different adjustments to the PIT capital requirements based on aggregate information (the rate of growth of the GDP, the rate of growth of bank credit, and the return of the stock market) and individual bank information (the rate of growth of banks' portfolios of commercial and industrial loans). The comparison of the different procedures is based on the criterion of

[9] See also the discussion in Committee of European Banking Supervisors (2009).

minimizing the root mean square deviations of each smoothed series with respect to the trend of the original series. This trend is computed by applying the Hodrick–Prescott (HP) filter, which is the procedure customarily used by macroeconomists to separate cycle from trend. Thus, our approach aims at smoothing just the cyclical component of the Basel II capital requirements.

The results show that the best procedures in terms of approaching the HP trend are either to smooth the input of the Basel II formula using TTC PDs, or to smooth the output with a simple multiplier of the PIT capital requirements that depends on the deviation of the rate of growth of the GDP with respect to its long-run average. Our discussion of the pros and cons of these two procedures concludes that the latter is better in terms of simplicity, transparency, low cost of implementation, and consistency with banks' risk pricing and risk management systems.

The remainder of the paper is structured as follows. Section 2 provides a broader perspective of the rationale for the approach developed in the paper. Section 3 presents the empirical model of PDs using data from the Credit Register of the Bank of Spain on commercial and industrial loans for the period 1987–2008. In Section 4 we use the estimated PDs to compute the corresponding Basel II capital requirements and its trend using the HP filter, and then compare different smoothing procedures using root mean square deviations from the HP trend. Section 5 contains our discussion of these results. Section 6 extends the analysis to adjustments using individual bank data and to the case where the loss given default moves along the business cycle, and also considers the cyclical adjustment of expected losses. Section 7 concludes. The Appendix contains the tables with the estimation results and the analysis of performance of the empirical model.

2. DEALING WITH THE PRO-CYCLICALITY OF BASEL II

In approaching the issue of how to deal with the pro-cyclical effects of Basel II it is important to stress that this regulation is not derived from a framework in which the costs and benefits of bank capital regulation are traded off. Instead, Basel II is derived from an ad hoc requirement that capital must cover credit losses with a confidence level of 99.9%, where the underlying probability distribution of loan losses is computed using a particular credit risk model. Thus there is no presumption that the resulting requirement is 'optimal' from a social welfare perspective.

Of course, designing optimal capital requirements is not an easy task, because one would require a proper economic model of the above-mentioned trade-off. A simple starting point could be the conceptual framework put forward by Kashyap and Stein (2004). In this framework, bank capital regulation is justified by the externalities associated with bank failures (losses to the deposit insurer, break-up of lending relationships, disruption to other players in the financial system, etc.). Bank capital regulation may serve to correct this externality, but if it is expensive for banks to raise and/or hold capital this will have a cost in terms of a reduction in the funding of positive Net Present Value (NPV) projects. Optimal regulation would trade off the reduction in the social costs of bank failures against the underinvestment of bank-dependent borrowers.

Using this framework, Kashyap and Stein (2004) argue that if the shadow value of bank capital is low in expansions and high in recessions, optimal capital charges for each type of risk should depend on the state of the business cycle. Without such adjustments, capital requirements would be too low in expansions, when bank capital is relatively plentiful and has a low shadow value, and too high in recessions, when the shadow value of bank capital goes up, leading to the amplification of business cycle fluctuations. They conclude that optimality would require a family of capital charge curves, with each curve corresponding to a different shadow value of bank capital. In this way, the cross-sectional dimension of Basel II (that is, that riskier exposures carry a higher capital charge) would be maintained, but without undesirable side-effects in the time series dimension.

One important issue that is not addressed in Kashyap and Stein (2004) is whether in the presence of risk-sensitive capital regulation banks have an incentive to build sufficient capital buffers (capital in excess of regulatory requirements) that could neutralize the effect of the cyclical variation in capital requirements. This was the view of many regulators before the onset of the current crisis. For example, Greenspan (2002) noted that 'the supervisory leg of Basel II is being structured to supplement market pressures in urging banks to build capital considerably over minimum levels in expansions as a buffer that can be drawn down in adversity and still maintain adequate capital.'

To address this issue, Repullo and Suarez (2009) construct a model that shows that banks have an incentive to hold capital buffers, but that the buffers maintained in expansions are typically insufficient to prevent a contraction in the supply of credit to bank-dependent borrowers at the arrival of a recession. They also show that Basel II leads to a substantial increase in the pro-cyclicality induced by bank capital regulation, with credit rationing at the beginning of a recession jumping from 1.4% to 10.7% on average in the baseline scenario. Finally they show that some simple cyclical adjustments in the 99.9% confidence level used to derive the Basel II capital requirements may significantly reduce its pro-cyclical effects.

In contrast with the normative approach of Kashyap and Stein (2004), the approach of Repullo and Suarez (2009) is positive. They take as given the Basel II regulation, and compute the associated costs in terms of credit rationing in different states of the credit cycle. This paper follows the latter approach. In particular, we do not attempt to provide a social welfare rationale for the various ad hoc adjustments that we compare, although we think that they could be related to the arguments in Kashyap and Stein (2004). Our focus is on how counter-cyclical regulation should be implemented in practice.

It could be argued that these adjustments should be left to the discretion of supervisors, in the context of the so-called 'supervisory review process' (Pillar 2) of Basel II. However, we believe that having a rule for counter-cyclical adjustments is better from the perspective of ensuring a level-playing field at the international level, and also for correcting possible biases in the objective function of supervisors, who would normally put extra weight on the avoidance of bank failures at the expense of the funding of positive NPV projects.

The rules that we consider imply changing the Basel II capital requirement k_{jt} for bank j at date t to a cyclically adjusted capital requirement $\hat{k}_{jt}$. The objective would be to remove the cyclical component of k_{jt} using a simple procedure that would be applied to all the banks (as opposed to using a different procedure for each bank). The natural benchmark for doing this adjustment is the trend of the k_{jt} series, which we compute by applying the HP filter. The comparison of the different procedures is conducted in Section 4 for a single fictional bank that aggregates all commercial and industrial loans in Spain, although in Section 6 we test the robustness of our results using individual bank data.

Summing up, this is not a paper about how optimal bank capital regulation should deal with business cycle fluctuations. It is a paper that considers fixing in an ad hoc manner an ad hoc regulation. Nothing can be done on the latter: risk-based regulation *à la* Basel II is already in place. And we think that the former is very important from a policy perspective, because Basel II has the potential to induce severe contractions in the supply of credit in downturns. Not surprisingly, discussions on pro-cyclicality are at the centre of the ongoing regulatory review process.

3. EMPIRICAL MODEL OF FIRMS' PROBABILITIES OF DEFAULT

3.1. Empirical model

To compute how Basel II capital requirements would evolve over the business cycle we estimate a model of default for the firms that borrowed from Spanish banks over the period 1987–2008. The model provides estimates of the PDs for each firm and year, which are used to compute the corresponding Basel II capital charges.

This procedure, although in line with other recent approaches,[10] is obviously subject to the Lucas critique. Had Basel II been in place, banks' decisions over lending, and consequently the pool of borrowers, might have been different. However, the dominant role of universal banks in the Spanish financial system, the limited role of securitization, as well as the tight model of supervision implemented by the Bank of Spain, suggest that composition effects may not be very significant.

[10] See, for example, Committee of European Banking Supervisors (2009), Kashyap and Stein (2004), and Saurina and Trucharte (2007).

Based on direct information on firms' economic and financial conditions, banks grant loans with very different characteristics. Some of these differential features are, directly or indirectly, contained in the information included in the Credit Register of the Bank of Spain and constitute the basis for our empirical analysis.

The Credit Register also provides information on the default status of each loan. This allows us to construct the dependent variable for the regression (logit) model, y_{it+1}, which is a dichotomous (zero-one) variable that takes value 1 if borrower i defaults in year $t + 1$, and 0 otherwise.[11] A borrower is considered to have defaulted if it is 90 days overdue failing to meet its financial obligations on a certain loan or if, with a high probability, it is considered to be unable to meet its obligations. If a borrower has several loans, failure to meet payments on any of them means that the borrower is in default. The default event is conditional, requiring that a firm defaulting in a certain year shall not have defaulted during the previous year.

The next step is to specify the explanatory variables, all dated in year t, that include variables that describe the characteristics of the borrower and its risk profile, as well as macroeconomic controls and regional (Spanish province in which the firm is registered) and industry (NACE code) dummies.

$COLLATERAL_{it}$ represents the average (weighted by the size of the exposures) of the proportion of guarantees in a firm's borrowing.[12] The empirical evidence (Berger and Udell, 1990, Jiménez *et al.*, 2006) shows that banks ask for collateral to those firms perceived as riskier. $MATURITY_{it}$ represents the proportion of long-term exposures (more than one year) over total exposures. The longer the maturity of a loan, the more thorough will be the screening process of the quality of the borrower. Riskier borrowers will probably be granted only short-term loans. AGE_{it} tries to approximate the age of each firm, with the idea of capturing that firms of recent creation are more prone to disappear than older ones. Thus, higher rates of default are expected during the first years of activity. As the relationship is not likely to be linear, we have constructed a set of dummy variables each accounting for the number of years (one, two, three, and four or more) a borrower has been reporting to the Credit Register. $FIRM\_SIZE_{it}$ stands for the total amount of bank borrowing, and proxies for the size of each firm. The variable has been deflated by the consumer price index, and enters the model in logarithmic terms.

We also include in the model the variable $NUMBER\_BANKS_{it}$, representing the number of banks that have granted a loan to firm i in year t. We hypothesize that the more banks a firm is related to, the more constrained it may be in terms of liquidity and thus the higher its PD. We expect a non-linear relationship between this variable and the default event, so it enters the equation in logarithmic terms. We have also included a variable that accounts for the number of times a firm

[11] This definition is similar to that established in Basel II; see BCBS (2006, para. 452).

[12] Clearly, some of the explanatory variables (such as collateral) may be endogenous, but this is not a problem for our empirical model since we are interested in predicting default, not in estimating causal effects.

changes its main lender, *MAIN_LENDER_CHANGE*$_{it}$. It indicates the frequency with which a firm changes the bank that provides the largest amount of funding. High values of this variable imply high rates of rotation and hence possible constraints or even difficulties in securing finance, which suggest low creditworthiness. *UTILIZATION*$_{it}$ is the ratio between the amount of credit drawn by a borrower and the total available amount (credit line). For various reasons, firms extensively use credit line facilities where they can withdraw funds at any time. Collateral required, if any, remains pledged to the credit line. The rationale for this variable is that the more a borrower withdraws, the more liquidity constrained it may be. The empirical evidence in Jiménez *et al.* (2009a) shows that firms that eventually default draw down more intensely their credit lines.[13]

HISTORIC_DELINQUENCY$_{it}$ represents the borrowers' record of overdue loans that have been paid before the 90-day threshold (that is, before having defaulted) measured as the number of years in which the firm has been delinquent divided by the number of years it has been reporting to the Credit Register. The problems behind overdue loans are sometimes 'technical', spanning only a few days as a result of mismatches in cash flows, but in other cases they are good predictors of future defaults. *HISTORIC_DEFAULT*$_{it}$ is another risk profile variable that captures whether a certain borrower defaulted in the past.[14] As in the case of the delinquency variable, this variable is defined as the number of years in which the firm has been in default divided by the number of years it has been reporting to the Credit Register.[15]

The macroeconomic controls are the rate of growth of the gross domestic product, *GDP_GROWTH*$_t$, the rate of growth of the commercial and industrial loans in the Credit Register, *CREDIT_GROWTH*$_t$, and the return of the Spanish stock market index, *STOCK_MARKET_RETURN*$_t$. These variables proxy macroeconomic activity factors that affect credit risk, an essential ingredient for our analysis of the cyclical implications of Basel II.

3.2. Data

The database used in the estimation of the model of PDs is the Credit Register of the Bank of Spain (CIR). This Register records monthly information on all credit operations granted by all credit institutions operating in Spain for a value of over €6,000. The data distinguishes between loans to firms and to households. CIR includes information on the characteristics of each loan, including the following: instrument (trade credit, financial credit, leasing, etc.), currency denomination,

[13] In fact, utilization ratios are significantly different for defaulted and non-defaulted firms well in advance of the date of default (even 4 or 5 years before).

[14] The dates have to be $t-1$ or earlier to be consistent with the definition of default: failing to meet its financial obligations in year $t+1$ given that it was not in default in year t.

[15] Jiménez *et al.* (2009a) show that these two variables are good proxies for firms' financial condition. When they replace them by balance sheet and profit and loss data there is no significant change in the fit of the empirical model.

maturity, existence of guarantees or collateral, type of guarantor, coverage of the guarantee, amount drawn and undrawn of a credit commitment, and whether the loan is current in payment or past due, distinguishing in turn between delinquency and default status. CIR also includes information on the characteristics of borrowers: province of residence and, for firms, the industry in which they carry out their main economic activity.

Our analysis focuses on loans to firms. The sample period goes from 1984 to 2008, although for estimation purposes and to use explanatory variables such as age or historic delinquency and default it spans from 1987 to 2008. It should be noted that this time span includes the recession of the early 1990s and the subsequent upturn during the late 1990s and the first years of the current decade. The database contains a vast amount of information (about 10 million observations). To facilitate the analysis we have randomly selected a 10% sample, which leaves us with about 1 million observations. The main statistics of the sample (and in particular those referred to the default condition of borrowers) perfectly match those of the entire population.

3.3. Results

Table A1 in the Appendix presents the results of the estimation of the model. The results show that firms that post collateral when granted a loan have higher PDs. Lenders try to mitigate risks by requiring collateral to those firms that they consider riskier. Longer maturities are associated with lower default rates, and this is also the case for the age of the borrower. Big firms are safer than smaller ones. Firms that are two or three years old have, on average, lower credit quality, and as they grow older their default rate decreases. The more lenders a firm has and the higher rotation of its main lender the higher its PD. The higher the utilization of credit lines the higher the PD, so liquidity constraints also seem to play a role in firms' default. Regarding risk-profile variables, past overdue and past default events are a signal of future defaults. Finally, the macroeconomic controls show that firms' defaults increase during downturns, proxied by low GDP growth, credit growth, and stock market returns.

Tests of stability have been carried out by estimating the model without some of the variables, which does not change the signs and statistical significance of the remaining variables, and by omitting some years of the sample period, which leads to very small changes in the estimated coefficients. The model classifies correctly approximately 70% of the defaulted and non-defaulted firms in the sample (see Table A2 in the Appendix).[16] Finally, we tested the predictive power of the model

[16] Alternative performance measures confirm the predictive power of the model. In particular, the area under the ROC curve is over 76% which results in an Accuracy Ratio (AR) of 52%. These results are in line with those in the related literature; for example, Chava and Jarrow (2004) obtain an AR of 53%.

by using a second 10% sample of the population. The parameters estimated with the original sample were used to predict defaults in the validation sample. The results show that 68% of defaulted and 71% of non-defaulted firms were correctly classified.

4. CYCLICAL ADJUSTMENT OF BASEL II CAPITAL REQUIREMENTS

4.1. Point-in-time (PIT) capital requirements

The results reported in Section 3.3 allow us to compute the PIT capital requirements k_{it} for each borrower and each year using the Basel II formula for corporate exposures (BCBS, 2006, para. 272) included in Box 1, the estimated probability of default PD_{it}, and assuming an LGD of 45% (as in the foundation IRB approach of Basel II),[17] and a 1-year maturity. We then compute the aggregate PIT capital requirements per unit of loans for each year, that is

$$k_t = \frac{\Sigma_i k_{it}}{\Sigma_i l_{it}}, \tag{1}$$

where l_{it} denotes the value of the loans to firm i at the end of year t.

Figure 1 shows how aggregate PIT capital requirements per unit of loans would have evolved in Spain during the sample period had Basel II been in place, together with the Spanish GDP growth rate. Both series are highly negatively correlated (the correlation is –0.80), which suggests that GDP growth rates may be useful to mitigate the pro-cyclicality of Basel II. It is important to note that this result is not due to the fact that GDP growth is one of the explanatory variables in our empirical model. We also run cross-section regressions for each year of the sample (thus excluding the macroeconomic controls) and computed the PDs and the corresponding Basel II capital requirements, obtaining a cyclical profile very similar to that in Figure 1 (the correlation between both series was 0.94).

There is a very significant cyclical variation of the Basel II capital requirements when they are calculated with PIT PDs. In 1993, at the worst point in the business cycle, they would have been 11.9%, falling to around 8% at the peak of the cycle (8.07% in 2005, 7.63% in 2006, and 8.06% in 1986, three years of strong economic expansion). The variability of 57% in Basel II capital requirements from peak to trough contrasts with the flat 8% requirements of Basel I.[18]

It should be noted that the average capital requirement over the sample period is 9.37%, higher than the 8% of Basel I,[19] but this has little significance because

[17] Section 5.2 analyses the case where LGDs vary over the business cycle.

[18] It can be argued that this result is only for a specific portfolio (of loans to firms). However, Saurina and Trucharte (2007) show that PIT capital requirements also fluctuate significantly for mortgage portfolios in Spain. Loans to firms and mortgages represent close to 90% of total loan portfolios of Spanish banks.

[19] The actual capital requirement would have been 8%, since loans to firms had a 100% risk-weight under Basel I.

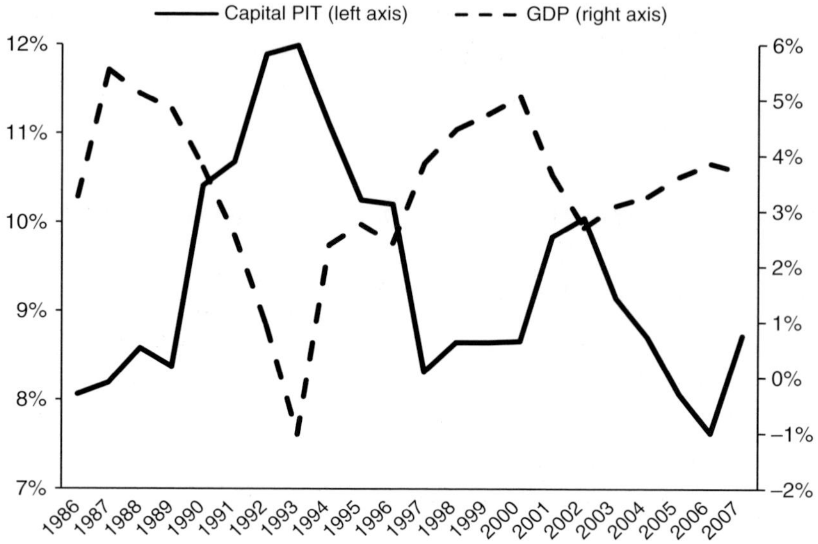

Figure 1. PIT capital requirements and GDP growth

Notes: This figure shows the aggregate PIT Basel II capital requirements per unit of loans for the portfolio of commercial and industrial loans of Spanish banks, together with the Spanish GDP growth rate.

Source: Authors' calculations (capital), Instituto Nacional Estadística, INE (GDP growth).

we are only looking at the portfolio of commercial and industrial loans that typically bears higher capital charges than other important parts of banks' portfolios such as mortgages. In fact, Basel II was calibrated so that banks would hold total capital equivalent to at least 8% of their risk-weighted assets.

4.2. The Hodrick–Prescott benchmark

To identify a trend in the PIT capital requirements series we apply a HP filter with a smoothing parameter $\lambda = 100$ (annual data).[20] Figure 2 shows the HP trend in dashed lines. As expected, the trend filters out the cyclical movements in the capital requirement series, being below the series in bad times and above the series in good times, but maintains the risk-sensitiveness of the capital requirements along the business cycle (i.e. they increase in downturns and decline in upturns). The purpose of computing this trend is to provide a benchmark for the comparison of different alternatives proposed in the literature to mitigate the cyclicality of the Basel II requirements.

[20] The choice of the smoothing parameter λ depends on the purpose of the exercise. Using the standard value for annual data ($\lambda = 6.25$) produces a trend that follows more closely the series and consequently leaves smaller cyclical variations of capital requirements. However, a number of people criticized this feature and suggested to us using a flat benchmark (see Section 6.3). For this reason, we chose to work with $\lambda = 100$. Nevertheless, the qualitative results are not very sensitive to the choice of λ.

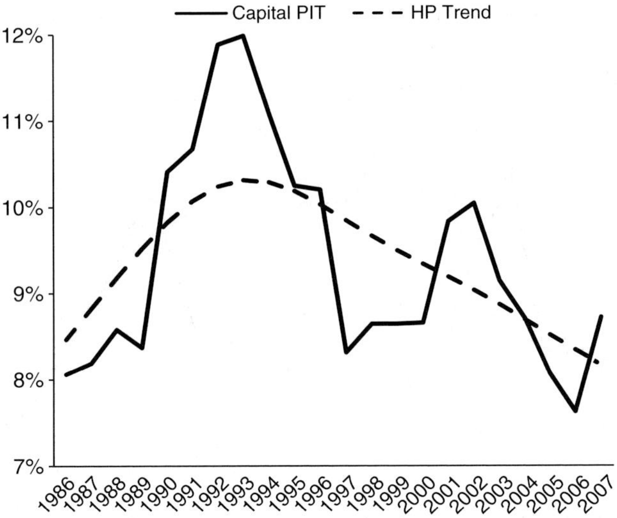

Figure 2. PIT capital requirements and HP trend

Notes: This figure shows the aggregate PIT Basel II capital requirements per unit of loans for the portfolio of commercial and industrial loans of Spanish banks, together with the HP trend.

Source: Authors' calculations.

4.3. Adjusting the input of the Basel II formula: TTC capital requirements

The first procedure that we analyse is to smooth the PD input of the Basel II formula by using TTC PDs. To estimate these PDs we follow the idea in Saurina and Trucharte (2007) of replacing the current values of the macroeconomic controls by their average values over the sample period. We then compute the capital requirements for each borrower and each year using the Basel II formula for corporate exposures, the estimated TTC PDs, an LGD of 45%, and a maturity of 1 year. Figure 3 shows the TTC capital requirements per unit of loans for each year of the sample.

In comparison with the PIT capital requirements, the cyclical variability of the TTC capital requirements series declines significantly. The maximum is reached in 1991, two years before the recession, at the level of 10.8%, while the minimum is 8.8% in 2005. The change in capital requirements from peak to trough goes down to 25%, which is less than half of the 57% figure obtained for the PIT series. Alternatively, the standard deviation of the TTC series is 0.62, while for the PIT series was 1.27. Figure 3 also shows that TTC PDs would have produced capital levels above those corresponding to PIT PDs during the boom of 2003–2007, with a very significant increase in 2005 and 2006.

4.4. Adjusting the output of the Basel II formula

The second procedure to adjust the Basel II capital requirements that we analyse is to apply to the PIT series a *business cycle multiplier* of the form:

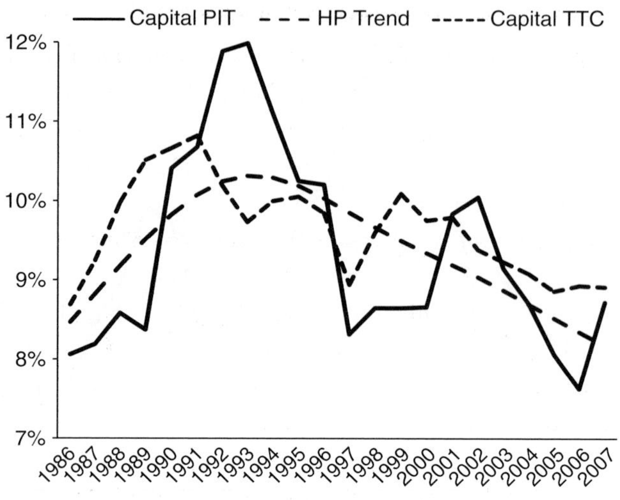

Figure 3. PIT and TTC capital requirements and HP trend

Notes: This figure shows the aggregate PIT and TTC Basel II capital requirements per unit of loans for the portfolio of commercial and industrial loans of Spanish banks, together with the HP trend of the PIT series.

Source: Authors' calculations.

$$\hat{k}_t = \mu_t k_t \tag{2}$$

where k_t is the original PIT capital requirements series, computed using the Basel II formula in Box 1, and $\hat{k}_t$ is the adjusted series. A convenient functional form for the multiplier μ_t is:

$$\mu_t = \mu(g_t, \alpha) = 2N\left(\frac{\alpha(g_t - \bar{g})}{\sigma_g}\right) \tag{3}$$

where g_t is the growth rate of some indicator variable of the business cycle, $\bar{g}$ its long-run average, σ_g its long-run standard deviation, $N(\cdot)$ is the standard normal cumulative distribution function, and α is a positive parameter. The multiplier μ_t in (3) has several key features: it is continuous and increasing in the proxy for the business cycle g_t, so capital requirements would be increased in good times and reduced in bad times, it is equal to 1 when $g_t = \bar{g}$, so there would be no adjustment at the average of the business cycle indicator, and it is bounded, so capital requirements do not increase without bound or become negative. The normalization of the business cycle indicator allows us to express changes of capital requirements (surcharges) in terms of standard deviation movements with respect to the average value of the indicator. Any functional form with these features could be an alternative, but (3) is a particularly simple one.

Two issues related to the proposed adjustment have to be addressed. First, what is the variable that should be chosen as indicator of the business cycle? Second, how does one choose parameter α? With respect to the first issue, we consider the three macroeconomic controls used in the empirical model, namely the rate of growth of the GDP, the rate of growth of bank credit, and the return of the stock market. With respect to the second, we propose as criterion for the choice of α (for each proxy for the business cycle) to minimize the root mean square deviations (RMSD) of the adjusted series with respect to the HP trend. In other words, we choose the value of α that is best in terms of smoothing the cyclical component of the PIT capital requirements series.

The results obtained are as follows. When the variable selected as indicator of the business cycle is the rate of growth of the GDP we get $\alpha(\text{GDP}) = 0.081$; when the variable is the rate of growth of bank credit we get $\alpha(\text{credit}) = 0.075$; and when the variable is the return of the stock market we get $\alpha(\text{stock market}) = 0.038$.

Figures 4, 5 and 6 show the adjustment of the PIT capital requirements for the three indicators of the business cycle and the optimally chosen values of parameter α, together with the HP trend. It can be readily seen that the stock market indicator does very poorly in terms of approaching the HP benchmark, while the other two are much better.

An alternative procedure to adjust the output of the Basel II formula is to follow the proposal of Gordy and Howells (2006) to use an autoregressive filter of the form

$$\hat{k}_t = \hat{k}_{t-1} + \phi(k_t - \hat{k}_{t-1}) \tag{4}$$

where k_t is the original PIT capital series and $\hat{k}_t$ is the adjusted series, and ϕ is a positive parameter. As in the case of parameter α, we propose as criterion for the choice of ϕ to minimize the RMSD of the adjusted series with respect to the HP trend, which gives $\phi = 0.306$.

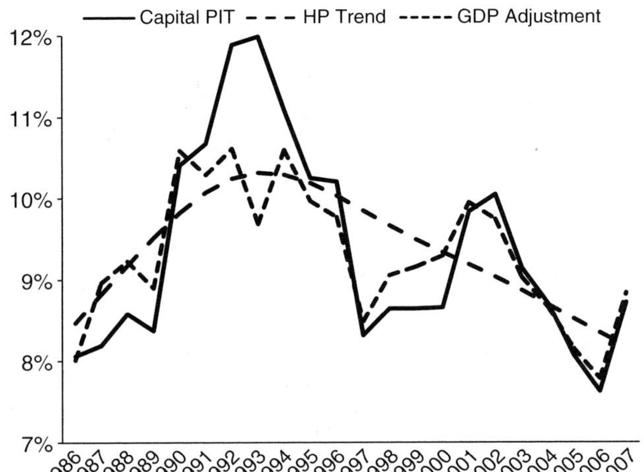

Figure 4. PIT capital requirements, GDP adjustment, and HP trend

Notes: This figure shows the aggregate PIT Basel II capital requirements per unit of loans for the portfolio of commercial and industrial loans of Spanish banks, the adjustment using a multiplier based on GDP growth, and the HP trend of the PIT series.

Source: Authors' calculations.

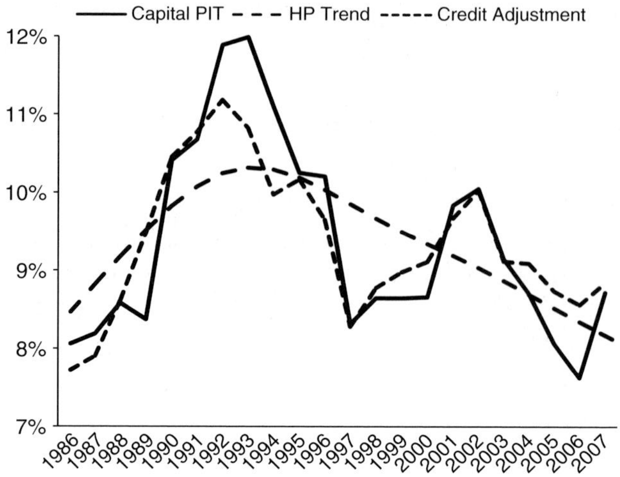

Figure 5. PIT capital requirements, credit adjustment, and HP trend

Notes: This figure shows the aggregate PIT Basel II capital requirements per unit of loans for the portfolio of commercial and industrial loans of Spanish banks, the adjustment using a multiplier based on credit growth, and the HP trend of the PIT series.

Source: Authors' calculations.

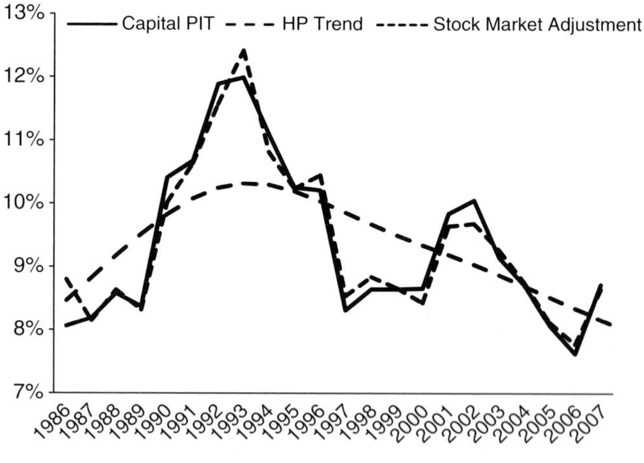

Figure 6. PIT capital requirements, stock market adjustment, and HP trend

Notes: This figure shows the aggregate PIT Basel II capital requirements per unit of loans for the portfolio of commercial and industrial loans of Spanish banks, the adjustment using a multiplier based on the return of the Spanish stock market, and the HP trend of the PIT series.

Source: Authors' calculations.

Figure 7 shows the autoregressive adjustment of the PIT capital requirements for the optimally chosen value of ϕ, together with the HP trend. As expected, this adjustment follows the original series with a lag. The results in Repullo and Suarez

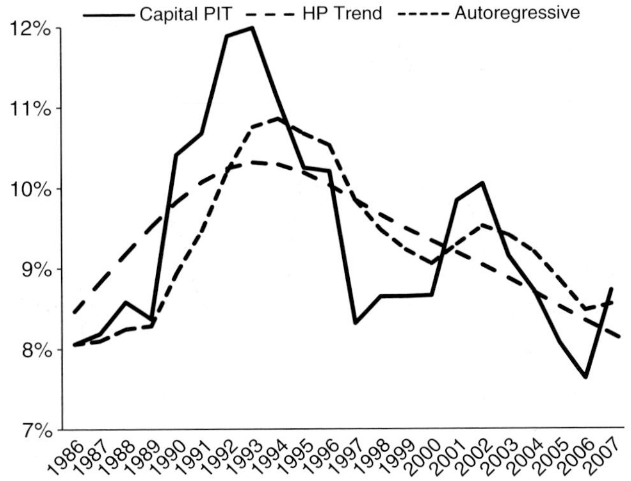

Figure 7. PIT capital requirements, autoregressive adjustment, and HP trend

Notes: This figure shows the aggregate PIT Basel II capital requirements per unit of loans for the portfolio of commercial and industrial loans of Spanish banks, the autoregressive adjustment, and the HP trend of the PIT series.

Source: Authors' calculations.

(2009) suggest that this is a significant shortcoming, especially in downturns, when capital requirements should be brought down in order to reduce the likelihood of a credit crunch. Another disadvantage of the autoregressive adjustment, noted by Gordy and Howells (2006, p. 415), is that 'it assumes that the bank's lending strategy is stationary. A weak bank would have the incentive to ramp up portfolio risk rapidly, because required capital would catch up only slowly'.

4.5. Comparing the different smoothing procedures

In line with the proposed HP benchmark, we compare the different smoothing procedures by computing the RMSD of the adjusted series with respect to the HP trend. Table 1 shows the results, together with the estimated values of parameters α and ϕ. It also shows a performance indicator given by the percentage reduction in the RMSD of the original series with respect to the HP trend that is achieved by each procedure (so the indicator would be 100% if the adjusted series coincided with the HP trend). Two procedures are clearly dominated according to this criterion, namely adjusting the output of the Basel II formula with a credit growth multiplier and with a stock market returns multiplier. The other three procedures are very similar in terms of RMSD. We have argued that there are good reasons to discard the autoregressive adjustment, so the final choice is between smoothing the input of the Basel II formula with TTC PDs and smoothing the output with a GDP growth multiplier. The discussion of the pros and cons of these two procedures is contained in the next section.

Table 1. Root mean square deviations from the HP trend for different adjustment procedures

Type of adjustment	α or ϕ	RMSD	Performance (%)
TTC PDs	–	0.0055	35.6
GDP growth	0.0810	0.0054	37.6
Credit growth	0.0745	0.0066	23.5
Stock market return	0.0382	0.0081	5.3
Autoregressive	0.3062	0.0054	36.9

Notes: This table compares the performance in terms of RMSDs from the HP trend of the following adjustment procedures: TTC PDs, multipliers based on GDP growth, credit growth, and stock market returns, and autoregressive adjustment. It also shows the relative performance of each procedure, measured by the reduction in the RMSDs of the original series with respect to the HP trend, and the value of parameter α for the multipliers based on GDP growth, credit growth and stock market return, and of parameter ϕ for the autoregressive adjustment.

Source: Authors' calculations.

It is interesting to note in Figure 5 the early tightening in the last years of the sample of the series adjusted with the credit growth multiplier. For this reason, we also tried a multiplier that used as inputs both GDP growth and credit growth. The results were only marginally better than those obtained with the GDP growth multiplier, with a RMSD of 0.0052 and a performance indicator of 39.6%. The disappointing result, together with the additional complexity involved, led us to discard this procedure.

Given the functional form (3) of the multiplier μ_t, the value α(GDP) = 0.081 implies that capital requirements should be increased in expansions and reduced in recessions by approximately 6.5% (since $\mu_t = 2\mathcal{N}(0.081) = 1.065$) for each standard deviation in GDP growth. The relatively low value of α(GDP) also implies that the multiplier is almost linear for reasonable values of GDP growth. In particular, we have $\mu_t = 1.13$ for two standard deviations and $\mu_t = 1.19$ for three standard deviations in GDP growth. This is a convenient property that allows us to easily translate changes in the business cycle indicator into capital surcharges.

It is important to note that during the second half of 1989 and the whole of 1990 there were binding credit growth limits in Spain. Those limits were an extraordinary measure to complement conventional monetary policy tools during a period in which inflation was hard to control. In order to avoid any potential bias in our results against the credit growth multiplier, we have rerun the whole exercise from 1991 onwards. RMSDs show almost no change. GDP growth is still better than credit growth, although now the TTC PDs adjustment is slightly better than the GDP growth adjustment.

It should be noted that the methodology presented in this paper may be used to assess other proposals to mitigate the pro-cyclicality of Basel II. For instance, it could be argued that one should focus on proxies for the business cycle that are more closely related to banks' business activity, such as loan losses or profitability. However, in both cases the results are disappointing. The RMSD corresponding to a multiplier based on the ratio of loan loss provisions to total loans is 0.0077,[21] while the RMSD corresponding to the multipliers based on ROA (return on assets) and ROE (return on equity) are 0.0075 and 0.0070, respectively, which are much higher than the figures in Table 1 for the GDP growth multiplier.[22]

Recently, macro-variables such as the ratio of credit to GDP have been proposed as a possible indicator to deal with the pro-cyclicality of capital requirements (see, for example, Borio and Drehmann, 2009, and Committee of the Global Financial System, 2010). The idea behind the use of this ratio is that increases in the value of the credit to GDP ratio are associated with higher leverage levels in the economy and could also imply lowering lending standards and thus higher credit risk. As the risk increases during rapid credit growth episodes (relative to the expansion of the economic activity), so should capital requirements. Jiménez and Saurina (2006) provide robust empirical evidence for the Spanish banking system of a close relationship between credit expansion and risk taking by banks. However, we are not convinced that the ratio of credit to GDP is the best variable to carry out the adjustment of the pro-cyclicality of capital requirements. First, this ratio is a variable that normally shows an increasing trend along time. In particular, in bad times the reduction in GDP will continue pressing the ratio upwards providing the wrong signal in terms of the required adjustment. Second, the performance of a multiplier based on the credit to GDP ratio is even worse than the multiplier based on the stock market return, with a RMSD of 0.0085.

Finally, some people have argued that the adjustment could be done using forward-looking credit market variables such as credit default swaps (CDS) indices or corporate bond spreads (see, for example, Gordy and Howells, 2006). However, it is not possible to find such variables for the Spanish market during the whole period under analysis. Even in the last few years, there is only a small number of Spanish non-financial companies for which CDS are traded, and there is not much information about the liquidity of those contracts (to figure out how reliable prices could be). A similar remark applies to corporate bond spreads.

5. DISCUSSION

5.1. What is the best procedure?

Our previous results show that the best procedures for mitigating the pro-cyclicality of the Basel II capital requirements are either to adjust the input of the Basel II formula using TTC PDs or to adjust the output with a multiplier based on GDP growth.

[21] We are using specific loan loss provisions, that is, provisions that cover individually identified losses.

[22] At any rate, we would be rather sceptical about making regulation contingent on a variable that may be easily manipulated by the regulated. See Beatty *et al.* (1995), Ahmed *et al.* (1999), and Pérez *et al.* (2008), among many others.

The use of TTC PDs has been criticized by Gordy and Howells (2006, pp. 414–15) on the grounds that 'changes in a bank's capital requirements over time would be only weakly correlated with changes in its economic capital, and there would be no means to infer economic capital from regulatory capital'. They also point out that 'through-the-cycle ratings are less sensitive to market conditions than point-in-time ones, [so] they are less useful for active portfolio management and as inputs to ratings-based pricing models'. Finally, they add (p. 406) that 'despite the ubiquity of the term "through-the-cycle" in descriptions of rating methods, there seems to be no consensus on precisely what is meant'.

As noted in Financial Services Authority (2009, p. 89) adjusting PDs so that they reflect 'an average experience across the cycle' involves a very significant challenge, since it requires 'the ability to differentiate changes in default experience that are due entirely to the economic cycle from those that are due to a changing level of non-cyclical risk in the portfolio'. As a result, they observe that 'in general firms have not developed TTC ratings systems whose technical challenges are typically greater than those of PIT approaches'. The UK Financial Services Authority has been working with the industry to develop a so-called 'quasi-TTC' rating approach, based on adjusting the PIT PDs by a cyclical scaling factor. However, calibrating such a factor seems a difficult task. From this perspective, doing the scaling with the output of the Basel II formula, along the lines that we have proposed above, seems much easier.

The difficulty in making precise the notion of TTC ratings implies that this adjustment procedure would be implemented very differently across banks in a single jurisdiction, and especially across banks in different jurisdictions, so level playing field issues are likely to emerge. These issues would be particularly difficult to resolve because of the lack of transparency of the procedure. From this perspective, it also seems better to do the adjustment with a single (and fully transparent) macro multiplier.

Finally, it has been argued that using one-year-ahead PDs is not appropriate for loans with longer maturities, and that for this reason a TTC procedure would be more appropriate. The reply to this objection is three-fold. First, the share of long-term loans in non-mortgage portfolios is relatively small.[23] Second, even for longer-term loans, a correct assessment of their risk should be done conditional on the state of the economy, not in an unconditional manner. Doing the latter, which is in the spirit of TTC ratings, contradicts the Basel II requirement of using 'all relevant and material information in assigning ratings' (BCBS, 2006, para. 426). Third, one should remember that the Basel II formula incorporates a maturity adjustment factor that is supposed to take care of possible downgrades during the life of the loan.

The distinction between conditional and unconditional assessments of risk deserves further discussion. To make it more precise, consider an economy with

[23] For example, the proportion of loans in our sample with an initial maturity over one year is only 28%.

two aggregate states, expansion (denoted by h) and recession (denoted by l). Let p_h and p_l denote the representative PDs in the two states, with $p_h < p_l$, and let q_{ij} denote the transition probability from state i to state j. From the transition probabilities one can derive the unconditional probabilities, q_h and q_l, of being in each state, which gives the unconditional probability of default $\bar{p} = q_h p_h + q_l p_l$. Now suppose that the economy is in an expansion state, and that we want to price a one-year loan. Clearly we should use the PIT p_h rather than the TTC $\bar{p}$. Similarly, for a two-year loan we should use p_h for the first year, and (if the loan does not default during the first year) $q_{hh}p_h + q_{hl}p_l$ for the second year. If q_{hh} is sufficiently high, that is, if expansions have a long duration, then this PD will be close to p_h, so using the (conditional on the state) one-year-ahead PD would be approximately correct for pricing purposes. And so on for longer maturity loans. The conclusion is that cyclically adjusting the PDs produces a distortion in the correct measurement of risk that makes them inadequate for risk pricing and risk management purposes.

This is especially relevant in the light of the requirements on the use of internal ratings specified by the BCBS (2006, para. 444): 'Internal ratings and default and loss estimates must play an essential role in the credit approval, risk management, internal capital allocations, and corporate governance functions of banks using the IRB approach.'

The preceding arguments suggest that adjusting the input of the IRB formula by using TTC PDs has many shortcomings. The alternative procedure, to adjust the output with a multiplier based on GDP growth, is much better in terms of simplicity, transparency, low cost of implementation, consistency with banks' risk pricing and risk management systems, and even consistency with the idea of a single aggregate risk factor that underlies the capital requirements of Basel II (see Gordy, 2003).

5.2. Alternative forms of the multiplier

The proposed multiplier could be adjusted in several ways. For example, the range of μ_t in (2) goes from 0 (when $g_t \to -\infty$) to 2 (when $g_t \to \infty$), but one could easily introduce alternative lower and an upper bounds so that $1 - \Delta \leq \mu_t \leq 1 + \Delta$. Alternatively, the multiplier could be redefined so that $\bar{g} = g_{\min}$ where $g_{\min}$ is the lowest value of GDP growth in the sample. In this way, it would be possible to generate a positive buffer of regulatory capital, so minimum capital requirements would be cyclically adjusted but would never be below the level specified by the Basel II formulas with PIT PDs.

5.3. Application to international banks

The procedure of adjusting the Basel II capital requirements with a multiplier based on GDP growth would be applied in each national jurisdiction, possibly with different multipliers for different portfolios, and only for banks that are under the

IRB approach of Basel II, on the grounds that the standardized approach is only minimally risk-sensitive. The procedure is very simple, since it only requires a readily available macroeconomic variable such as the rate of growth of the GDP, and very transparent, since it would be possible to ask the banks to report the unadjusted capital requirements (and the corresponding risk-weighted assets). It would of course imply having different capital requirements for different jurisdictions, but this is an inevitable feature of any procedure designed to correct the effect of the business cycle on risk-sensitive capital requirements. It should also be noted that with the increasing correlation in international business cycles these differences should not be very significant.

The procedure would involve some complexity in its application to international banks, especially those that have significant cross-border lending activities. To limit the possibility of regulatory arbitrage, which could lead to a concentration of lending from the jurisdiction with the lowest multiplier, some general criterion should be established. A possible approach would be to base the calculation of capital requirements on the geographic location of the credit exposures. The final requirement would be computed by adding all the adjustments in the jurisdictions in which the bank has a significant exposure. As commented above, the methodology is very simple and transparent and the required data are easily accessible in all countries.

5.4. GDP revisions

One relevant issue about the cyclical adjustment of capital requirements using a multiplier based on GDP growth is the fact that in many countries GDP statistics are usually revised, sometimes by significant amounts. The revisions are obviously more important for the quarter-on-quarter data, rather than the year-on-year data, so we would favour using the latter. We would also favour using the latest data corresponding to the second to last quarter, without making any subsequent adjustments in the multiplier. For example, in the United States the Bureau of Economic Analysis (BEA) releases three quarterly GDP reports: the advance report that comes out within one month after the end of the quarter, the second report (formerly called the preliminary report) that comes out within two months after the end of the quarter, and the third report (formerly called the final report) that comes out within three months after the end of the quarter. Thus for the United States we could use the final data for second to last quarter (for example, the end-of-2009 multiplier could have been set with the third quarter data released on 22 December), so the problem of revisions would not arise. Even when this is not the case, leaving unchanged the multiplier after revisions in GDP data should not generate significant deviations with respect to its final 'correct' value. For example, for $\alpha(\text{GDP}) = 0.081$ a revision amounting to 0.25 standard deviations of GDP growth would have a maximum impact on the multiplier of 1.6% (since $2\mathcal{N}(0.081/4) = 1.016$).

5.5. How would banks react to the adjustment?

The potential pro-cyclical effects of bank capital regulation depend not only on the design of the minimum capital requirements but also on the endogenous response of banks to the regulation, in terms of the characteristics of their portfolio and the incentives to hold capital above the minimum required by regulation. Repullo and Suarez (2009) analyse the effect on capital buffers of modifying the cyclical profile of the 99.9% confidence level of Basel II, and hence the corresponding capital requirements, so that they are lower in recessions and higher in expansions. The results show that this policy changes the cyclical behaviour of the capital buffers in a direction that partly offsets its intended effect (reducing them in expansions and increasing them in recessions), but the net effect is a significant reduction in the pro-cyclicality of the regulation.

5.6. Contingent capital: is it an alternative?

Contingent capital has recently emerged in policy discussions as an instrument that could be useful to deal with the pro-cyclicality problem.[24] Contingent capital is a debt instrument with the potential of converting into common equity during periods of financial strain. This property effectively helps banks to weather recession periods without having to resort to issuing equity in unfavourable conditions. At the same time, it could be a cost-effective way for banks to reduce their capital holdings, and hence its costs, in normal times. From a regulatory perspective there are two problems with using contingent capital as part of the regulatory framework. First, a number of important design issues should be resolved, especially in connection with the trigger points for conversion.[25] Second, there is the view that the new capital regulation should focus on core capital, playing down the role of hybrid securities such as subordinated debt.[26] The proposal of strengthening the current definition of capital could be blurred if a new hybrid instrument is brought into the picture. However, contingent capital could be useful as an instrument outside of the regulatory framework for banks to manage their capital over the business cycle. Design issues would be addressed by private contracting, and regulators would be able to focus on core capital. Obviously, the availability of such an instrument would alter banks' incentives to hold capital buffers, but this would not probably change the amplification effects of risk-sensitive capital regulation *à la* Basel II. This is an interesting topic that should be pursued in future work.

[24] See, for example, Kashyap *et al.* (2008) and Flannery (2009).

[25] As noted recently by Sundaresan and Wang (2010), the proposal for banks to issue contingent capital that is forced to convert into common equity when stock prices fall below a certain specified low threshold does not in general lead to a unique equilibrium, which opens the door to price manipulation.

[26] See, for example, Basel Committee on Banking Supervision (2009).

6. EXTENSIONS

6.1. Adjustments using individual bank data

The results obtained in Section 4 are based on an adjustment calibrated for the entire banking system, but they would be applied to individual banks. Therefore it is important to check the performance of the different procedures with individual bank data. In addition, this extension allows us to assess the performance of adjustments based on disaggregated data such as the credit growth of each bank.

In particular, we have chosen five Spanish banks that have opted for the IRB approach of Basel II, and that are currently calculating their minimum capital requirements using the IRB formulas. We compute the PIT capital requirements per unit of exposure for each of these five banks and for each year of the sample using the estimated PDs, an LGD of 45%, and a 1 year maturity.

The results show that there is significant heterogeneity across our sample of five banks, despite the fact that they all operate at the national level (i.e., there are no regional banks). The average value over the sample period of their Basel II capital requirements ranges from 4.5% to 8.2%, and the range of variation from peak to trough is between two and three times higher than the 57% figure obtained for the aggregate data. The significant heterogeneity among these banks makes the comparison of the different adjustment procedures much more interesting.

The analysis is carried out with the PIT capital requirements series data of the five selected banks plus a sixth fictitious bank that comprises all the other banks in the system. To provide a benchmark for the comparison of the different procedures, we compute for each of these six banks the HP trend of each capital requirements series.

Following the steps in Section 4, we first consider adjusting the PD input of the Basel II formula by using TTC PDs estimated by replacing in the regression model the current values of the macroeconomic controls by their average values over the sample period. In this way we get the TTC capital requirements for each of the six banks. Second, we apply to the PIT series of each bank the business cycle multiplier (3), where the value of parameter α (for each proxy for the business cycle) is chosen to minimize the sum for the six banks of the RMSD of the adjusted series with respect to the HP trends.[27] As proxies for the business cycle, we use the rate of growth of the GDP, the rate of growth of the credit of each bank, and the return of the stock market. Finally, we also compute for each bank the autoregressive adjustment (4), where the value of parameter ϕ is chosen to minimize the sum for the six banks of the RMSDs of the adjusted series with respect to the HP trends.

In line with this approach, we compare the different procedures in terms of the sum for the six banks of the RMSDs of the adjusted series with respect to their HP

[27] Although parameter α could be estimated for each bank, we restrict attention to multipliers that have the same α for all banks within a jurisdiction.

Table 2. Root mean square deviations from the HP trend for different adjustment procedures using individual bank data

Type of adjustment	α or ϕ	RMSD	Performance (%)
TTC PDs		0.0048	52.0
GDP growth	0.1237	0.0066	33.8
Individual credit growth	0.0796	0.0091	9.2
Stock market return	0.0239	0.0098	1.8
Autoregressive	0.3654	0.0070	29.6

Notes: This table compares the performance of the adjustment procedures in terms of the sum for six banks (five banks that have opted for the IRB approach of Basel II plus a sixth fictitious bank which is the aggregate of all the other banks in the system) of the RMSDs from the HP trend of each bank's series. It also shows the relative performance of each procedure, measured by the reduction in the sum of RMSDs of the original series with respect to their HP trends, and the value of parameter α for the multipliers based on GDP growth, individual credit growth and stock market return, and of parameter ϕ for the autoregressive adjustment.

Source: Authors' calculations.

trends. Table 2 shows the results, together with the estimated values of parameters α and ϕ. It also shows a performance indicator given by the percentage reduction in the sum of RMSDs of the original series with respect to the HP trends that is achieved by each procedure (so the indicator would be 100% if all adjusted series coincided with their HP trends). The best procedure is now to adjust the input of the Basel II formula with TTC PDs, with the procedure based on a GDP growth multiplier coming second, and the autoregressive procedure coming third. The other two procedures are clearly dominated, including the one based on individual credit growth. In fact, comparing Tables 1 and 2 we conclude that the relative performance of the credit growth multiplier worsens when moving from aggregate to disaggregated data. Thus, our results raise doubts about the proposal of Goodhart and Persaud (2008) to adjust Basel II capital requirements 'by a ratio linked to the growth of the value of bank assets, bank by bank'. The values of parameters α and ϕ in Table 2 are broadly in line with those in Table 1, although interestingly α(GDP) jumps from 0.081 to 0.124. This implies an increase in the corresponding multiplier from 6.5% to 9.8% (since $2N(0.124) = 1.098$) for each standard deviation in GDP growth.

The superiority of the TTC PDs procedure may be explained by the fact that it approaches more closely the characteristics of the portfolio of each bank, instead of using a common adjustment for all banks. However, despite its better statistical performance, we believe that the arguments in Section 5 are sufficiently strong to favour using the multiplier based on GDP growth.

To the extent that GDP data could be available at the (domestic) regional level, it would be possible to compute regional multipliers, with a treatment of national banks similar to that proposed for international banks in Section 4. However, we would not favour this approach because the high correlation in regional business cycles does not justify the additional complexity that would be introduced in the regulation of bank capital.

6.2. Cyclically varying LGDs

We have assumed so far a constant LGD fixed at the 45% level specified in the foundation IRB approach of Basel II. However, banks in the advanced IRB approach must input their estimated LGDs, which clearly vary over the business cycle (they are typically higher in recessions when asset prices are depressed than in expansions).[28] This means that for those banks there is further cyclicality of the PIT capital requirements.

A problem to assess the impact of cyclically varying LGDs on the procedures to smooth the Basel II capital requirements is that we do not have data on the LGDs of the loans in our sample. For this reason, in what follows we simply postulate a linear relationship between LGD_t and PD_t with the same slope as in Altman *et al.* (2005) and with an intercept such that when the PD is at its average level over the sample period then the LGD equals the reference value of 45%,[29] that is:

$$LGD_t = 0.45 + 2.61(PD_t - \overline{PD}) \tag{5}$$

where PD_t is the weighted average PD in year t (with weights equal to the borrowers' exposures), and $\overline{\text{PD}}$ is the average of PD_t over the sample period. Figure 8 represents the values of weighted average PDs and cyclically varying LGDs. The fluctuation in LGDs ranges between 40% and 55%.

Figure 9 shows PIT capital requirements when LGDs vary over time in this manner and PIT capital requirements calculated using a fixed 45% LGD. The cyclicality of capital requirements increases significantly. From peak to trough, they range from almost 7% to more than 14%, which is twice the variation that we had before.

With this data we proceed to perform the same analysis as in Section 4, comparing the different procedures by computing the RMSD of the adjusted series with respect to the HP trend. The results in Table 3 show that the best procedures are either to smooth the input of the Basel II formula with TTC PDs (and a constant 45% LGD) or to smooth the output with a GDP growth multiplier. The performance of the autoregressive adjustment worsens relative to the case with a fixed 45% LGD, while as before the other two procedures are clearly dominated.

Thus, the introduction of cyclically varying LGDs does not affect the relative performance of the different procedures to adjust the Basel II capital requirements. However, the value of the multipliers is higher. In particular, the jump in the value of α(GDP) from 0.081 to 0.133 implies an increase in the corresponding multiplier

[28] For example, Altman *et al.* (2005) show that there is a positive relationship between PDs and LGDs. In particular, they regress average bond recovery rates ($1 - LGD$) on average bond default rates (PD), obtaining a slope coefficient of –2.61.

[29] There is not much justification in the literature for this assumption. Araten *et al.* (2004) estimate LGDs in the interval between 39.8% and 50.5%, while Gupton (2000) estimates LGDs between 30.5% and 47.9%. Frye (2000) finds similar results for senior secured corporate loans. Data collected during the calibration processes leading to Basel II (Quantitative Impact Studies or QIS exercises) do not settle the question because those exercises were carried out under benign economic conditions. Thus it is not unreasonable to take the 45% benchmark set by the Basel Committee for the IRB foundation approach.

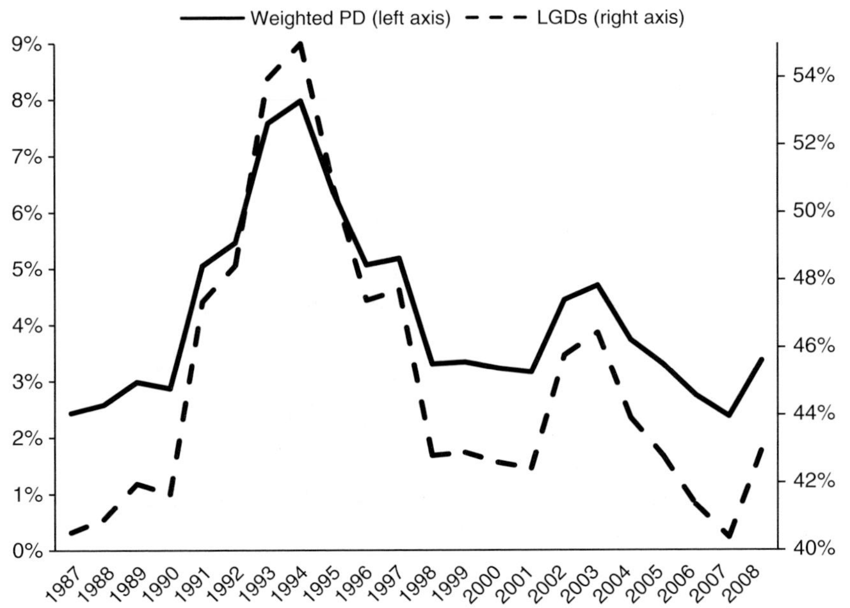

Figure 8. Weighted average PDs and cyclically varying LGDs

Notes: This figure shows the average (weighted by the size of the exposures) PD for the portfolio of commercial and industrial loans of Spanish banks, and the cyclically varying LGD computed by assuming that it is increasing in PD according to Equation (5).

Source: Authors' calculations.

from 6.5% to 10.6% (since $2N(0.133) = 1.106$) for each standard deviation in GDP growth.

Obviously, these results should be taken with care, since they are based on the ad hoc linear relationship between LGDs and PDs postulated in (5). On the other hand, there is an additional factor that increases the sensitivity of PIT capital requirements to the business cycle, namely that exposures at default (EADs) also move in parallel with PDs (see, for example, the evidence in Jiménez *et al.*, 2009b). It is not easy to simulate the impact of EADs on capital requirements, so we will not pursue this here. But the fact that EADs vary over the business cycle makes the proposed cyclical adjustment of capital requirements even more compelling.

6.3. A flat benchmark

It could be argued that our results might depend on the filtering procedure used. Although the HP filter is the standard procedure used by macroeconomists to separate cycle from trend, to check the robustness of our results we tried an alternative benchmark, namely a constant requirement at the average level of the estimated PIT capital requirements over the sample period, which is 9.37%. We then

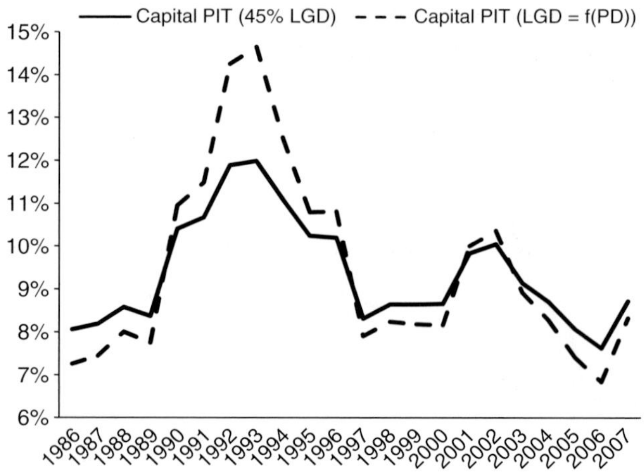

Figure 9. PIT capital requirements with and without variable LGDs

Notes: This figure shows the aggregate PIT Basel II capital requirements per unit of loans for the portfolio of commercial and industrial loans of Spanish banks using a 45% LGD and a cyclically varying LGD.

Source: Authors' calculations.

Table 3. Root mean square deviations from the HP trend for different adjustment procedures using cyclically varying LGDs

Type of adjustment	α or ϕ	RMSD	Performance (%)
TTC PDs		0.0086	42.7
GDP growth	0.1330	0.0084	43.8
Credit growth	0.1329	0.0108	27.8
Stock market return	0.0489	0.0146	2.6
Autoregressive	0.2984	0.0095	37.0

Notes: This table compares the performance in terms of RMSDs from the HP trend of the adjustment procedures when LGDs are a linear function of weighted average PDs according to equation (5) in the text. It also shows the relative performance of each procedure, measured by the reduction in the RMSDs of the original series with respect to the HP trend, and the value of parameter α for the multipliers based on GDP growth, credit growth and stock market return, and of parameter ϕ for the autoregressive adjustment.

Source: Authors' calculations.

perform the same analysis as in Section 4 with a flat benchmark replacing the HP trend.[30]

For this benchmark the best adjustment is obtained with the autoregressive procedure, because starting at the 9.37% level and setting the autoregressive parameter ϕ equal to zero we get a zero RMSD. However, risk-sensitivity is completely eliminated by making the capital requirement equal to the flat benchmark. This is effectively throwing out the baby with the bath water, and adds to the previous

[30] One way to rationalize this filter is to think of it as Basel I-type benchmark.

drawbacks noted in Section 4.4. As for the other procedures, smoothing the input of the Basel II formula with TTC PDs dominates the adjustment based on GDP growth (RMSD = 0.0066 and 0.0074, respectively), which in turn is better than the adjustments based on credit growth and stock market returns (RMSD = 0.0085 and 0.012, respectively). The main conclusion from this exercise is that the performance of the different procedures does not seem to depend on the selected benchmark, but on their ability to smooth cyclical patterns in the original PIT capital requirements series.

6.4. Adjustment of expected losses

Regulatory capital under Basel II is set aside to cover unexpected losses, while expected losses must be covered with loan loss provisions. Assuming an LGD of 45%, our empirical model allows us to compute the expected losses for each borrower and each year of the sample. From here we may obtain an estimation of the expected losses per unit of loans for each year of the sample. Figure 10 shows expected losses and capital requirements per unit of loans over the sample period. Both series exhibit a very similar pattern, driven by the cyclical behaviour of PDs. It is also worth noting that the average level of expected losses (2%) is significantly lower than the average level of capital requirements (9%). This means that in order to mitigate the pro-cyclical effects of regulation, acting on the capital requirements front is much more important than acting on the expected losses front.

Figure 10. PIT expected and unexpected losses

Notes: This figure shows the aggregate PIT Basel II capital requirements per unit of loans for the portfolio of commercial and industrial loans of Spanish banks using a 45% LGD, and the corresponding expected losses per unit of loans computed by multiplying the LGD by the average (weighted by the size of the exposures) PD.

Source: Authors' calculations.

As a response to the current financial crisis, there is a growing consensus among academics and policy-makers about the need to build buffers in good times that can be drawn down when conditions deteriorate.[31] One way to build up these buffers would be to implement an explicit cyclical adjustment of loan loss provisions similar to the adjustment of capital requirements discussed above. For example, a multiplier of expected losses based on GDP growth could be designed to smooth the provisioning requirements over the business cycle. Thus, during expansion phases, when expected losses are below their cyclically adjusted value, the buffer would be built up, while in recessions, when the opposite obtains, the buffer would be drawn down. This Economic Cycle Reserve (Turner Review, 2009), could be implemented by either adjusting the P&L figures (as in the case of the Spanish dynamic provisioning system[32]) or by restricting distributable profits. The choice between these two alternatives would require an agreement between prudential and accounting regulators.

7. CONCLUSION

This paper provides clear evidence that Basel II capital requirements based on PIT PDs move significantly along the business cycle. According to our results, from peak to trough capital requirements for loans to firms may vary by more than 50%, a figure that could reach 100% with cyclically varying LGDs. This variation in capital requirements could lead to a significant amplification of business cycle fluctuations. Therefore, a very important question that is in the front line of current discussions among policy-makers is: How should the pro-cyclical effects of risk-sensitive bank capital regulation *à la* Basel II be mitigated? To the best of our knowledge this is the first paper that presents a framework to address this issue.

We propose a benchmark for comparing different procedures and apply it to the adjustment of the estimated Basel II capital requirements for commercial and industrial loans in Spain over the period 1987–2008. The comparison is based on the minimization of the RMSD of each adjusted series with respect to the trend of the original series computed by applying the HP filter.

The results show that adjusting the output of the Basel II formula with a credit growth multiplier (based on aggregate or individual bank data) or with a stock market return multiplier is suboptimal, as it is also the case when the multiplier is based on profits (e.g., ROA, ROE) or specific loan loss provisions. The autoregressive adjustment performs better, but we argue that its lagged response is an impor-

[31] See, for example, Brunnermeier *et al.* (2009) and the G20 Leaders' Declaration on Strengthening the Financial System of 2 April 2009.

[32] Jiménez and Saurina (2006) explain the rationale for anti-cyclical or dynamic provisions. Such provisions were introduced in Spain in 2000, and were adjusted in 2005 when the International Financial Reporting Standards (IFRS) came into effect.

tant shortcoming, especially in downturns. Consequently, the final choice is between smoothing the input of the Basel II formula by using TTC PDs or smoothing the output with a multiplier based on GDP growth. Our discussion of the pros and cons of these two procedures concludes that the latter is better in terms of simplicity, transparency, low cost of implementation, and consistency with banks' risk pricing and risk management systems.

We also show that for the portfolio of commercial and industrial loans in Spain and for banks using the foundation IRB approach (with an LGD set at 45%), the multiplier would amount to a 6.5% surcharge for each standard deviation in GDP growth. The surcharge would be significantly higher for banks using cyclically varying LGDs. Applying these results to the current crisis, where GDP growth in many countries is three or more standard deviations below its long-run average, would imply a reduction in capital requirements of the order of at least 20%. The analytical framework presented in the paper could also be applied to expected losses, so it can be used to calibrate economic cycle reserves or dynamic provisions.

To conclude, it is important to stress that the proposed adjustment maintains the risk-sensitivity of the Basel II capital requirements in the cross-section, so banks with riskier portfolios would bear a higher capital charge, but a cyclically-varying scaling factor would be introduced to increase capital requirements in good times and to reduce them in bad times. Such changes should contribute to reduce the incidence and magnitude of both credit bubbles and credit crunches.

Discussion

Morten O. Ravn

University College London and the CEPR

This is a timely, relevant, insightful, and potentially very important contribution to the debate on how to ameliorate the pro-cyclicality of bank capital requirements built into Basel II. The issue addressed by the authors is that the first pillar of Basel II introduces risk-sensitive capital requirements which essentially imply that banks that engage in more risky lending activities are required to hold more capital. This seems like a sensible requirement in a cross-sectional sense but can induce 'too much' (more on this later) pro-cyclicality in a time-series implying more restrictive regulation when credit may be more needed, therefore potentially contributing to business cycle volatility. Thus, the authors examine whether there are simple, transparent and sensible adjustments that can be made to the capital requirements of Basel II that will help address this problem.

Repullo, Saurina and Trucharte's (hereafter RST) paper makes real headwind on this issue and one can only hope that higher powers (regulators) take this paper serious. RST do the following:

1. As a first stage, RST estimate a logit model for the one-year-ahead default probability of Spanish bank loan portfolios using data for the sample period 1987–2008. The logit model assumes that the one-year-ahead default probability is a function of the characteristics of the lender, the borrower, macroeconomic conditions allowing for regional and industry specific fixed effects. This estimation is carried out using a most impressive dataset which is a 10% sample drawn (1 million observations) from the universe of Spanish bank loans made to firms (of a value of €6,000 or more).

2. In the second step, the estimated default probabilities are fed into a Basel II formula assuming a loan maturity of 1 year and a loss given default rate of 45%. This produces time-series estimates of point-in-time capital requirements that would be induced by Basel II had banks carried out the same procedure to estimate default probabilities. These estimates are then averaged over lenders and creditors to produce an aggregate time-series for the capital requirements.

3. In the third step RST produces a cyclically adjusted measure of this capital requirement estimate by fitting a HP trend. This trend is the benchmark to which they compare various methods for cyclical adjustments.

4. Finally, RST compute simple adjustments to the estimated capital requirement time-series and evaluate their fit with the HP trend. These adjustments include a through-the-cycle adjustment which essentially amounts to replacing the current values of the macroeconomic aggregates in step 2 with their average values. The second method is a business cycle multiplier approach which amounts to adjusting the estimated capital requirements with a factor that depends upon (the growth rate of) a business cycle indicator's current value relative to trend. When above trend, this procedure adjusts upwards the capital requirement thereby mitigating procyclicality. This clearly leaves open issues regarding the appropriate macroeconomic factor and the elasticity of the adjustment. The latter of these issues is addressed by estimating the elasticity which allows for the minimal root-mean-square-error (RMSE) relative to the HP trend of step 4. The first issue is instead addressed by comparing the outcomes produced by using either GDP growth rates, credit growth rates, or stock market returns. Finally, the authors look at an adjustment which smoothes the capital requirement over time using a first order autoregressive filter with a persistence measure estimated as the one that minimizes the RMSE relative to the HP trend.

RST conclude from their analysis that the autoregressive adjustment and the business cycle multiplier approach using GDP growth perform the best. They point out that the former of these methods is backward looking so their preferred adjustment method is the latter of these two methods. Their estimates imply that a one standard deviation increase in GDP growth should amount to a 6.5% surcharge on the Basel II capital requirement.

The analysis therefore produces a clear and applicable result that could be adopted by banking regulators. This is extremely useful and I would very much like to applaud the authors for writing this paper.

My discussion is going to concentrate upon three issues. These will concern details of the analysis outlined above, the question of 'too much' pro-cyclicality, and the impact of adjustments to Basel II. To be fair, I think that the authors do not necessarily disagree with any of the points that I will make and I stress that I think that this is a really excellent paper.

The benchmark

In step 3 of the procedure RST estimate an HP trend for the aggregate estimate of the capital requirement for the Spanish data. This HP trend is the benchmark to which they compare the various adjustment methods. One could ask at this point why they do not simply implement the HP filter as the adjustment method rather than asking how close other methods get to the HP trend. After all, the HP filter is easily applicable. I will make two points of this issue, one of which I will expand further upon below.

First, and this is the point that I shall return to, there is a fundamental question as the sense in which Basel II is 'too pro-cyclical'. Leaving this aside, if we accept that this is the case, the question is whether the HP trend is an appropriate benchmark. I admit that I am a fan of using HP filters for measuring deviations from trend (and therefore also for using them as measures of trend). When applied to macroeconomic time-series, the HP filter produces measures of the deviations from trend that look reasonable and with second moments that are useful for thinking about business cycles.

The easiest way of understanding what this procedure does is think in the frequency domain. Fluctuations in a time-series can be thought of as being the product of fluctuations with many different periodicities ranging from permanent to completely random. The HP filter estimates a trend by removing high frequency movements from the time-series in question. It leaves in the trend all permanent components and share of all other components with frequency weights that depend negatively on the periodicity. Thus, the product will be a trend that moves over time with the degree of smoothness depending on a parameter known as the smoothing parameter. When this parameter goes to zero, the trend is the data, while a very high value of the smoothing parameter produces a linear trend. I shall restrain myself from going into the technical details but simply point to the fact that this is a purely statistical procedure for making a trend-cycle decomposition. By contrast, as I return to below, theory makes predictions on how to correct the Basel II requirements and these are likely to be orthogonal in nature to the reasons why one might want to implement HP filters. Nonetheless, as I have mentioned, the HP filter has been shown to work rather well in practice but this is simply from the point of view of producing 'reasonable' results.

However, there is one point that is important. When the HP filter is translated into the time-domain, it implies a two-sided filter. What I mean by this is that the

HP-filter estimate of the trend component of some time-series y at date t, say y_t^{HP}, depends on past and future values of y. This is not necessarily a bad thing but it has one consequence that is important, which is that the properties of the HP trend near the end-points (the beginning and the end of the sample) are different than further away from the end-points. Suppose that $y_{T,T}^{HP}$ is the HP estimate of the trend component at data T when we have data for the sample period $t = 1,..,T$. Now suppose that we add one more observation, re-estimate the HP trend and ask about the value of $y_{T,T+1}^{HP}$ (the HP trend estimate for y_T when we have data for the sample $1,\ldots,T + 1$)? This value is very likely to be quite different from $y_{T,T}^{HP}$ because of this end-point problem. In other words, the HP filter is – because of its two-sided nature – not a very good method to produce stable 'real-time' estimates of trend components.

From this perspective, I think the authors make a wise choice in not proposing to use the HP trend as the proposed adjustment method as it would create the problem of how to communicate the fact that trend estimates (of the same data point) potentially change significantly over time as data is added.

Why 'too much' pro-cyclicality

The authors are very upfront about the fact that the paper is not about optimal banking regulation but instead about how to deal with business cycle fluctuations. Nonetheless, let me make a few remarks (which I am sure that the authors would not disagree with).

When dealing with the question of banking regulation one needs, of course, to have in mind some theory of why regulation is needed. There is a host of reasons for why this is the case and the recent financial crisis has added to many economists' priors about the relevance of this issue. Reasons span from moral hazard issues (the belief that *ex ante* threats of no-bail-out are empty, moral hazard due to costly state verification etc.) to issues of contagion due to cross-bank spill-overs. In general, each of these issues will call for different aspects of banking regulation and each would therefore need to be considered when asking about optimal design of banking regulation.

Let me – without going into details – outline one theory as proposed by Kashyap and Stein (2004). These authors study a model of financial intermediation in which banks engage in lending to firms. Firms use the loans to produce output and are subject to an aggregate productivity shock. Each bank may default with some probability that depends on its loan portfolio and its capital holdings. However, it is assumed that the default of one bank has a spill-over on the probability of default of other banks that any individual bank ignores. Without regulation, banks would therefore hold too little capital as they do not internalize the externality. A regulator can address this problem by imposing capital requirements which relate capital requirements to the risk of the loan portfolio. In particular, Kashyap and Stein (2004) show that the social optimum can be implemented by imposing capital requirements that depend on three aspects: (1) the contagion factor, (2) the shadow value of capital, and (3) the marginal impact of loans on the default probability.

It follows from this that – in a cross-sectional sense – banks that make more risky loans (loans that have a greater impact on the default probability) should hold more capital. This is the essence of the first pillar of Basel II. However, the optimal regulatory policy also calls for time-series dependence of the capital requirements. In particular, the shadow value of capital is likely to be higher in recessions than in booms, therefore implying that lack of cyclical adjustment of the capital requirements imply 'too much' pro-cyclicality.

Two remarks are warranted. First, nothing guarantees that the HP trend would provide anything close to the cyclical adjustment called for by theory so we would very easily end up in a second best environment. Secondly, and probably more importantly, variations in the shadow value of capital are not the only source of cyclical adjustment. It is also perceivable that the factor relating to contagion is cyclical and my prior would be that there is more scope for contagion in recessions than in booms. This would call for stricter standards in recessions than in booms in the time-series dimension. Whether this would potentially undo the impact of changes in the shadow value of capital is not clear so it might still be the case that Basel II has too much pro-cyclicality built into it. But the point is that the case for cyclical adjustments to the Basel II capital requirements is an empirical question that needs structural models to be answered.

Let me add a final twist to this. I think it would have been instructive if the authors would have reported some statistics on Spanish banks' actual capital holdings. The reason why this is interesting is that there is some evidence that banks actually have held more capital than prescribed by Basel I and II. As mentioned above, the nature of the regulatory policies would depend upon the type of environment that we envisage banks living in. The fact that banks may hold excessive capital would seem consistent with settings with moral hazard due to costly state verification in which banks use capital holdings to signal to investors that they are 'sound'. This may seem futile given the events of the financial crisis but one should perhaps not forget the role played by banks basically insuring themselves by effectively attempting to sell off the risk associated with their loans portfolios.

None of these comments are meant to detriment the value of the current paper. The authors are very clear in stating their objective as not being related to questions of optimal banking regulation. The issues I have highlighted, however, do imply that one needs to be somewhat careful when arguing about the appropriate cyclical adjustment of the Basel II capital requirements.

Summary

I would like to repeat what I started with: This is a really excellent and highly relevant paper that adds important insights to the debate on the first pillar of Basel II.

The authors' careful analysis comes to a result that should be of interest to policymakers and academics alike. There is little doubt that we will see a lot interest in financial sector regulation over the coming years and this paper makes real progress.

I would also like to add one more positive note. The estimates of the one-year-ahead default probabilities of Spanish banks are of independent value. The data are truly remarkable and I think that this part of the paper could be further developed by the authors. Of course, to the extent that banks react to regulation – as we would expect, it would be of much interest to take one more step and make this part of the paper fully structural so that we make sure that regulatory interventions do not impact on the parameter estimates, but this is surely something better left for future research.

I very much look forward to seeing future work from the authors on this very important topic.

Panel discussion

Hans-Werner Sinn acknowledged the paper's focus was on the fine tuning of the Basel II system but he believed the issue of pro-cyclicality arose out of the mark to market accounting principle which is embedded in the IFRS approach. He contended that a much more radical solution beyond reforming the Basel II is needed. He recounted the Prussian experience in the nineteenth century where the mark to market principle was introduced in 1861 and contributed to the stock market collapse (founders' crisis) in 1873. Prussia quickly returned to the tried and tested lowest value principle in 1874.

Ray Rees believed greater consideration should be given to the use of alternative policy instruments which are proposed in the literature instead of capital requirement ratios to mitigate the problem of systemic externalities which arise out of increased bank defaults. Georges de Ménil noted that macroeconomic moral hazard was another important motivation for regulation. In the face of a major shock, he suggested it may be necessary to distinguish between the optimal *ex ante* and *ex post* regulatory approach.

Peter Dolton wondered about the significance of the estimated results given the use of predicted regressors in their modelling approach. He also raised concerns on the modelling of the probability of loan default and suggested the use of a hazard model where the probability of a loan default now is conditional on not having defaulted up to this point and also on the macroeconomic conditions at the time of issuing the loan. Although the time coverage of the data is short, he emphasized that it was important to correctly estimate the structural endogenous breaks in the data. Alberto Pozzolo noted that the aggregate variables used in their model contain a cyclical component which they should adjust for.

Fabrizio Perri pointed out that every crisis is different and in this context wondered if a fixed rule approach based on past experience is more appropriate than an approach which allows the regulator some room for discretion. Silvana Tenreyro believed the arguments for and against pro-cyclicality are well known and thought the development of a quantitative model, although very difficult to construct, could provide new and important insights. She suggested the authors could use real time GDP data and a one-sided filter to compute the multiplier and compare results with the paper's findings.

Richard Portes suggested the authors should relate the papers to the leverage cycle literature. He wondered had the regulators already decided on how to reform Basel II, which he felt was the view of the authors.

Rafael Repullo reiterated that the paper was about fine tuning the Basel II system not about designing the optimal capital regulation. On the forecasting of defaults, he accepted that the approach taken to calculate the probability of default did not correspond to the approach taken by banks; however, he maintained that their primary aim was to forecast the actual behaviour of defaults as accurately as possible. He commented that the inclusion of GDP and credit growth in their model could be useful in capturing the impact of business cycle.

APPENDIX: EMPIRICAL RESULTS

Table A1. Estimation results

Dependent variable (0/1): Borrowers' default in $t + 1$	Coefficient*	S.E.
Borrower variables (t)		
COLLATERAL	0.169	0.017
MATURITY	–0.251	0.016
AGE dummy 2	0.868	0.023
AGE dummy 3	0.756	0.024
AGE dummy 4	–0.100	0.023
FIRM_SIZE	–0.254	0.005
NUMBER_BANKS	0.488	0.013
MAIN_LENDER_CHANGE	0.660	0.029
UTILIZATION	2.655	0.034
HISTORIC_DELINQUENCY	2.133	0.024
HISTORIC_DEFAULT	2.858	0.058
Macro variables (t)		
GDP_GROWTH	–0.148	0.005
CREDIT_GROWTH	–1.596	0.087
STOCK_MARKET_RETURN	–0.248	0.023
Control_Variables (t)		
Regional_dummies	Yes	
Industry_dummies	Yes	
Constant	–4.829	0.046
Number of observations	996,885	
Sample period (annual)	1987–2008	

Table A1. (Continued)

Dependent variable (0/1): Borrowers' default in $t + 1$	Coefficient*	S.E.
Pseudo R^2	10.28%	
Log pseudolikelihood	−145,548.960	
LR $chi^2(47)$	33,349.380	
Prob > chi^2	0.000	

Notes: This table reports the estimation of the logistic model of firms' default. The dependent variable takes value 1 if borrower i defaults in year $t + 1$, and zero otherwise. $COLLATERAL_{it}$ represents average (weighted by the size of exposures) of the proportion of guarantees in a firm's borrowing. $MATURITY_{it}$ represents the proportion of long-term exposures (more than one year) over total exposures. AGE_{it} accounts for the number of years a borrower has been reporting to the Credit Register. $FIRM\_SIZE_{it}$ is the log of a firm's borrowing deflated by the consumer price index. $NUMBER\_BANKS_{it}$ is the number of banks with which a firm has lending relationships. $MAIN\_LENDER\_CHANGE_{it}$ indicates the frequency with which firms change the bank which provides them with the largest amount of funding. $UTILIZATION_{it}$ is the ratio between the amount of credit drawn by a borrower and the total available amount (credit line). $HISTORIC\_DELINQUENCY_{it}$ is the number of years in which a firm has been delinquent divided by the number of years it has been reporting to the Credit Register. $HISTORIC\_DEFAULT_{it}$ is the number of years in which a firm has been in default divided by the number of years it has been reporting to the Credit Register. GDP_GROWTH_t is the rate of growth of the gross domestic product, $CREDIT\_GROWTH_t$ is the rate of growth of the commercial and industrial loans in the Credit Register, and $STOCK\_MARKET\_RETURN_t$ is the rate of change of the Spanish stock market index.

*All coefficients are statistically significant at the 99% level.

Source: Authors' calculations.

Table A2. Model performance

	Classification table In-sample model		Classification table Out-of-sample model	
Classification Power	Predicted defaults (%)	Predicted non-defaults (%)	Predicted defaults (%)	Predicted non-defaults (%)
Observed defaults	68.01	30.27	68.05	29.54
Observed non-defaults	31.99	69.73	31.95	70.46
	Area under ROC curve = 0.76		Area under ROC curve = 0.76	
	Accuracy ratio = 52%		Accuracy ratio = 52%	

Notes: This table reports the performance of the estimated logit model for an in-sample (a random 10% of the population) and an out-of-sample set of observations (another random 10% of the population) in terms of observed and predicted defaults, areas under the Receiver Operating Characteristic (ROC) curve, and Accuracy Ratios (AR). The AR measure determines the performance enhancement over the random model. For references on these performance statistics see, for example, Sobehart *et al.* (2000), Sobehart and Keenan (2001), and Engelmann *et al.* (2003).

Source: Authors' calculations.

REFERENCES

Ahmed, A.S., C. Takeda and S. Thomas (1999). 'Bank loan loss provisions: a re-examination of capital management, earnings management and signalling effects', *Journal of Accounting and Economics*, 28, 1–25.

Altman, E.I., B. Brady, A. Resti and A. Sironi (2005). 'The link between default and recovery rates: theory, empirical evidence, and implications', *Journal of Business*, 78, 2203–28.

Araten, M., M. Jacobs and P. Varshney (2004). 'Measuring LGD on commercial loans: an 18-year internal study', *RMA Journal*, May 28–35.
Basel Committee on Banking Supervision (2006). *International Convergence of Capital Measurement and Capital Standards. A Revised Framework*, Bank for International Settlements, Basel.
—— (2008). 'Comprehensive strategy to address the lessons of the banking crisis', Press Release, 20 November.
—— (2009). 'Strengthening the resilience of the banking sector', Consultative Document, 17 December.
Beatty, A., S. L. Chamberlain and J. Magliolo (1995). 'Managing financial reports of commercial banks: the influence of taxes, regulatory capital, and earnings', *Journal of Accounting Research*, 33, 231–61.
Berger, A. N. and G. F. Udell (1990). 'Collateral, loan quality, and bank risk', *Journal of Monetary Economics*, 25, 21–42.
—— (1994). 'Did Risk-based capital allocate bank credit and cause a "credit crunch" in the US?' *Journal of Money, Credit, and Banking*, 26, 585–628.
Bernanke, B. (2009). 'The crisis and the policy response', Stamp Lecture, London School of Economics, 13 January.
Bernanke, B.S. and C.S. Lown (1991). 'The credit crunch', *Brookings Papers on Economics Activity*, 2, 205–48.
Borio, C., C. Furfine and P. Lowe (2001). 'Pro-cyclicality of the financial system and financial stability: issues and policy options', *BIS papers*, 1, 1–57.
Borio, C. and M. Drehmann (2009). 'Towards an operational framework for financial stability: "fuzzy" measurement and its consequences', *BIS Working Papers*, 284, June.
Brunnermeier, M., A. Crocket, C. Goodhart, A. D. Persaud and H. Shin (2009). *The Fundamental Principles of Financial Regulation*, Geneva Report on the World Economy 11, ICMB-CEPR.
Chava, S. and R. A. Jarrow (2004). 'Bankruptcy prediction with industry effects', *Review of Finance*, 8, 537–69.
Committee of European Banking Supervisors (2009). 'Position paper on a countercyclical capital buffer', 17 July.
Committee on the Global Financial System (2010). 'Macro-prudential instruments and frameworks: a stocktaking of issues and experiences', *CGFS Publications*, 38, May.
Council of the European Union (2009). 'Council conclusions on pro-cyclicality', Press release 2954th Economic and Financial Affairs, 7 July.
Engelmann, B., E. Hayden and D. Tasche (2003). 'Measuring the discriminative power of rating systems', Deutsche Bundesbank, Discussion Paper Series 2: Banking and Financial Supervision, 01/2003.
EU Economic and Financial Committee (EFC) Working Group on Pro-cyclicality (2009). 'Final Report of the EFC Working Group on Pro-cyclicality', 29 June.
Financial Services Authority (2009). 'A regulatory response to the global banking crisis', Discussion Paper 09/02.
Financial Stability Board (FSB) (2009). 'Report of the Financial Stability Forum on addressing procyclicality in the financial system', 2 April 2.
Flannery, M. (2009). 'Stabilizing large financial institutions with contingent capital', mimeo.
Frye, J. (2000). 'Depressing recoveries', *Risk*, November, 108–111.
G-20 Washington Summit (2008). 'Declaration on Financial Markets and the World Economy', *Washington*, 15 November.
G-20 Pittsburgh Summit (2009). 'Leaders' Statement', 24–25 September.
Gambacorta, L. and P. E. Mistrulli (2004). 'Does bank capital affect lending behaviour?' *Journal of Financial Intermediation*, 13, 436–57.
Goodhart, C. and A. Persaud (2008). 'A party popper's guide to financial stability', *Financial Times*, 4 June.
Gordy, M. (2003). 'A risk-factor model foundation for ratings-based bank capital rules', *Journal of Financial Intermediation*, 12, 199–232.
Gordy, M. and B. Howells (2006). 'Pro-cyclicality in Basel II: can we treat the disease without killing the patient?' *Journal of Financial Intermediation*, 15, 395–417.
Greenspan, A. (2002). 'Cyclicality and banking regulation', Conference on Bank Structure and Competition, Federal Reserve Bank of Chicago, 10 May.

Gupton, G.M. (2000). 'Bank loan loss given default', Special Comment, Moody's Investors Service, November.

Hancock, D. and J. A. Wilcox (1994). 'Bank capital, loan delinquencies, and real estate lending', *Journal of Housing Economics*, 4, 121–46.

Hancock, D., A. J. Laing and J.A. Wilcox (1995). 'Bank capital shocks: dynamic effects on securities, loans, and capital', *Journal of Banking and Finance*, 19, 661–77.

High-Level Group on Financial Supervision in the European Union, (De Larosière Group) (2009). Report, 25 February.

Jackson, P. (1999). 'Capital requirements and bank behaviour: the impact of the Basel Accord', Basel Committee on Banking Supervision, Working Paper 1.

Jiménez, G. and J. Saurina (2006). 'Credit cycles, credit risk, and prudential regulation', *International Journal of Central Banking*, 2, 65–98.

Jiménez, G., V. Salas and J. Saurina (2006). 'Determinants of collateral', *Journal of Financial Economics*, 81, 255–81.

Jiménez, G., J. A. Lopez and J. Saurina (2009a). 'Empirical analysis of corporate credit lines', *Review of Financial Studies*, 22, 5069–98.

—— (2009b). 'EAD calibration for corporate credit lines', *Journal of Risk Management of Financial Institutions*, 2, 121–29.

Kashyap, A., R. Rajan and J. Stein (2008). 'Rethinking capital regulation', Federal Reserve Bank of Kansas City Symposium on Maintaining Stability in a Changing Financial System.

Kashyap, A. and J. Stein (2004). 'Cyclical implications of Basel II capital standards', Federal Reserve Bank of Chicago, Economic Perspectives, 1st Quarter, 18–31.

Panetta, F. and P. Angelini (2009). 'Financial sector pro-cyclicality. lessons from the crisis'. Occasional Paper 44, Banca D'Italia, April.

Peek, J. and E. S. Rosengren (1995a). 'The capital crunch: neither a borrower nor a lender be', *Journal of Money, Credit, and Banking*, 27, 621–38.

Peek, J. and E. S. Rosengren (1995b). 'Bank regulation and the credit crunch', *Journal of Banking and Finance*, 19, 679–92.

Pérez, D., V. Salas-Fumás and J. Saurina (2008). 'Earnings and capital management in alternative loan loss provision regulatory regimes', *European Accounting Review*, 17, 423–45.

Repullo, R. and J. Suarez (2009). 'The procyclical effects of Basel II', CEPR Discussion Paper 6862.

Saurina, J. and C. Trucharte (2007). 'An assessment of Basel II pro-cyclicality in mortgage portfolios', *Journal of Financial Services Research*, 32, 81–101.

Sobehart, J., S. Keenan and R. Stein (2000). 'Benchmarking quantitative default risk models: a validation methodology', Moody's Investor Service.

Sobehart, J. and S. Keenan (2001). 'Measuring default accurately', *Risk*, 14, 31–33.

Sundaresan, S. and Z. Wang (2010). 'Design of contingent capital with stock price trigger for conversion', mimeo.

Turner, A. (2009). 'The financial crisis and the future of financial regulation', The Economist's Inaugural City Lecture, 21 January.

Turner Review (2009). *A Regulatory Response to the Global Banking Crisis*, Financial Services Authority, London.

US Treasury (2009). 'Principles for reforming the U.S. and international regulatory capital framework for banking firms', US Treasury Department Policy Statement, 3 September.

Multinational banks

SUMMARY

This paper examines whether multinational banks have a stabilizing or a destabilizing role during times of financial distress. With a focus on Europe, it looks at how these banks' foreign affiliates have been faring during the recent financial crisis. It finds that retail and corporate lending of these foreign affiliates has been stable and even increasing between 2007 and 2009. This pattern is related to the functioning of the internal capital market through which these banks funnel funds across their units. The internal capital market has been an effective tool to support foreign affiliates in distress and to isolate their lending from the local availability of financial resources, notwithstanding the systemic nature of the recent crisis. This effect has been particularly large within the EU integrated financial market and for the EMU countries, thus showing complementarity between economic integration and multinational banks' internal capital markets. In light of these findings, this paper supports the call for an integration of the European supervisory and regulatory framework overseeing multinational banks. The analysis is based on an analytical framework which derives the main conditions under which the internal capital market can perform this support function under idiosyncratic and systemic stresses. The empirical evidence uses both aggregate evidence on foreign claims worldwide, and firm-level evidence on the behaviour of banking groups' affiliates, compared to stand-alone national banks.

— *Giorgio Barba Navaretti, Giacomo Calzolari, Alberto Franco Pozzolo and Micol Levi*

Economic Policy October 2010 Printed in Great Britain

Multinational banking in Europe – financial stability and regulatory implications: lessons from the financial crisis

Giorgio Barba Navaretti, Giacomo Calzolari, Alberto Franco Pozzolo and Micol Levi

University of Milan and Centro Studi Luca d'Agliano; University of Bologna, CEPR and Centro Studi Luca d'Agliano; University of Molise, Centro Studi Luca d'Agliano and MoFiR; Centro Studi Luca d'Agliano

1. INTRODUCTION

Multinational banks (MNBs) have been growing fast, especially within the EU. The size and the global interconnectedness of their activities have raised serious concerns about their potential systemic effects. They have been considered as being among the main culprits of the present financial crisis. Many of the financial institutions that had to be bailed out or supported with public funds in 2008 and 2009 in Europe and in the United States were MNBs.[1] Special supervisory mechanisms and prudential requirements for these banks are at the core of most reform proposals of regulation and supervision of financial markets.[2]

We would like to thank the Editor (Philippe Martin), Giorgio Basevi, Nicola Cetorelli, Paolo Manasse, Giancarlo Spagnolo, the discussants (Dalia Marin and Gianmarco Ottaviano), the panellists at the Economic Policy Meeting in Madrid, and four anonymous referees for their very helpful comments and suggestions on the previous versions of this paper. All remaining errors are of course our own.
The Managing Editor in charge of this paper was Philippe Martin.

[1] For example, the Royal Bank of Scotland, Lloyds, ING, Fortis, Dexia, Merril Lynch, Citigroup and several others.

[2] See, for example, the proposal for the European Banking Authority by the EU and Turner (2009).

Economic Policy October 2010 pp. 703–753 Printed in Great Britain

However, these concerns often rest on a superficial assessment of the role and the activities of MNBs. The aim of this paper is to provide a comprehensive assessment of the behaviour of MNBs in the last decade and during the recent crisis. The analysis will be based on an in-depth theoretical evaluation of the functioning of the *internal capital market* (ICM), through which MNBs funnel funds across their global operations, and on macro and firm level evidence. We will address the question of whether MNBs have a stabilizing or destabilizing role during times of financial distress. There are several well-grounded economic arguments supporting the claim that this type of bank can rather have a stabilizing effect on global financial markets and on the economies of the host countries where they operate. Also, the empirical evidence, including the period of the recent financial crisis, shows that these banks have kept being a substantial and stable source of financial resources for host economies.

The analysis is especially focused on the operations that MNBs carry out in the host countries, where they have foreign affiliates. Indeed, these banks have increasingly been competing with domestic institutions in activities which are to a large extent non-tradable, like retail banking and corporate loans to small businesses, and which imply a high degree of local intermediation of funds through affiliates based in host countries (McCauley *et al.*, 2010). Their role has been growing especially fast within the integrated financial market of the EU and in emerging economies, where domestic institutions are weak. The financial claims towards residents in host countries held by MNBs through their affiliates account today for more than half of the total foreign claims of the banking system worldwide (which also include the cross-country operations of national, stand-alone banks).

This type of banking is of course similar to what domestic institutions do and inherently less volatile and more intertwined with the real economy than wholesale cross-border activities. However, it is also quite clear that MNBs have greater ease than domestic banks in channelling funds across their units world-wide, because of their role in the wholesale market and through internal transfers of liquidity and assets, indeed the ICM. In this respect, their deep involvement in the retail and corporate market of local economies, associated with a high potential for mobilizing activities cross border, has raised concerns that these financial institutions might be a cause of volatility and instability in the countries where they operate.[3]

The availability of a global ICM can indeed affect stability in both directions: MNBs can either support foreign affiliates in distress or, rather, funnel resources away, thereby creating potential distress. The theoretical framework we develop here, though, shows that it is possible to identify clearly the conditions under which the bright side of ICMs (i.e. their ability to support affiliates in distress and to allocate resources efficiently on the basis of global returns) is more likely to emerge.

[3] For example Ostry *et al.* (2010) have recently argued that FDI in the financial sector in emerging economies may be disguising a build-up of intragroup debt in the financial sector and increase the riskiness of local financial systems.

The empirical analysis we carry out on a large panel of banks in the EU27 countries between 2000 and 2008 provides robust evidence that foreign affiliates of MNBs, compared to stand-alone domestic banks and domestic banking groups, actively use the ICM to isolate the rate of growth of loans in host countries from available local resources (measured by the rate of growth of local deposits). During this period ICMs have indeed been functioning so as to isolate lending activities of foreign affiliates from *idiosyncratic* shocks in the local availability of funding. But our evidence of the limited volatility of aggregate claims during the recent financial crisis supports the view that MNBs can enhance financial stability also in times of *systemic* financial distress. Indeed, even in 2007 and 2008 ICMs helped to isolate lending activities of foreign affiliates from the local availability of funding.

Both the analytical framework and the empirical analyses developed in this paper are consistent with the claim that the activities carried out by MNBs through their affiliates have not been a source of financial instability in host economies. Rather, they have enhanced the supply of resources in those local markets.

Although it provides a general framework for analysis and evidence on worldwide trends in multinational banking, this paper focuses mostly on the EU. Our results show that the ICM is particularly effective when banks operate within the integrated EU financial market. This is not surprising, since retail activities and corporate lending and support to local businesses are non-tradable and in this domain market integration can only be fostered through the activities of MNBs. To this extent the ICMs and the external capital markets are to some degree *complementary*. When the external capital markets are less integrated, for regulations or because they involve different currencies, then the ICMs of MNBs are *de facto* operating to a very limited extent or even inactive, with no differences with respect to domestic banks. Consequently, even though some of the top MNBs in the world are non-European, the largest share of multinational banking activities are carried out within the EU and by European banks.

Within an integrated financial market our results also imply that there is a special urgency for reforming regulations and supervision, so as to deal with groups operating cross-border. Based on our analysis on the working of ICMs, in the final section we then discuss how a reformed European regulatory framework could enhance the stabilizing role of MNBs. We support the call for an integrated European supervision of MNBs and for an increased harmonization of national regulatory frameworks.

European countries should contemplate a new and specific framework for European MNBs that would allow these banks to set up truly integrated organizations with well-functioning ICMs. This framework would define the responsibilities and the powers of the parent company and its foreign affiliates, providing due protections to minorities and creditors. A specific treatment for MNBs in terms of regulation and supervision should be contemplated, along the lines of the proposals that have already been discussed in Europe (i.e., enhancing coordination among countries through strengthened colleges of supervisors overseen by a newly created

European Banking Authority and also possibly defining rules for the allocation of the costs of rescuing those banks in case of distress). A sensible revision of the current framework should seriously keep into account the organizational format that MNBs adopt for their ICMs. And also that the effectiveness of any regulatory reform strictly depends on the level of financial integration between the countries where the bank is active.

Several other works have been looking at the functioning of the ICM for global corporations in general and specifically for banks (see, for example, Houston *et al.*, 1997; Houston and James, 1998; Morgan *et al.*, 2004; Kroszner and Strahan, 2006; Kroszner, 2008; de Haas and van Lelyveld, 2010). These works are discussed in Sections 3 and 4. Also, a very large number of recent contributions have discussed regulatory and supervisory reforms to deal with MNBs (see, for example, Eisenbeis and Kaufman, 2006; Dermine, 2005; Freixas, 2009). The novelty of this paper is combining the analytical insights on the functioning of the ICM with empirical evidence which compares the performance of MNBs to the one of stand-alone national banks, and thus delivering some insights for policy reforms.

The remainder of this paper is organized as follows. The next section sets the scene and provides aggregate descriptive evidence on worldwide trends in multinational banking. Section 3 outlines an analytical framework for the functioning of the ICM, highlighting several testable implications on the conditions under which the 'bright side' of ICMs (e.g., their ability to support affiliates in distress) is more likely to emerge and taking them to the data. Section 4 is devoted to the assessment of the effects of the crisis on the behaviour of MNBs with particular reference (although not only) to Europe. Finally, Section 5 concludes and develops some policy implications of our analysis that may be useful in particular for the current debate in Europe.

2. KEY FACTS ON MULTINATIONAL BANKS

This section examines the key facts of the main global trends in the activities of MNBs since 2000, as emerging from aggregate statistics. It sets the scene for the subsequent analysis of the behaviour of these banks during the crisis. We examine how large these activities are with respect to the size of host countries' economies and how fast they have been growing in the last decade. In particular, we look at the patterns of the assets and liabilities of foreign affiliates (for a precise definition see n. 9), as these are the distinctive activities of MNBs, those likely to have a larger long-term impact on the economies of the host countries. We defer to Section 4 the assessment of how these activities have been faring since the outset of the financial crisis.

Two key facts emerge from the data. First, total claims of foreign affiliates[4] of banks have been rising worldwide, in absolute terms and with respect to the total

[4] See Box 1 for a definition.

banking assets and the GDP of host economies. Second, the rise has been especially large in the EU and particularly within the euro area.

2.1. The rise of multinational banking

The activities of MNBs' affiliates in host countries differ from cross-border financial transactions, which could also be undertaken by non-MNBs. These activities are mostly non-tradable, as they include retail banking and loans towards local businesses. As argued by McCauley *et al.* (2010), international banking has evolved for many countries from a model essentially based on centralized patterns of resource allocation (involving a large share of cross-border transactions), whereby headquarters pool funds and then reallocate them within the group, to a more decentralized pattern, where affiliates are allowed to raise funds locally to finance assets in each location. As we will discuss extensively in the next section, both models of multinational banking can be more or less efficiently supported by an ICM channelling funds across countries within the group. However, the decentralized model implies that a larger share of funds is directly intermediated by foreign affiliates.

The increasing role of foreign affiliates in local markets indeed emerges from the aggregate cross-country data provided by the Bank for International Settlements' (BIS) Banking Statistics, discussed in detail in Box 1. These statistics provide data on the claims of foreign affiliates in *host countries* vis-à-vis local residents (families, firms and other financial institutions) – defined as local claims – denominated in local and foreign currency.[5] These include loans, but also securities such as stocks and bonds. BIS statistics also provide data on total foreign claims, which include all the foreign assets held abroad by banks (domestic and MNBs), that is, summing up the local claims held through local affiliates with those held through cross-border transactions.

Trends in local and foreign claims are reported in Figure 1. Local claims in local currency (measured in current US dollars) rose in absolute terms to a value of more than \$10 trillion and almost doubled between 2000 and 2009 with respect to world GDP (from roughly 10% to 20%). Also local claims in foreign currency followed a similar pattern, although they can only be estimated as of March 2005. Both types of local claims summed up to \$17 trillion in 2009, accounting for more than 55% of total foreign claims, also reported. Notice that in the last two years (December 2007–December 2009) total foreign claims experienced a more pronounced decline compared to local claims. We will further discuss this point in Section 4, which deals specifically with the crisis.

[5] The BIS Banking Statistics report separate statistics for local claims in local currency only, whereas local claims in foreign currency are summed up with cross-border claims, and thus are not immediately identifiable. Following McCauley *et al.* (2010) they can be estimated starting from March 2005 as the difference between total international claims on an immediate borrower basis and cross-border claims on an ultimate risk basis (further details and a discussion on the bias introduced by this estimation are in Box 1).

Box 1. The banking statistics of the Bank for International Settlements (BIS)

The BIS Banking Statistics report financial claims and liabilities of banks towards the rest of the world.

Data are compiled on a consolidated (*Consolidated Statistics*) and on an unconsolidated basis (*Locational Statistics*).

The *Consolidated Statistics* report banks' on-balance sheet financial claims on the rest of the world and thereby provide a measure of the risk exposures of lenders' national banking systems. The quarterly data cover contractual lending by the head office and all its branches and subsidiaries on a worldwide consolidated basis, that is, net of inter-office accounts. Total claims are broken down by maturity, sector (banks, non-bank private sector and public sector) as well as vis-à-vis country. It is therefore possible to construct statistics on total foreign claims by destination (vis-à-vis) country. These statistics also provide separate data on claims and liabilities of foreign affiliates (branches and subsidiaries, see note 9 for a discussion of these two types of foreign affiliates), located outside the reporting countries, towards residents of the host country, on an unconsolidated basis (defined as '*Local Claims*', see below).

The *Locational Statistics* report the aggregate international claims and liabilities of all banks resident in the 41 reporting countries broken down by instrument, currency, sector, country of residence of counterparty, and nationality of reporting banks. In this system, both domestic and foreign-owned banking offices in the reporting countries record their positions on a gross basis (except for derivative contracts for which a master netting agreement is in place) and on an unconsolidated basis, including those vis-à-vis own affiliates, which is consistent with the principles of national accounts, money and banking, balance of payments and external debt statistics. As locational statistics combine foreign activities of both national and multinational banks, it is not possible to disentangle separate data for foreign affiliates.

From a risk reallocation perspective, BIS provides information either on an *immediate borrower basis* or on an *ultimate risk basis*. Within the former, the claim is allocated directly to the country of immediate risk; the latter reallocates claims to the country of ultimate risk which is defined as the country where the guarantor of a claim resides. The use of derivative transactions, for instance, often implies a mismatch between risk allocated on a borrower or on an ultimate risk basis: suppose an Italian bank acquires a bond issued by a German issuer but guaranteed by a US insurance company on the basis of a derivative transaction written on the top of the bond; in this case, Germany is the country of the immediate guarantor, while the United States is the country where the ultimate risk resides.

Most of the data used in Section 2 are derived from the Consolidated Statistics and expressed on an immediate borrower basis, as per the following definitions:

- *Foreign Claims* are the sum of cross-border claims of banks (domestic and multinationals) plus the local claims in all currencies of banks' foreign affiliates. Claims comprise financial assets (items reported on balance sheets only) including, as a minimum, deposits and balances with other banks, loans and advances to other banks and non-banks, and holdings of debt securities. It excludes derivatives and off balance sheet transactions. In the BIS statistics foreign claims are reported as the sum of international claims (A + B) and local claims in local currency (C).
- *International Claims* (A + B) are banks' cross-border claims (A) plus local claims of foreign affiliates in foreign currencies (B).
- *Local Claims* (C) are the claims denominated in local currency of foreign affiliates on the residents of the host country (i.e., country of residence of affiliates).

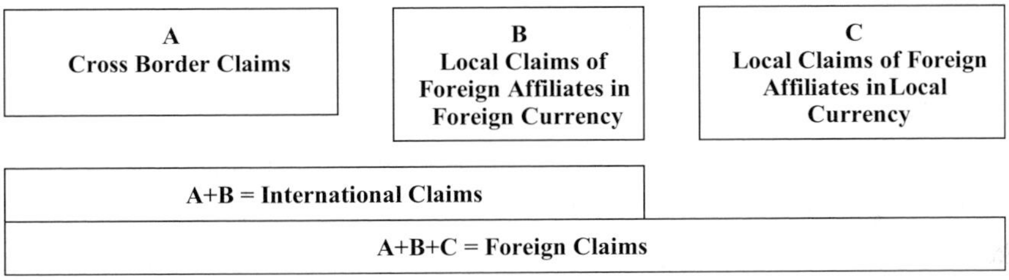

Local Claims of foreign affiliates is the key variable used in the analysis of this paper, as it measures the claims of foreign affiliates towards residents in the host country. However, consolidated statistics on an immediate borrower basis provide separate data only on local claims in local currency and not on local claims in foreign currencies. Therefore, local claims in foreign currency are estimated as the difference between total international claims on an immediate borrower basis (Table 9AA BIS Statistics) and cross-border claims on an ultimate risk basis (Table 9CT BIS Statistics; see McCauley *et al.*, 2010). Estimates for local claims in foreign currency at the country level therefore include a bias which is larger, the larger the ultimate transfer risk.

Local Liabilities refer to liabilities of foreign affiliates of domestic banks in local currency vis-à-vis local residents.

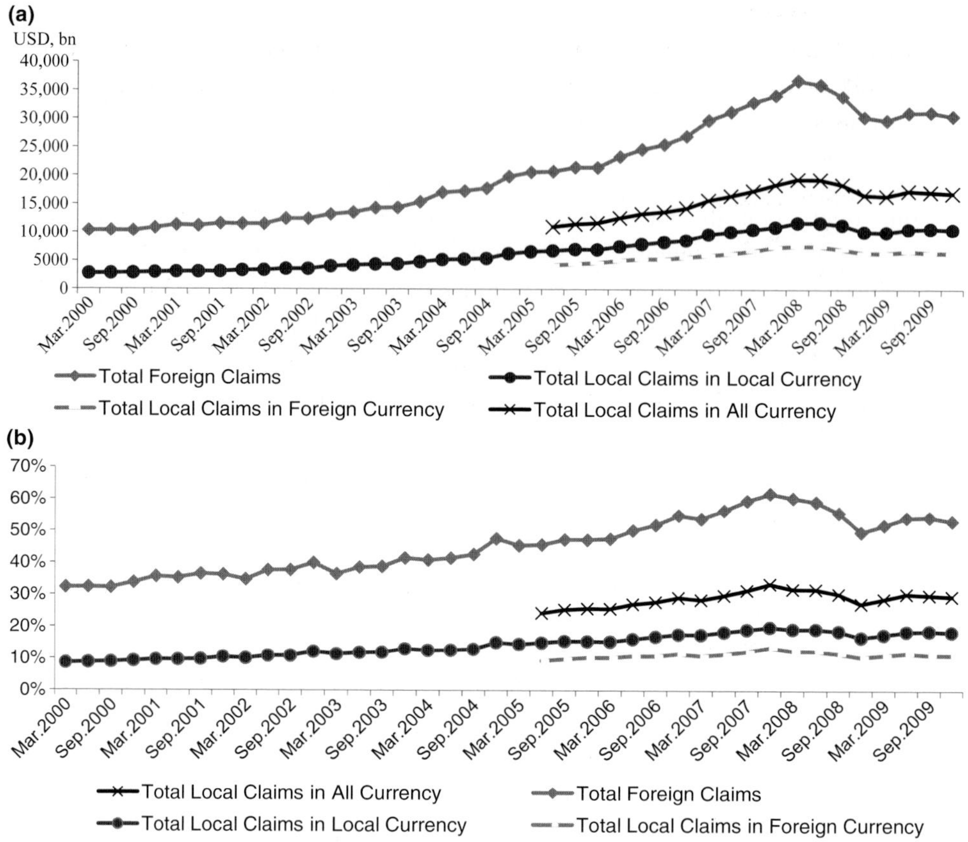

Figure 1. Total foreign and local claims in (a) nominal values and (b) percentage of GDP

Source: BIS Consolidated Statistics for claims and World Bank Statistics for GDP.

2.2. The rise of multinational banking within the EU single market

Decomposing the BIS data by regions of destination, we notice that the value of local claims of foreign affiliates denominated in local currency (converted in current US dollars in the BIS statistics) have been rising especially fast in the EU, particularly among the EMU12 countries (Figure 2), reaching the other advanced economies, including the United States and Japan, by the end of the period.[6]

These trends are also the outcome of severe exchange rate fluctuations in the period analysed. The yen roughly devalued by 30% with respect to the euro between 2000 and 2009 and the dollar by almost 50%. To better gauge the

[6] Here we restrict our analysis to claims denominated in local currency, as the bias in the estimates of those in foreign currency is particularly severe at the level of a country or a group of countries.

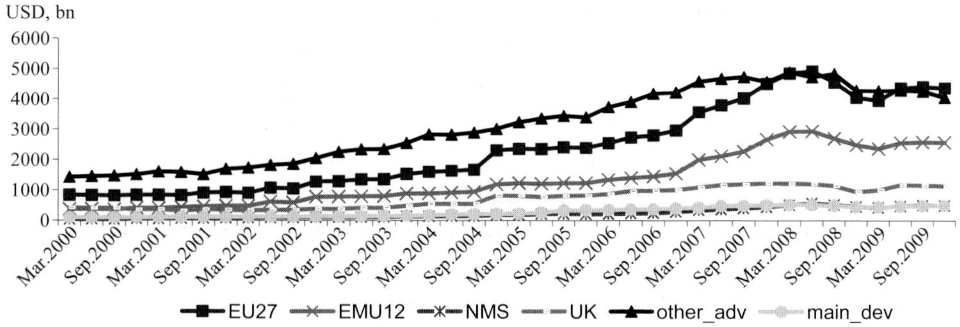

Figure 2. Nominal total local claims of foreign affiliates by host region

Note: Other advanced: United States, Canada, Japan, Australia, New Zealand, Switzerland. NMS: Bulgaria, Cyprus, Czech Republic, Hungary, Latvia, Lithuania, Malta, Poland, Romania, Slovakia, Slovenia. Main Developing: China, India, Malaysia, South Korea, South Africa, Singapore, United Arab Emirates.

Source: BIS Consolidated Statistics.

Table 1. Total local claims in local currency on total assets (%)

	avg 2001–2003	avg 2004–2006	2007	2008-I	2008-II	2008-III	2008-IV	2009-I	2009-II
EU27	9.8	13.3	17.9	17.8	17.7	17.8	16.4	16.6	16.9
EMU12	7.5	9.9	15.1	15.4	15.2	15.2	14.1	13.8	13.8
UK	16.5	21.7	23.0	21.7	21.3	21.5	21.0	22.9	23.4
NMS	35.7	43.1	50.2	49.4	50.6	48.9	44.7	46.6	47.4
other_adv	4.1	5.1	6.0	6.3	6.0	6.3	5.6	5.9	5.9

Notes: Other advanced: United States, Canada, Japan, Australia, New Zealand, Switzerland. NMS: Bulgaria, Cyprus, Czech Republic, Hungary, Latvia, Lithuania, Malta, Poland, Romania, Slovakia, Slovenia.

Source: BIS Consolidated Statistics for Local Claims. IMF, International Financial Statistics for Total Assets.

increasing role of multinational banking it is therefore necessary to relate local claims to the value of total banking assets in the countries of destination. This is done in Table 1.

The especially important role of foreign affiliates in the EU stands out clearly when the size of their assets is normalized with the total banking assets of each country. By mid-2009 these were 16.9% with respect to total assets, compared to a mere 5.9% for the other industrialized economies. The ratio for the EU has also risen considerably (and at a faster pace than for other advanced economies) from early 2000, when it was lower than 10%. The picture is fairly heterogeneous within the Union. Foreign affiliates have an especially large role in the United Kingdom and in the new member states (NMSs), particularly in those that have adopted the euro, where they account for a very large share of total assets. These particularly high shares reflect of course the role of the United Kingdom as an international financial centre and, for the NMSs, their relatively weak local financial institutions which were acquired by large European banks during the transition years. As for the EMU12, the share of assets held by foreign banks is lower than for the EU average. However, given the size of this area, in nominal values the EMU12 countries account collectively for the largest amount of local claims held by foreign affiliates.

The evidence that MNBs have become increasingly active within the EU, particularly through mergers and acquisitions, requires some qualifications.[7] In principle, an integrated financial market should provide an ideal ground for cross-border market transactions, reducing the need to rely on the ICM to move resources across countries, as it would be the case with MNBs. Yet, we know that retail activities are non-tradable even within integrated markets. Therefore, tapping the European retail market requires having local operations in foreign countries anyway. But within an integrated financial area and particularly with a single currency, those local operations can likely benefit from easier and smoother intra-bank cross-border transactions, taking place through the ICM. We will discuss extensively these results in Sections 3 and 4.

The argument that the ICM is likely to work more smoothly within integrated financial areas is also supported by the evidence that most foreign banking activity in the Union is intra-European. This can be gauged by ECB data, where total banking assets of member countries are decomposed by the nationality of ownership of the bank and by whether foreign affiliates are independent subsidiaries or branches.[8] As we will further discuss below, the distinction between subsidiaries and branches is important both from the point of view of the organization of the internal capital market and of the regulatory framework in the EU (see Calzolari and Loranth, 2010, for an analysis of regulation of MNBs in terms of their organization).[9] This decomposition is reported in Figure 3. Differences in definitions of

[7] M&A activity within the EU banking sector experienced a boom at the beginning of the new century. In 2000 there were approximately 140 M&A transactions in the EU, of which intra EU 25 M&A deals involving a non-domestic acquirer represented almost 30% of the total (European Central Bank, 2006).

[8] Assets of credit institutions under the ECB definition comprise any asset that is (i) cash; or (ii) a contractual right to receive cash or another financial instrument from another enterprise; or (iii) a contractual right to exchange financial instruments with another enterprise under conditions that are potentially favourable; or (iv) an equity instrument of another enterprise. Total assets are calculated on a residential basis, meaning that for each Member State the credit institutions under the law of that Member State are included (regardless of whether or not they are a subsidiary of a foreign bank). However, the activity of the foreign branches of these credit institutions is not included, as this is reported by the host country. Credit institutions include any institution covered by the definition contained in Article 4(1) of Directive 2006/48/EC (recast). Accordingly, a credit institution is '(i) an undertaking whose business is to receive deposits or other repayable funds from the public and to grant credits for its own account; or (ii) an electronic money institution within the meaning of Directive 2000/46/EC. The most common types of credit institutions are banks and savings banks'.

[9] Foreign affiliates set up as subsidiaries are stand-alone companies, where local management has a high degree of decisional autonomy within the group. In the current European regulatory framework they are subject to host country supervisory authorities. Branches instead are part of the foreign group and not stand-alone companies, normally with less decisional autonomy than subsidiaries. They are subject to the home country supervisory authorities. Branches are used more frequently by MNBs to carry out wholesale activities. Subsidiaries are normally used to carry out retail activities, given that they collect deposits and that a large part of their transactions have to be carried out face to face with local customers. The largest share of foreign assets is held by EU banks through subsidiaries. This reflects the recent spur of cross-border acquisitions, where acquired banks become autonomous foreign subsidiaries and also the fact that within Europe foreign affiliates are generally used to carry out non-tradable activities like retail.

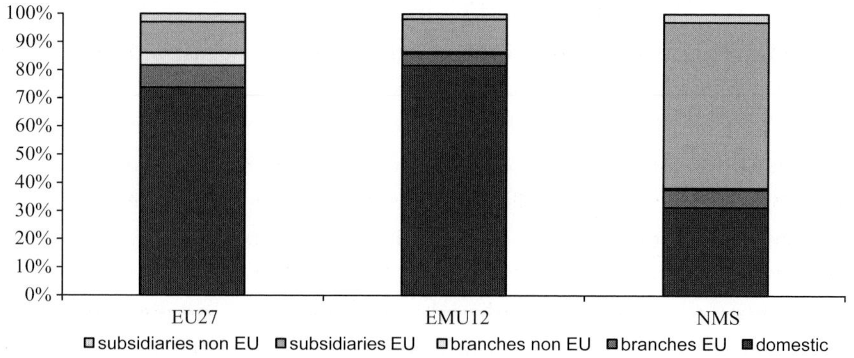

Figure 3. Distribution of total banking assets EU27 (2008)

Note: NMS: Bulgaria, Cyprus, Czech Republic, Hungary, Latvia, Lithuania, Malta, Poland, Romania, Slovakia, Slovenia.

Source: ECB Statistics.

asset categories explain why the ECB figures do not match precisely the BIS figures reported above.[10]

If we consider the aggregate of the EU countries, we notice that foreign banks account for roughly 29% of total assets, held through either subsidiaries or branches. Foreign banks' assets can further be decomposed into EU and extra-EU institutions. Notice that by far the largest share of these assets are owned by EU banks. This share is especially large within the EMU aggregate.

The EU is therefore an especially interesting case to look at for assessing the role of MNBs and the functioning of their ICMs, particularly during the financial crisis. This justifies our focus on the EU in the micro analysis of the following sections.

3. MULTINATIONAL BANKS AND INTERNAL CAPITAL MARKETS: IMPLICATION FOR EFFICIENCY AND FINANCIAL STABILITY

This section examines how the availability of an ICM affects the behaviour of MNBs, and their possible reactions during a crisis. It is indeed the ICM that makes the activities of foreign affiliates in host economies distinctly different from those of stand-alone national banks. Large corporations can establish ICMs that allocate scarce capital, liquidity and risk across the many units belonging to the holding (Box 2 briefly describes the functioning of ICMs and summarizes the literature in finance and economics that have analysed their working, both theoretically and empirically).

[10] Note that the share of the assets held by foreign banks (29%) is larger than the share of local claims on total assets (15%) and smaller than the share of foreign claims (60%) reported in Table 1. The reason is that the definitions of assets are different for the two institutions. Foreign assets under the ECB include claims towards residents and non-residents in the host country held by foreign subsidiaries and branches based in a given EU host country (but not those held through other foreign subsidiaries or branches based abroad). Local claims under the BIS have a strictly host country perspective and only include claims of foreign branches and subsidiaries vis-à-vis residents in the host country. Foreign claims in BIS statistics also include cross-border transactions.

Box 2. Internal capital markets: the bright and the dark side

Financial and non-financial institutions are often organized in divisions or affiliated units, by product or by location. Consider, for example, a bank with its parent company P and two affiliates A1 and A2, each with some internal funding, collaterals, pledgeable income and investment opportunities (see Figure 4 for a graphical representation). A1 can be financed as a stand-alone entity using funds internal to A1 or raised directly by A1 in the external credit market. Alternatively, in the absence of constraining regulation, A1 can be financed in an ICM in which A1 approaches P for funding. The parent P in turn can directly raise external funds against its own and the combined collateral of affiliates A1 and A2, centralize the funds individually raised by the affiliates and, finally, allocate them to A1, A2 and P according to some criteria. In the end, this allocation is similar to the task performed by the credit market, although it takes place within the 'internal' capital market of the bank. The central question for ICMs is whether this internal process is more or less efficient and profitable for the bank than an external market for credit. Clearly, if the capital market were fully efficient, ICMs would be irrelevant, but we know this is almost never the case. First, raising external funds in a centralized way may allow increasing the total amount of funds (the '*more-money effect*' of ICMs). Second, funds may be allocated more efficiently and profitably to all investment opportunities when the process is centralized and information asymmetries are overcome (the '*smarter-money effect*' of ICMs). Clearly the two effects, which are known as the '*bright side*' of ICMs, are related (smarter money may lead to more money) and depend on the ICM's organization. In particular, more money may take place since the control power attributed to the internal capital market should induce more screening and monitoring of the projects to be financed. Furthermore, an ICM may create value in financially constrained firms, since affiliates' projects compete for scarce internal funds and are jointly screened within the ICM. However, badly organized ICMs may show up with a '*dark side*': competition for funding may turn out to be wasteful rent-seeking, funds may be spread among affiliates with no reference to relative merit, thus dampening incentives and with the affiliates' manager feeling expropriated. The empirical literature has shown that ICMs do operate in large corporations since one observes that shocks in one affiliate affect investments in other affiliates and investments in small units are positively related to cash flow of other units. ICMs have also been shown to deliver more and smarter money when the external capital market is less developed (e.g. for weak legal enforcement, inadequate accounting and disclosure practices); when divisions have not sharply divergent investment prospects; when the firm is able to control the agency issues intrinsic to ICMs using high-powered incentives such as management ownership. These results have been shown by a significant theoretical and empirical academic literature while that on ICMs for banks is instead less developed and that on MNBs even less so, as discussed in the main text.

Some relevant theoretical papers related to the more-money and smarter-money effects are Williamson (1975), Gertner *et al.* (1994), Stein (1997, 2002), and Carletti *et al.* (2007). Scharfstein and Stein (2000), Rajan *et al.* (2000), Hart and Holmstrom (2010), and Brusco and Panunzi (2005) have studied the dark side of ICMs. For empirical analyses see, among others, Lamont (1997), Scharfstein (1998), Shin and Stulz (1998), Rajan *et al.* (2000), Chevalier (2004), Khanna and Tice (2001), Whited (2001), Billett and Mauer (2003), Ozbas and Scharfstein (2008).

This analysis is important to our aims since MNBs have the possibility to diversify risk internationally, to optimally allocate funds across their network of international affiliates in search of higher returns, and to efficiently share liquidity. We are also particularly interested in understanding whether ICMs in cross-border banks have stabilizing or destabilizing effects in home and host countries, in normal times and in times of crisis. In particular, as for the effects of shocks affecting banks and host countries, in this section we will deal with *idiosyncratic* ones, while the next section will be devoted to the *systemic* shocks of the present crisis. Here we will develop a theoretical framework for MNBs and their ICMs which will deliver a number of 'claims'. Considering the set of all these claims, we will then derive some testable implications that will be explicitly verified with the empirical analysis in the next section.

Affiliates of an MNB located in different countries may well face different costs of external funds. These banks may thus collect deposits, say in country 1 and 2, and finance a project in country 2 by pooling deposits in an ICM. In addition, by pooling liquidity from affiliates in different countries, when affiliates' liquidity shocks are not positively correlated, an MNB may then be able to keep lower liquidity to take care of the duration mismatch of assets and liabilities typical of the transformation activity of banks. For given regulatory constraints that national authorities impose to banks on liquidity, this possibility allows an MNB to reduce overall costs. Although diversification can also be obtained in a large national group, it is clear that cross-border activities may well increase diversification. On the other hand, one should also consider that the functioning of an ICM operating across countries may be hindered by factors such as limited economic and regulatory integration, differences in (business) culture, in languages and by distance among the units belonging to the ICM, as we will further illustrate.

From these arguments it is possible to derive some important consequences of an ICM in a banking group and, in particular, for an MNB. As explained in Box 2,

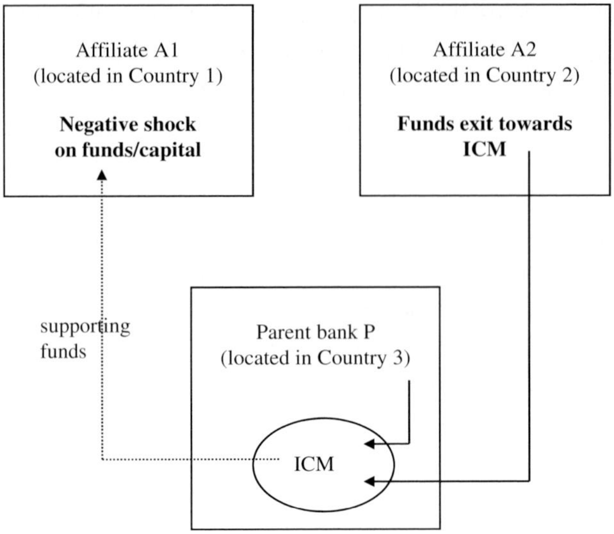

Figure 4. Functioning of ICM of an MNB when affiliate A1 is hit by shock on capital

the organization of an ICM and its functioning are responsible for the possible realization of 'smarter money', according to which funds, risk and liquidity are allocated to the MNB's affiliates that are better at managing them. This process of relocation leads to a *support* effect and a *substitution* effect which are described next (this useful taxonomy is due to Morgan *et al.*, 2004).

Consider Figure 4 and a shock that is local in country 1, deteriorating capital (assets or loans) or reducing funds availability (with a reduction of deposits) of affiliate A1 of the MNB. This negative shock may force the affiliate either to obtain new equity, to satisfy its capital adequacy ratio and/or its strategies, or to reduce its loans. This would certainly be the case were the bank a single entity. When belonging to an MNB, instead, the shock may be reduced by the capital and the liquidity provided by home or other affiliates in foreign countries, through the ICM. An MNB may then be able and willing to *support* its affiliates in cases of country-specific shocks, thus watering down the effect of these local shocks: *the support effect makes an affiliate's lending capacity less responsive to local shocks on capital and deposits, i.e. on the availability of local funds* (*Claim 1*).

In addition to the support effect, an ICM determines capital and liquidity movements looking for the best remuneration within the MNB (the 'smarter money'), that might lead to a *substitution* effect. Consider now a real shock hitting the economy in the country of an affiliate (say country 1 in the previous figure), thus reducing the returns of investments in that country. Then, the ICM would substitute the activities of that affiliate relocating funds towards the parent bank and other affiliates with better investment opportunities. This makes an affiliate's lending in a banking group more responsive to shocks affecting the returns of its investments. *Hence, the substitution effect weakens the link between funds availability and lending. This is more so for banking groups operating in countries with little correlated real shocks and it is definitely less relevant for domestic banking groups operating in a single country* (*Claim 2*).

The support and substitution effects emerge from the 'smarter money' of an ICM (which ultimately may enhance efficiency and profitability of an MNB). We are now interested to see the role of 'more money' that a banking group may generate if its ICM works properly (see again Box 2). If this is the case, then an ICM has much more information and control on a troubled affiliate than the external capital market which, instead, may be completely impaired due to lack of information. On a similar vein, the functioning and the effects of ICMs are closely related to the organization and the incentives that are used in setting up an MNB's ICM. On the one hand, affiliates may be tightly integrated to form a unique ICM, such as for branches of a bank which are *de facto* (and *de jure*) parts of the holding company. Alternatively, even though they take part in an ICM, affiliates may keep some independence and responsibility in their decisions, as it is often the case for MNBs' subsidiaries (which are *de jure* independent legal entities controlled by the holding). We are mainly interested in the organization of groups with subsidiaries, which are the predominant form of foreign affiliates in Europe (with the exception of the United Kingdom), also because, as explained in the sequel, data on single affiliates are only available for subsidiaries. It has been emphasized (Shah and Thakor, 1987; Kahn and Winton, 2004; Boot and Schmeits, 2000) that a subsidiary structure may allow external investors to better evaluate the different projects in the holding by clearly associating projects to single units so that higher transparency translates into smaller cost for external funding. Hence, *a well-organized ICM of domestic and international banking groups may generate 'more money' available to address any kind of shock, thus smoothening the link between funds and lending* (*Claim 3*).

Overall, Claims 1–3 all point to a reduction of correlation between available funds and a bank's lending capacity.

As explained in Box 2, however, an ICM can deliver its desirable properties that lead to Claims 1–3 when showing its bright side. Support/substitution is strictly related to the information that is made available within the organization, since an ICM involves a decision process that requires information.[11] Hence, a more integrated ICM with intense information sharing may lead to more substitution and support effects. However, for an ICM to work smoothly there must not be impediments which can emerge as external constraints. These constraints may

[11] A decentralized MNB with more independent units still belonging to the ICM (i.e. a flatter organization) is most likely to be an attractive option when information about individual projects is 'soft' and cannot be easily and credibly transmitted upstream through the hierarchy. In contrast, a large and hierarchical MNB with multiple layers composed of units of limited independence and a strongly integrated ICM is best when information can be 'hardened' and passed along the hierarchy.

emerge because of an inadequate organization and incentive mechanism of the ICM, but also by the regulatory and economic environment. Pooling resources into an ICM and relocating internationally to the affiliate in need of support requires that the MNB satisfies a set of rules imposed by possibly many different countries (since a fully harmonized or integrated regulatory authority is still missing in the international banking sector) thus leading to a 'regulatory risk'. Pooling resources also exposes the MNB to a 'transfer risk', for example associated with the exchange rate swings of the currencies in use in the different countries. On a similar vein, the literature on the ICM has shown that this should operate better when the participating units have not sharply divergent investment prospects, as it is the case in related economies. Thus, *MNBs operating in an integrated area, both in terms of regulations and in terms of currencies, may make a more intense use of their ICMs* (*Claim 4*). Furthermore, one may expect that *units that are located in distant countries with different languages or different cultural environments may find it difficult to actively take part into a cross-border ICM of an MNB* (*Claim 5*).

In light of Claims 2, 4 and 5, it will be particularly interesting to understand whether the ICMs are substitutes or complements of the process of market integration taking place at different stages in Europe. On the one hand, as illustrated above, the need for an ICM may be limited in very well-integrated economies with correlated real shocks, since the external and the integrated internal capital markets may function as substitutes and the scope for the substitution effect is limited. On the other hand, differences in terms of cultures, languages, banks' regulations and currencies may obstruct the kind of integration within the MNB that is needed for an ICM to work smoothly.

That ICMs operate in large banks is a documented fact. It has been shown that loan growth of an affiliate of domestic holdings is more sensitive to the parent's cash flow and capital than the affiliate's own capital (Houston *et al.*, 1997; Houston and James, 1998; Morgan *et al.*, 2004; Kroszner and Strahan, 2006; Kroszner, 2008; Carlson and Mitchener, 2009).[12] As for cross-border banks, De Haas and van Lelyveld (2010) have recently documented the functioning of ICMs in the top 45 MNBs around the world (see also Chan-Lau *et al.*, 2008), showing that they are more active (in terms of support and substitution effects) in foreign units that are less independent (e.g. that have been established with green field investment instead of takeover).[13] In this case, they find evidence that the substitution effect is at play, since foreign lending is negatively related to the business cycle of the home country of the parent holding, and that the support effect shows up mainly for dependent

[12] Carletti *et al.* (2007) set up a theoretical model of banks merging in different regions and explicitly account for their liquidity decisions. They show that merged banks have lower liquidity risk and financing costs and are more efficient but also that merges may have adverse macro effects reducing liquidity of the interbank market.

[13] Havrylchyk and Jurzyk (2006) show that greenfield banks are much more embedded in an MNB group's internal capital market, whereas acquired banks within the group seem to be organized as rather independent capital units.

units of MNBs that reduce lending less than independent banks when the foreign economy is hit by a negative shock.[14]

3.1. Empirical evidence on the functioning of internal capital markets: a European perspective

Following the five claims we identified above, we now turn to an empirical analysis of the effects of ICMs on the link between bank lending and funds availability in Europe. To do so, we consider how, in a given bank, deposits co-vary with loans, focusing therefore on one specific effect of the availability of an ICM, its impact on the correlation between funding and the use of resources. The advantage of using this simple index is that it requires no assumptions on the direction of causality between deposit and loan growth. We focus instead on the possible differences in their correlation between banks that do have internal capital markets and banks that do not. Clearly, this exercise is only possible by retaining a control group of stand-alone units, which represents our benchmark for banks that have no access to ICMs.

The existing empirical literature has not explicitly considered domestic banks and domestic banking groups as controls for a direct comparison for the effects of national and international ICMs. Our strategy is therefore complementary to that of De Haas and van Lelyveld (2010), who show that the lending behaviour of bank affiliates is affected by their parents' financial conditions, but only control for the contemporaneous behaviour of very large stand-alone units, that might not be fully comparable with typically smaller foreign affiliates.

Comparing the correlation between loans and deposit of MNBs and a counterfactual of national banks is also justified by the fact that we are focusing our analysis on Europe, where the number of country-specific crises is very limited. Consequently, in our case, contrary to De Haas and van Lelyveld (2010), we cannot test for the existence of the ICM by looking at how national banking crises affect the lending strategies of affiliates based in other countries.[15]

Finally, since we will concentrate on banks operating in Europe, we have the possibility to consider banks active in an economic area with a significant level of integration both for the real economy, thus being characterized by correlated real shocks, and for the financial sector. We will then study the interplay between international integration and the functioning of ICMs. As explained above, *a priori*

[14] On anecdotal evidence, during the 2003 crisis of Norwegian banks, it has been observed that Noredea Norway, although hit by significant losses (accounting for 1.17% of its gross lending in 2003), was able to limit the reduction of its capital by borrowing from the Nordea Group. Looking at the crisis of Japanese banks in the early 1990s, units in the United States experienced reduction of lending where they were units more dependent on the parent banks but they were almost unaffected when they were more independent (Peek and Rosengren, 1997).

[15] According to the reliable and updated dataset on banking crises by Laeven and Valencia (2008) – the one used, for example, in De Haas and van Lelyveld (2010) – there are no national crises in our sample, except for the crisis hitting the United Kingdom in 2007, which is however the first year of a global crisis.

the relationship could be one of complements or substitutes. Discriminating between the two cases is critical in particular in the current period of revision of the European environment for supervision and regulation of MNBs.

Our analysis is based on balance sheet information of a large sample of European banks, collected by the commercial data provider Bureau Van Dijk, in its Bankscope data base. We started by considering all affiliates in the EU27 countries of the 100 largest European banks (that are likely to be those that will be more directly supervised by European colleges of supervisors) between 2000 and 2008, distinguishing between domestic and foreign affiliates (i.e. dependent subsidiary banks that operate, respectively, in the same country and in a different one from that of incorporation of the parent bank), on the basis of their ownership structure.[16] In addition, we have checked the shareholding structure of all other banks in our sample, that includes all institutions in EU27 countries with total assets above US$100 million, to identify additional affiliates of domestic or foreign institutions. Summary statistics for our sample are presented in Table 2.

We have 7,326 banks, 637 affiliates of which 529 foreign, and 213 parent banks of which 148 MNBs.[17] The average size of the banks in our sample, measured by their total assets, is US$17 billion, while the median is less than US$1 billion, suggesting a significant skewness, as it is quite common when using company data. Affiliates and parent banks are larger (US$31.3 billion and US$204.0 billion, respectively). The average yearly rate of growth of nominal customer loans in our sample period is 20%, and it is smaller than average for parent banks (18%) and larger for affiliates (26%). Similarly, the average rate of growth of demand deposits is 19% (22% for affiliates and 15% for parent banks). Affiliates are also more profitable and are more leveraged than both parents and stand-alones. Finally, foreign affiliates within EMU and EU15 are larger than average, less leveraged and less profitable.

As a preliminary step, we have calculated the total correlations between the rate of growth of customer loans and of deposits, distinguishing between stand-alone banks, domestic and multinational parent banks and domestic and foreign affiliates. Table 3 shows that the average correlation between the loan and deposit growth is 0.54, and it is statistically significant at the 1% level. Consistent with our Claim 1 (*the support effect makes an affiliate's lending capacity less responsive to local shocks on capital and deposits, i.e. on the availability of local funds*) and Claim 2 (*the substitution effect weakens the link between funds availability and lending. This is more so for banking groups operating in countries with little correlated real shocks and definitely less relevant for domestic banking groups operating in a single country*), the correlation is slightly smaller than average for

[16] As it is common in this literature, we have not been able to extend our analysis to the behaviour of foreign branches, because with very few exceptions their activities are recorded only in confidential supervisory data, and not by all countries.

[17] The largest number of banks in our sample is from Germany, Italy and France; the largest number of affiliates is from Luxemburg, Poland and Spain.

Table 2. Summary statistics

Variables	Observations	Mean	Coefficient of variation	Median
Full sample				
Total assets (US$ bn)	7326	17.00	5.76	0.79
Customer loans (%)	6732	0.20	1.61	0.18
Demand deposits (%)	6584	0.19	1.53	0.17
Bank total assets – Country (%)	9239	0.17	0.44	0.18
Returns on assets (%)	7311	0.58	4.05	0.47
Customer loans/total assets	7263	0.58	0.38	0.62
Bank deposits/total assets	7058	0.18	1.08	0.12
Equity/total assets (%)	7316	10.27	1.51	7.26
Loan loss prov./Net int. margin	7311	0.58	4.05	0.47
Net interest margin (%)	6862	0.17	4.91	0.14
GDP (%)	7201	2.85	1.99	2.70
Stand-alones				
Total assets	6535	11.00	5.59	0.66
Customer loans (%)	6026	0.20	1.66	0.18
Demand deposits (%)	5893	0.19	1.54	0.17
Bank total assets – Country (%)	8445	0.17	0.40	0.18
Returns on assets (%)	6523	0.57	4.26	0.45
Customer loans/total assets	6479	0.58	0.36	0.63
Bank deposits/total assets	6285	0.17	1.12	0.11
Equity/total assets (%)	6525	10.33	1.56	7.27
Loan loss prov./Net int. margin	6137	0.17	5.17	0.14
Net interest margin (%)	6433	2.87	2.06	2.73
Affiliates				
Total assets	637	31.30	4.29	32.79
Customer loans (%)	570	0.26	1.28	0.25
Demand deposits (%)	556	0.22	1.43	−0.22
Bank total assets – Country (%)	633	0.23	0.53	−0.21
Returns on assets (%)	634	0.70	2.76	0.69
Customer loans/total assets	630	0.50	0.50	0.53
Bank deposits/total assets	621	0.29	0.79	0.23
Equity/total assets (%)	637	10.53	0.96	7.64
Loan loss prov./Net int. margin	634	0.70	2.76	0.69
Net interest margin (%)	574	0.17	1.97	−0.12
Parent banks				
Total assets	213	204.00	2.00	37.70
Customer loans (%)	192	0.18	1.11	0.18
Demand deposits (%)	191	0.15	1.67	0.13
Bank total assets – Country (%)	219	0.19	0.64	0.18
Returns on assets (%)	213	0.66	1.04	0.57
Customer loans/total assets	213	0.53	0.40	0.57
Bank deposits/total assets	211	0.20	0.80	0.16
Equity/total assets (%)	213	7.04	0.98	5.85
Loan loss prov./Net int. margin	213	0.66	1.04	0.57
Net interest margin (%)	210	0.16	1.14	0.14
Foreign affiliates				
Total assets	529	21.40	5.08	2.95
Customer loans (Δ%)	483	0.26	1.27	0.27
Demand deposits (Δ%)	471	0.22	1.45	0.23
Bank total assets – Country (Δ%)	530	0.24	0.52	0.23
Returns on assets (%)	527	0.67	2.52	0.67
Customer loans/total assets	522	0.50	0.49	0.53

Table 2. (Continued)

Variables	Observations	Mean	Coefficient of variation	Median
Bank deposits/total assets	520	0.29	0.80	0.23
Equity/total assets (%)	529	10.76	1.00	7.60
Loan loss prov./Net int. margin	527	0.67	2.52	0.67
Net interest margin (%)	475	0.17	2.07	0.12
Foreign parent banks				
Total assets	148	251.00	1.80	52.30
Customer loans (Δ%)	135	0.16	1.11	0.17
Demand deposits (Δ%)	134	0.13	1.68	0.13
Bank total assets – Country (Δ%)	153	0.18	0.70	0.18
Returns on assets (%)	148	0.66	1.04	0.56
Customer loans/total assets	148	0.51	0.41	0.54
Bank deposits/total assets	148	0.22	0.77	0.17
Equity/total assets (%)	148	6.37	0.78	5.50
Loan loss prov./Net int. margin	148	0.66	1.04	0.56
Net interest margin (%)	146	0.16	1.12	0.14
Banks chartered in EMU				
Total assets	6087	15.40	6.05	0.74
Customer loans (Δ%)	5614	0.19	1.59	0.18
Demand deposits (Δ%)	5515	0.18	1.52	0.17
Bank total assets – Country (Δ%)	7629	0.16	0.34	0.18
Returns on assets (%)	6082	0.53	3.82	0.43
Customer loans/total assets	6040	0.58	0.37	0.62
Bank deposits/total assets	5914	0.18	1.08	0.12
Equity/total assets (%)	6077	10.07	1.12	6.97
Loan loss prov./Net int. margin	6082	0.53	3.82	0.43
Net interest margin (%)	5826	0.18	4.93	0.15
Banks chartered in EU15				
Total assets	6826	18.10	5.62	0.78
Customer loans (Δ%)	6283	0.19	1.66	0.18
Demand deposits (Δ%)	6142	0.18	1.55	0.17
Bank total assets – Country (Δ%)	8654	0.16	0.35	0.18
Returns on assets (%)	6812	0.58	3.58	0.45
Customer loans/total assets	6764	0.58	0.38	0.63
Bank deposits/total assets	6576	0.18	1.09	0.12
Equity/total assets (%)	6816	10.11	1.57	7.05
Loan loss prov./Net int. margin	6812	0.58	3.58	0.45
Net interest margin (%)	6406	0.17	4.99	0.14
Foreign subsidiaries in EMU				
Total assets	283	33.00	4.41	5.49
Customer loans (Δ%)	258	0.22	1.57	0.22
Demand deposits (Δ%)	247	0.19	1.71	0.19
Bank total assets – Country (Δ%)	291	0.20	0.52	0.20
Returns on assets (%)	282	0.49	2.83	0.51
Customer loans/total assets	278	0.48	0.59	0.50
Bank deposits/total assets	281	0.34	0.74	0.28
Equity/total assets (%)	283	9.01	1.14	5.94
Loan loss prov./Net int. margin	282	0.49	2.83	0.51
Net interest margin (%)	256	0.19	2.30	0.13
Foreign subsidiaries in EU15				
Total assets	314	33.40	4.19	5.28
Customer loans (Δ%)	284	0.21	1.62	0.21
Demand deposits (Δ%)	274	0.18	1.91	0.18
Bank total assets – Country (Δ%)	325	0.19	0.55	0.19

Table 2. (Continued)

Variables	Observations	Mean	Coefficient of variation	Median
Returns on assets (%)	312	0.52	2.55	0.53
Customer loans/total assets	308	0.46	0.61	0.47
Bank deposits/total assets	309	0.33	0.74	0.28
Equity/total assets (%)	314	9.52	1.17	5.94
Loan loss prov./Net int. margin	312	0.52	2.55	0.53
Net interest margin (%)	275	0.18	2.39	0.12

Source: Data are from Bankscope.

Table 3. Correlations between the rate of growth of customer loans and of demand deposits

Sample	Correlations
All banks	0.54
Stand-alones	0.54
Affiliates	0.42
Domestic affiliates	0.46
Foreign affiliates	0.42
Foreign affiliates (EMU)	0.26
Foreign affiliates (EU15)	0.26
Foreign affiliates (non-EU15)	0.66
Parent companies	0.82
Domestic parent companies	0.83
Multinational parent companies	0.82

Note: EMU and EU15 foreign affiliates are defined as those with their parent company within EMU and EU15, respectively. Non-EU15 foreign affiliates can have their parent company in any other EU27 country. All correlations are statistically significant at the 99% level.

Source: Data are from Bankscope.

affiliates, and it is even smaller for foreign affiliates. Further, the correlation is even smaller for foreign affiliates located within more integrated areas, such as EMU and EU15, providing convincing evidence to Claim 4 (*MNBs operating in an integrated area, both in terms of regulations and in terms of currencies, may make a more intense use of their ICMs*). Only in the case of foreign affiliates located in the NMSs of Central and Eastern Europe and of the few foreign banks in Malta and Cyprus (non-EU15 countries), the correlation is significantly higher, consistent with the hypothesis that regulatory and monetary integration is an important ingredient fostering the functioning of ICMs. The correlation is higher than average also for parents, both domestic and MNBs. A possible explanation is that parents are themselves very large banks composed with several dependent units (e.g. branches) and since they normally organize the ICM of the group, they smooth out the balance between loans and deposit of their affiliates, but on average keep stable their own relation between loans and deposits.

The indications of the simple correlations are that banks that may use ICMs can afford a more independent management of their assets and liabilities, thus smoothing the effects of potential idiosyncratic shocks. Furthermore, this is even more the case for those banks operating an ICM internationally.[18] To strengthen this preliminary evidence, in the following we will present the results of a more robust econometric analysis, capable of providing further support of our previous claims.

Our econometric framework exploits thoroughly the information contained in the correlations between each bank's growth of deposits and customer loans, using a two-step procedure. First, we estimate the time series correlation between each bank's rates of growth of deposits and of customer loans. Due to the frictions in our data set, we lose information for about 2,000 banks, obtaining a sample of 5,665 bank specific correlations. Second, we use the bank specific correlations as a dependent variable in a standard regression model, where the explanatory variables are: a set of dummies for foreign affiliates, in some specifications distinguishing those located within EMU and EU15; a set of bank specific characteristics; and country dummies.[19] In practice, our most general specification is the following:

$$\begin{aligned}\Delta Correl_{ij} = a_1 &+ a_2 DUM\_DomS_{ij} + a_3 DUM\_ForS_{ij}\\ &+ a_4 DUM\_ForS\_EMU_{ij} + a_5 DUM\_For\_EU15_{ij}\\ &+ a_6 DUM\_For\_EU15nEMU_{ij} + a_7 Char_{ij} + a_8 Country_j + \varepsilon_{ij}\end{aligned} \tag{1}$$

where: $\Delta Correl_{ij}$ is the correlation between the rate of growth (calculated as the annual change of the natural logarithm) of customer loans and of customer deposits of bank i in country j between 2000 and 2008; DUM_DomS_{ij} is a dummy variable for domestic affiliates; DUM_ForS_{ij} is a dummy variable for foreign affiliates; $DUM\_ForS\_EMU_{ij}$, $DUM\_For\_EU15_{ij}$, and $DUM\_For\_EU15nEMU_{ij}$ are dummies for foreign affiliates operating in EMU, in EU15 and in EU15 countries that are not EMU members, respectively;[20] $Char_{ij}$ are average characteristics of bank i of country j between 2000 and 2008; $Country_j$ is a set of country dummies; and ε_{ij} is a standard error term. The model is estimated using weighted least squares, to account for the different time span over which bank specific correlations have been calculated. As bank characteristics we have considered a measure of specialization (the share of customer loans over total assets), since banks active in traditional activities are more likely to have a strong matching between retail funding and lending; a measure of interbank liquidity (the share of bank deposits over total assets),

[18] It might be argued that MNBs are better at insuring idiosyncratic shocks because they are more efficient than domestic banks. Indeed, our results can be interpreted as showing that MNBs are more efficient precisely in the sense that they have an organization that allows them to make a better use of ICMs.

[19] We have chosen to focus on affiliates because, in a number of unreported regressions we have verified that the behavior of holding companies is not too dissimilar from that of average standalones, giving insignificant coefficients of the associated dummies.

[20] We considered banks that changed their status during the sample period as different institutions.

because easier access to the interbank market reduces the need for a strict matching of customer deposits and loans; leverage (the equity to total assets ratio), because more leveraged banks are typically those with better access to funding in capital markets; and size (the logarithm of total assets). To limit the effect of outliers we have run the estimates excluding observations below the 1st and above the 99th percentile of the sample distribution.[21]

The tests of our earlier claims are based on the signs and significance of the coefficients a_2 to a_5, associated with the dummies for the domestic affiliates and for the foreign affiliates in the different groups of countries. In particular, Claims 1–3 are generically consistent with a negative coefficient for the dummies of domestic and of foreign affiliates (a_2 and a_3); Claims 4 and 5 imply negative coefficients of the dummies for EMU and possibly non-EMU-EU15 affiliates (a_4 and a_5), consistent with an even lower correlation in the case of foreign affiliates, the more so if they operate within more integrated areas.

Table 4 presents the results of different specifications of model (1).

In column 1 we have included among the explanatory variables only the dummies for domestic and foreign affiliates, and the country dummies. As expected, both coefficients are negative, although only the coefficient of foreign affiliates, that is larger in absolute value, is statistically significant. Although the difference between the two is statistically insignificant, this provides some evidence consistent with the hypothesis of stronger incentives to use ICMs within a multinational group. Indeed, the aggregate result is likely to be the outcome of two opposing forces. In the case of domestic affiliates, ICMs may operate more smoothly, but they are used only when support is needed, since substitution is much less relevant within banks operating in the same country. In the case of foreign affiliates, both the support and the substitution effects are at work. Recall that both effects when at work should reduce the correlation between deposits and loans. But their relative magnitude is likely to vary, depending on the degree of market integration. Among highly integrated economies, on the one hand funds can be transferred more smoothly, but on the other hand business cycles are more correlated. Depending which of the two forces prevail, the support and the substitution functions are stronger or weaker within integrated areas. Columns 2 to 4 test precisely this hypothesis.

In column 2 we have included an additional dummy for MNBs operating within EMU. Consistent with Claim 4, we find strong evidence that foreign affiliates of EMU holding companies operating in another EMU country have an economic and statistically significant lower correlation between the rates of growth of deposits and of customer loans, with a coefficient of –0.197. Controlling for this effect, the coefficient of foreign affiliates becomes positive (0.007), although not statistically significant. For EMU foreign subsidiaries, the cumulative effect obtained summing

[21] Our results hold in unreported regressions where we use other trimming strategies.

Table 4. Correlation between loan and deposit growth – baseline specification

	(1)	(2)	(3)	(4)	(5)	(6)
Domestic affiliate (dummy)	−0.035	−0.036	−0.037	−0.037	−0.037	0.018
	0.038	0.038	0.038	0.038	0.038	0.035
Foreign affiliate (dummy)	−0.070***	0.007	0.067**	0.067**	0.067**	0.084**
	0.021	0.027	0.03	0.031	0.031	0.029
EMU foreign affiliate (dummy)		−0.197***		−0.264***	−0.258***	−0.193***
		0.042		0.045	0.045	0.042
EU15 foreign affiliate (dummy)			−0.266***			
			0.042			
EU15 non-EMU foreign affiliate (dummy)				−0.265***		
				0.064		
EU15 non-EMU non-UK foreign affiliate (dummy)					−0.091	−0.083
					0.101	0.093
UK foreign affiliate (dummy)					−0.355***	−0.233***
					0.076	0.07
Loans / total assets						0.364***
						0.018
Interbank deposits						−0.462***
						0.022
Leverage						−0.006***
						0.001
Total assets (log)						0.006**
						0.002
Observations	5665	5665	5665	5665	5665	5539
R^2	0.12	0.12	0.12	0.12	0.13	0.26

Notes: The dependent variable is the correlation between the annual percentage change of loans to customers and demand deposits at the bank level. Estimates are made using weighted least squares, using the number of years used to calculate the correlations as weights. All regressions include country dummies. Standard errors are reported in parentheses. The symbol *** indicates a significance level of 1% or less; ** between 1 and 5%; * between 5 and 10%.

Source: Data for balance sheet information is from Bankscope.

the two coefficients of the dummy for foreign subsidiaries and of the interaction term is negative and it is statistically significant at the 1% level.

This first evidence is further strengthened by the results reported in column 3, showing that MNBs operating within the larger group of EU15 countries (that includes EMU members) also benefit significantly from the functioning of ICMs. The coefficient for the dummy of EU15 foreign affiliates is −0.266 and it is statistically significant at the 1% level; as in the case of EMU, the cumulative effect obtained summing the two coefficients of the dummy for EU15 foreign subsidiaries and of the interaction term is negative and statistically significant. The coefficient of foreign affiliates remains positive (0.067) and it becomes statistically significant, suggesting that for the foreign affiliates operating in countries outside the EU15, mainly the NMSs of Central and Eastern Europe, the correlation between the rates of growth of deposits and of customer loans is even stronger than that of stand-alones. In this case, therefore, ICMs do work less smoothly, dampening the impact of potential support and substitution effects. This is not entirely surprising, since non-EU15 countries in our sample include mostly those recently admitted to the EU, that have typically higher cultural, linguistic and institutional barriers, as well as less-developed financial markets.

In column 4 we have distinguished between affiliates within EMU and affiliates within other EU15 countries, but outside EMU, with the aim of verifying the role of the monetary union in facilitating the functioning of internal capital markets for MNBs. On the one hand, sharing a common monetary policy and a common currency should facilitate intra-group fund transfers; on the other hand, it is possible that the support and substitution effects are in this case less relevant, due to the higher synchronization of the business cycles within EMU. The evidence of column 4 suggests that the two effects compensate each other, and the coefficients of the dummies for foreign affiliates in EMU and in the other EU15 countries are both economically and statistically significant, and very similar in size (−0.264 and −0.265, respectively). Again, the cumulative effects obtained summing the two coefficients of the dummy for foreign subsidiaries and of the interaction terms are economically and statistically significant.

In column 5 we have further distinguished between foreign affiliates operating in the United Kingdom and those operating in the other EU15 countries that are not members of EMU. The United Kingdom has a key role as a major financial centre, and its financial institutions have a large share of transactions denominated in the common European currency. Fund transfers with foreign affiliates operating in the United Kingdom might therefore be much smoother than with other non-EMU European countries, and therefore be the drivers of the coefficient of the dummy for the non-EMU-EU15 countries in the previous specification. Indeed, the results provide evidence in favour of this: the coefficient of the dummy for UK affiliates is negative and larger than that for EMU in absolute size (−0.355), while that for the other non-EMU-EU15 affiliates remains negative, but it becomes statistically insignificant.[22]

Finally, in column 6 we have added some bank specific controls to our previous specification. Our previous findings on the smoothness of the functioning of ICMs for foreign affiliates operating in different economic areas are substantially confirmed. As expected, we also find that the correlation between the rate of growth of deposits and of customer loans is on average higher for banks specialized in traditional lending activities, less leveraged, and less active in interbank markets. Bank size has a positive but negligible effect.

The evidence presented in Table 4 provides strong support to our claims on the functioning of ICMs for MNBs operating within well-integrated areas. In Table 5 we have further analysed the role of integration, including among the explanatory variables some measures of economic and institutional proximity, to test our earlier

[22] Indeed, our sample includes very few instances of foreign affiliates operating in non-EMU-EU15 countries other than the United Kingdom. In unreported regressions we have also analysed separately the role of Luxemburg, another important banking centre, finding that it also has no significant impact on our results.

Table 5. Correlation between loan and deposit growth – the role of proximity

	(1)	(2)	(3)	(4)
Domestic affiliate (dummy)	0.018	0.018	0.018	0.018
	0.035	0.035	0.035	0.035
Foreign affiliate (dummy)	0.060*	0.084**	0.038	0.111***
	0.031	0.029	0.033	0.032
EMU foreign affiliate (dummy)	−0.210***	−0.206***	−0.197***	−0.207***
	0.043	0.043	0.042	0.043
EU15 non-EMU non-UK affiliate (dummy)	−0.056	−0.087	−0.057	−0.108
	0.094	0.093	0.094	0.094
UK foreign affiliate (dummy)	−0.226***	−0.277***	−0.246***	−0.261***
	0.07	0.076	0.070	0.072
Loans / total assets	0.363***	0.363***	0.362***	0.363***
	0.018	0.018	0.018	0.018
Interbank deposits	−0.462***	−0.461***	−0.462***	−0.462***
	0.022	0.022	0.022	0.022
Leverage	−0.006***	−0.006***	−0.006***	−0.006***
	0.001	0.001	0.001	0.001
Total assets (log)	0.006**	0.006**	0.006**	0.006**
	0.002	0.002	0.002	0.002
Common border (dummy)	0.072*			
	0.037			
Common language (dummy)		0.121		
		0.079		
Low distance countries (dummy)			0.094*	
			0.035	
Low GDP correlation (dummy)				−0.086*
				0.046
Observations	5539	5539	5539	5539
R^2	0.26	0.26	0.26	0.26

Notes: The dependent variable is the correlation between the annual percentage change of loans to customers and demand deposits at the bank level. Estimates are obtained from weighted least squares, using the number of years used to calculate the correlations as weights. Low distance and low GDP correlation is defined as below the median of the sample distribution. All regressions include country dummies. Standard errors are reported in parentheses. The symbol *** indicates a significance level of 1% or less; ** between 1 and 5%; * between 5 and 10%.

Source: Data for balance sheet information is from Bankscope and data for GDP growth is from IFS.

Claim 5, that *units that are located in distant countries with different languages or different cultural environment may find more difficulties in actively taking part into a cross-border ICM of an MNB.*

In columns 1 and 2 we have included a dummy for foreign affiliates operating in countries sharing a border with that of the holding company (column 1), or where the same language is spoken (column 2). In both cases the estimated coefficient is positive, suggesting that stronger proximity has mainly the effect of reducing the impact of the substitution effect, but this result is only significant in the case of countries sharing a border and not for those with a common language.

In column 3 we have disentangled the effect for foreign affiliates operating in the countries that have a distance from that of the holding company that is below the median of the sample distribution. Closer countries are typically more integrated and have more synchronous business cycles, therefore reducing the scope for the substitution effect, but they are also more likely to permit a smoother working of

ICMs, for example by facilitating personal contacts. It turns out that the first effect prevails, since foreign affiliates operating in geographically closer countries have a higher correlation between the rates of growth of deposits and of customer loans.

Finally, to test the second part of our earlier Claim 2, that the substitution effect weakens the link between funds availability and lending especially for banking groups operating in countries with less correlated real shocks, in column 4 we have analysed the effect of the synchronization of the business cycles, disentangling the average effect of ICMs for affiliates operating in countries that have a bilateral correlation of the rate of growth of GDP with the country of the holding company that is below the first quartile of the sample distribution. Consistent with our expectation, the larger scope for the substitution effect in the case of less synchronized countries increases the role of ICMs, determining a reduction in the correlation between the rates of growth of deposits and of customer loans. Reassuringly, even when we include these controls, the EMU and EU dummies, which capture the degree of integration of financial markets, keep their negative and significant sign.[23]

4. MNBs AND THE SYSTEMIC CRISIS

In the previous section we have analysed how ICMs are expected to function under idiosyncratic financial distress and we have shown empirically that they have indeed been functioning so as to isolate lending activities of foreign affiliates from the local availability of funding. This finding is in line with the claim that ICMs may be used to support and stabilize financial markets, but it is not a direct test of how they have functioned in times of distress. Of particular concern is how they behaved during the current crisis, given its pervasiveness and that it impacted all players in the financial sector in Europe and all over the world.

In this section we turn precisely to the assessment of the effects of the recent crisis. We first discuss how the claims outlined in Section 3 hold in the case of a systemic crisis and then analyse empirically how the lending policies of foreign affiliates have been faring during the crisis. We do so first by using aggregate BIS world data and then our sample of European banks. Clearly, in this setting it is not our intention to provide an interpretation of the causes and consequences of the crisis itself, that have been and are being extensively analysed elsewhere (see, e.g., Acharya and Richardson, 2009).

Previous studies have shown that the presence of MNBs tend to increase stability in host developing countries during times of financial distress since domestic lending dropped during crises much more for domestic banks than for affiliates of MNBs

[23] Following the suggestion of one of the panellists, Martin Brown, we have also verified if the correlation between customer deposits and loans diminishes when a previously independent bank is acquired and becomes a foreign affiliate. Unfortunately, there are only few such operations in our sample with a time span before and after the acquisition sufficiently long to allow for the estimation of the correlations. Despite some weak evidence in favour of our hypothesis of a reduction in the correlation, we were unable to detect any statistically significant effect.

(see, for example, Clarke *et al.*, 2003, Detragiache *et al.*, 2006). Referring to the United States, Morgan *et al.* (2004) and Kroszner and Strahan (2006) have shown that when in a state there is a significant activity of a banking group that operates across states, then important macro variables in the state (e.g. growth and employment) tend to be less volatile, the size of the business cycle tends to be reduced and at the micro level loan availability becomes less related to the local banks' capital.

But all that these works do is show that banking groups seem to have a stabilizing role during *idiosyncratic* shocks. Our aim in this section is instead to verify the behaviour of MNBs in the current *systemic* crisis, in which the shocks are highly correlated among the countries in which the MNBs are active. To our knowledge, only two papers have focused on the behaviour of MNBs during the recent crisis. Using aggregate BIS and IMF data, Cetorelli and Goldberg (2010) show that foreign banks reduced the rate of growth of loans with respect to the pre-crisis period more than domestic banks. However, since their lending activity was much more buoyant than that of domestic intermediaries, their evidence confirms that the rate of growth of loans granted by foreign banks remained positive and stronger than that of domestic banks also after the crisis. Popov and Udell (2010) analyse instead a sample of medium and small firms in Eastern European countries, showing that firms that are located in provinces with a stronger presence of foreign intermediaries have a higher probability of being denied credit or to have renounced applying for bank loans because they feared to be denied. However, their data (based on a questionnaire) do not allow linking each firm to a potential lender, and the results are also consistent with the alternative hypothesis that MNBs are more efficient to screen troubled borrowers than domestic banks (thus relating to the 'smarter money' effect discussed above).

Despite the lack of analytical research, a well-shared perception during the crisis was that MNBs were heavily contributing to a credit crunch. The argument was that, by operating across borders, MNBs had quickly created a dramatic drop in lending in all countries where they were active, notwithstanding (substantially) stable deposits.

However, a deeper investigation of the functioning of ICMs reveals that this is a simplistic view. Two contradictory claims can emerge here. First, *if the shock is systemic, then one may expect that being an MNB may not help that much since the ICM cannot activate the support and substitution effect* (*Claim 6*). Second, if ICMs are well organized and functioning, they may attract more external funds relatively to stand-alone banks (i.e., the 'more money' effect described in Box 2). Depositors, for example, may behave differently when the bank belongs to an MNB: the 'more money' effect may significantly reduce the negative impact of the shock since the MNB may still be considered a safe harbour.[24] Hence, *if ICMs make the allocation of resources more*

[24] Indeed, De Haas and van Lelyveld (2010) illustrate this effect showing that in a crisis affecting a national banking system, foreign subsidiaries increase their deposits, contrary to domestic banks.

efficient within MNBs, they may help relaxing the nexus between local lending and funds also during a systemic crisis. MNBs would then have a stabilizing effect (Claim 7).

4.1. Aggregate evidence on the effects of the crisis on the activities of MNBs

A first test of Claims 6 and 7 can be performed by extending the analysis of Section 2 and looking at the aggregate trends in the activities of MNBs. Specifically, we focus on how local claims of these banks have behaved during the recent financial crisis, from the last term of 2007 to the fourth term of 2009. The key question is whether during the crisis MNBs have been unwinding their assets held through their foreign affiliates in host countries, or, in contrast, whether they have been channelling liquidity to their subsidiaries to support them.

We argued in Section 2 that local claims had been more stable than total foreign claims in 2008 and 2009. If we consider the EU27, the total value of local claims denominated in local currency, once converted in US dollars (as reported above in Figure 2 of Section 2) amounted roughly to $4.500 billion at the end of 2007, it declined by about $450 billion by the end of 2008, but was already at $4.370 billion dllars by the end of 2009. This pattern is consistent in all subgroups of EU countries, including the United Kingdom. In the NMS the absolute value of local claims by mid-2009 is even larger than at the end of 2007. This trend is also similar in the non-EU advanced economies like the United States.

The stability of local claims stands out even more clearly if we adjust for exchange rate fluctuations, by constructing index numbers measured in national currencies for the EMU12 aggregate and for the most significant NMS in terms of absolute values of foreign claims (Figure 5a). In all the country groups the value of local claims measured in local currency was higher at the end of 2009 than at the beginning of 2007. This is also true for Hungary and Poland, countries where foreign banks were the major players in the financial crisis and which have been through a particularly severe recession in 2008 and 2009.

In Figure 5b we also report local claims denominated in foreign currency. These figures should be taken as proxies for likely trends, because, as mentioned above, they are estimated and their allocation to individual countries is likely to be biased. Moreover, since the currency basket of these claims is not reported, we keep them in current US dollars (as BIS does). Also in this case, claims are higher at the end of 2009 than at the beginning of 2007 in the EMU12 countries, Hungary and Poland.[25]

To better understand investment policies of foreign banks during the crisis, and particularly whether these banks have been instrumental in channelling financial resources towards host countries rather than the opposite, it is useful to relate

[25] Figures for the Czech Republic are negligible and therefore have not been reported.

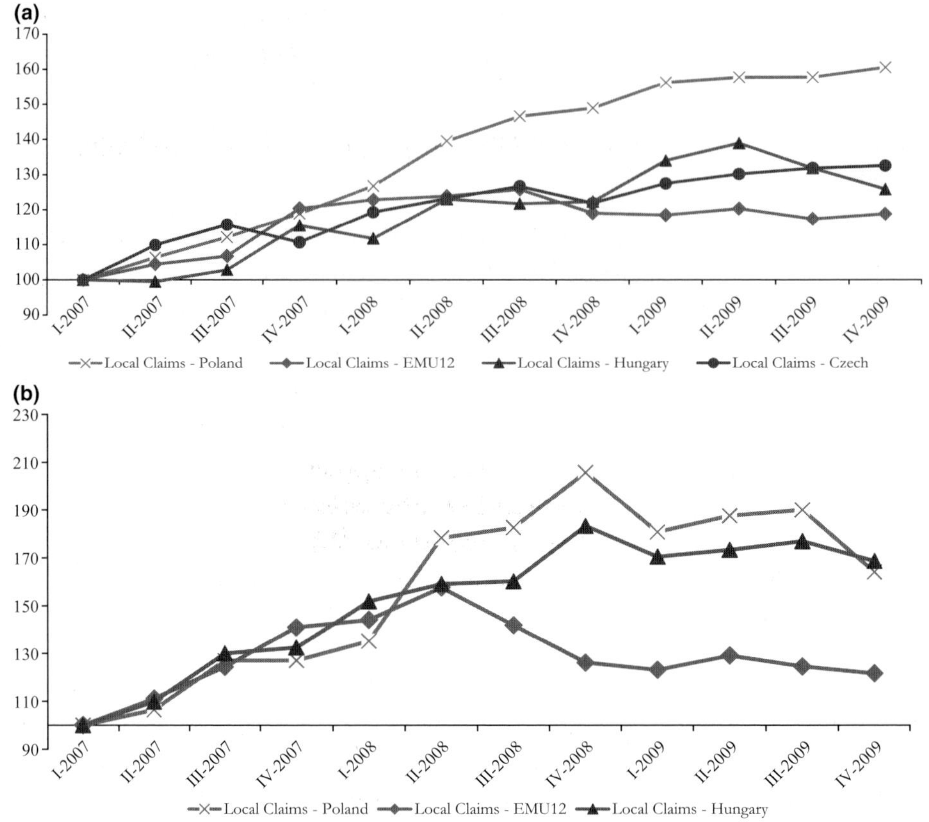

Figure 5. Total local claims in (a) local currency expressed in national currencies, and (b) foreign currency

Note: EMU12 and specific countries. I-2007 = 100

Source: BIS Consolidated Statistics.

trends in assets to trends in liabilities in local currency towards local residents (see Box 1 above for the definitions). The issue here is understanding, first, how much claims in local currency are strictly funded by local deposits and other liabilities and, second, whether during the crisis resources acquired in a given country have been transferred to affiliates based in other countries or to headquarters. Figure 6 reports the ratio between these assets and liabilities for the EMU12 and the other countries reported in Figure 5 from the first term of 2007 to the fourth term of 2009. The evidence is particularly interesting and in line with the hypothesis that foreign banks have been supporting local assets through cross-border funding.

Indeed it stands out that this ratio is always larger than one. In Hungary it is the highest, almost at 1.8. Also, this ratio is stable and even increasing for most countries. Now local assets not funded by local liabilities in local currency can either be funded by local liabilities in foreign currency (not reported in the BIS statistics but

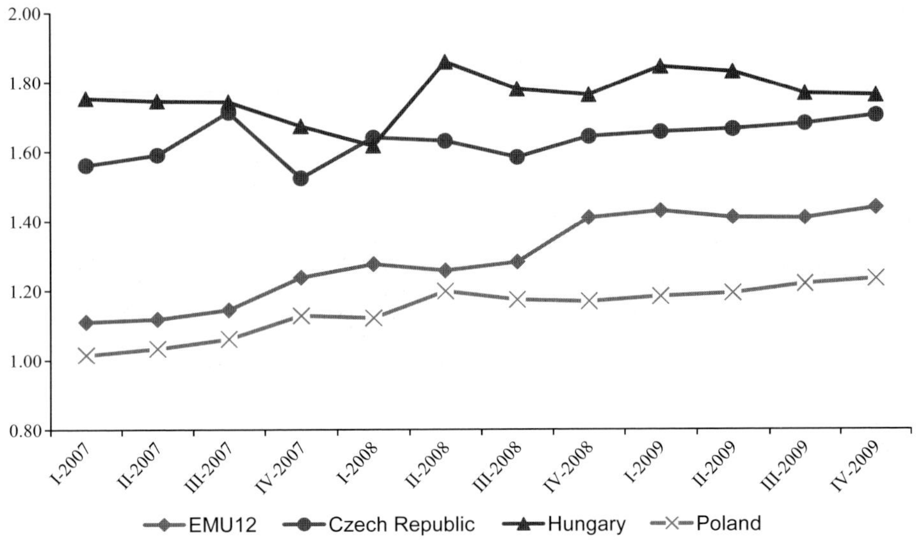

Figure 6. Ratio total claims over total liabilities in local currency

Source: BIS Consolidated Statistics.

likely to be pretty small) or by cross-border funds, channelled either through the global market or through the ICM. In other words, during the crisis an increasing share of the local assets of foreign subsidiaries have been funded by cross-border financial flows.

This preliminary descriptive evidence that lending and investment policies of MNBs have been stable, if not rising, during the period of the crisis is now tested econometrically. Using the same quarterly data described above for the period between 1999 and 2009 and for a sample of 49 developed and developing countries, we look at whether the time trends of local claims denominated in domestic currencies of foreign affiliates is affected by the crisis, taking them as a ratio of local liabilities denominated in domestic currencies, or of total financial assets in the country, obtained from IMF data.

The results are reported in Table 6. Since both ratios show a high cross-country dispersion, we used a quantile regression technique evaluated at the median, also including country fixed effects. Column 1 shows that on average the ratio of local claims to local liabilities has increased since 1999, as shown by the positive and significant coefficient of a linear time trend. Moreover, the growth has accelerated in the post-crisis period, as shown by the positive and statistically significant coefficient of the post crisis dummy, that takes the value of one from the fourth quarter of 2007 (column 2). In column 3 we have further specialized our analysis, interacting the post-crisis dummy with a set of dummies for different groupings of countries, to see if the effect of the crisis has been heterogeneous across regions. The results show that the ratio of local claims to local liabilities has increased in all geographic

Table 6. Claims-liabilities ratio: the effect of the crisis

	Claims/total liabilities			Claims/total assets		
	(1)	(2)	(3)	(4)	(5)	(6)
Time trend	0.004***	0.003***		0.004***	0.004***	
	0.001	0.001		0.000	0.000	
Post crisis (dummy)		0.058*			−0.003	
		0.022			0.006	
Time trend * EMU countries			−0.004**			0.007***
			0.001			0.000
Time trend * EU-no-EMU-no-NMS countries			0.003			0.003***
			0.002			0.000
Time trend * NMS countries			0.008***			0.003***
			0.002			0.000
Time trend * CEECs-no-NMS countries			0.038***			
			0.002			
Time trend * Main developing countries			0.001			0.001***
			0.002			0.000
Time trend * Other countries			−0.004**			0.002***
			0.002			0.000
Post crisis * EMU countries			0.129***			0.013*
			0.037			0.008
Post crisis * EU-no-EMU-no-NMS countries			0.027			−0.010
			0.060			0.011
Post crisis * NMS countries			0.116***			−0.011
			0.045			0.009
Post crisis * CEECs-no-NMS countries			−0.614***			
			0.042			
Post crisis * Main developing countries			0.159***			0.060***
			0.044			0.011
Post crisis * Other countries			0.047			0.047***
			0.054			0.011
Observations	2074	2074	2074	1471	1471	1471
Pseudo R^2	0.27	0.27	0.28	0.63	0.63	0.63

Notes: In columns 1–3, the dependent variable is the ratio between total claims and total liabilities denominated in local currencies, of foreign affiliates; in columns 4–7 it is the ratio between total claims by foreign affiliates and total credit to the private sector in the country. All estimates are conducted using quantile regression technique, evaluated at the median, and include country dummies. EMU countries include: Austria, Belgium, Finland, France, Germany, Greece, Ireland, Italy, Luxembourg, Netherlands, Portugal, Spain, Slovenia; NMS countries include Bulgaria, Czech Republic, Estonia, Hungary, Latvia, Lithuania, Poland, Romania and Slovakia; CEEC countries excluding NMSs include: Albania, Armenia, Bosnia and Herzegovina, Croatia, Georgia, Kazakhstan, Moldova, Montenegro, Russia, Serbia, Turkey, Ukraine, Uzbekistan; Main developing countries include China, India, Malaysia, South Korea, South Africa, Singapore, United Arab Emirates; other countries are Australia, Canada, Japan, New Zealand, Switzerland, USA. Since data on total financial assets in the post-crisis period for Central and Eastern European countries outside EU are available only for Turkey, in Column 6 it is included in the group of NMSs. The symbol *** indicates a significance level of 1% or less; ** between 1 and 5%; * between 5 and 10%.

Source: Data for claims and liabilities is from BIS, and data for private credit is from IMF.

areas, with the only exception of Central and Eastern European countries (CEECs) that are not members of EU. The effect has been stronger in the NMSs and in the EMU countries, smaller and not statistically significant in the EU countries that are not EMU members, neither NMSs and in the other main developed countries.

The results are broadly confirmed by the analysis of the evolution of the local claims of foreign affiliates as a ratio of total financial assets in the country. Also this ratio has been increasing since 1999, as shown by the positive and statistically significant nature of the coefficient of the time trend, in column 4. However, the crisis has not significantly altered its evolution, as shown by the insignificant coefficient of the post-crisis dummy in column 5. Finally, analysing separately the effect of the crisis across different groups of countries shows that this ratio has significantly risen within affiliates in EMU and in the other main developed and developing countries outside the EU. It has not changed significantly in the group including NMSs and Turkey.[26]

The role played by MNBs in NMSs during the recent crisis, and in particular the decisions of the parent companies to support their foreign affiliates, might have been influenced by the international initiatives of financial support decided at the multilateral level and by the ring-fencing policies that some of these countries might have put in place. Indeed, it is legitimate to question whether foreign parent companies have stabilized and even increased local lending because of: (a) ring fencing policies decided by host governments; (b) indirect resources provided by multilateral institutions to some NMSs. However, the evidence is controversial. On the one hand, there is no evidence of a tightening of formal regulatory ring fencing in NMSs during the crisis. On the other hand, it is true that a coordinated international effort to financially support the regions provided resources to banks with a local presence.[27] But although these interventions had effects that cannot be disentangled in our data, a number of facts suggest that they cannot be the sole explanation of our findings. First, they do not explain the increase in the lending to deposit ratio of foreign affiliates relative to that of domestic banks, which were all the same entitled to receive part of the financial resources provided on the basis of these multilateral agreements. Second, the financial support only became operative in the first quarter of 2009, and our evidence does not show a substantial reduction in the lending to the deposit ratio in the previous quarters. Third, all the main support measures undertaken in favour of Central and Eastern European countries are not legally binding agreements, but they are made on a voluntary basis, including

[26] Since data on total financial assets in the post-crisis period for Central and Eastern European countries outside EU are available only for Turkey, we have included it in the group of NMSs.

[27] During the crisis the IMF and the EU committed to extensive balance of payments support packages of over €50 billion (the commitment was sealed at the end of March 2009). In addition, on the basis of a joint agreement (the so-called IFI Action Plan) the European Bank for Reconstruction and Development, the European Investment Bank and the World Bank committed to make available up to $25 billion on a 2-year horizon programme to support banking sector stability and lending to the real economy; $19 billion have been already delivered (the commitment was sealed in February 2009).

the so-called Vienna Initiative.[28] Finally, our data show that also in other European markets, where such measures were not implemented, foreign banks have neither reduced lending nor behaved differently from domestic banks.

4.2. Micro effects of the crisis

Since our bank specific micro-data cover the period from 2000 to 2008, we have also investigated the effects of the financial crisis on the relationship between deposits and customer loans. Unfortunately, the empirical model of Equation (1) is unsuitable to analyse the effects of the crisis, because it is impossible to calculate the correlation between the rates of growth of deposits and loans at the bank level, with only two years' observations since the summer of 2007. For this reason, we have chosen a specification similar to the one adopted for the analysis at the aggregate level, verifying if the bank specific ratio of customer loans to deposits has changed significantly during the crisis, and in particular if these changes have been different for foreign affiliates operating in different areas (which we couldn't test with aggregate data). In practice, we have estimated the following specification of a difference in difference model around the event of the crisis:

$$\begin{aligned} Ratio_{ijt} = {} & a_1 + a_2 DUM\_Crisis * DUM\_ForS\_EMU_{ij} \\ & + a_3 DUM\_Crisis * DUM\_For\_EU15nEMU_{ij} \\ & + a_4 DUM\_Crisis * DUM\_For\_nEU15_{ij} \\ & + a_5 DUM\_ForS\_EMU_{ij} + a_6 DUM\_For\_EU15nEMU_{ij} \\ & + a_7 DUM\_For\_nEU15_{ij} + a_8 Char_{ijt-1} + a_9 Year_t + a_{10} Country_j + \varepsilon_{ijt} \end{aligned} \quad (2)$$

where $ratio_{ijt}$ is the ratio between customer loans and customer deposits of bank i in country j at time t; *DUM_Crisis* is a dummy taking the value of one in 2007 and 2008; $DUM\_ForS\_EMU_{ij}$, $DUM\_For\_EU15nEMU_{ij}$ and $DUM\_For\_nEU15_{ij}$ are dummy variables that take the value of one if bank i of country j at time t is a foreign subsidiary of a holding company located, respectively, in EMU, in EU15 countries that are not EMU members, and in the remaining EU27 countries; $Char_{ijt-1}$ are characteristics of bank i of country j at time $t-1$ (the logarithm of total assets and leverage); $Year_t$ is a yearly time dummy; $Country_j$ is a country dummy; and ε_{ijt} is a standard error term. Due to the extremely high kurtosis of the dependent variable, we have run the estimates excluding observations below the 10th and above the 90th percentile of the sample distribution.

[28] Following the IFI Action Plan (see previous footnote), country-based policy coordination has evolved in voluntary agreements (known as the Vienna Initiative) according to which the parent banks of affiliates operating in countries that have received support from IMF programmes (co-financed by the EC in the case of EU members) committed to maintain constant their exposures in the host nations and to recapitalize their subsidiaries as long as IMF/EC programmes are on track. So far, such agreements have been reached in Romania, Hungary, Serbia, Bosnia Herzegovina, and most recently in Latvia.

The test of the effect of the financial crisis on the functioning of ICMs for cross-border groups is based on the sign and significance of coefficients a_2 to a_4. A positive and significant value would imply that foreign banks with access to ICMs reduced their loans-deposits ratio less than the control group of banks, and therefore had a stabilizing effect after the shock induced by the financial crisis. Clearly, a negative coefficient would imply the opposite.

Table 7 presents the results of the estimation of Equation (2). Column 1 presents the estimates obtained using an OLS specification, including unreported country dummies. The negative values of the coefficients for the year dummies in 2007 and 2008 show that the ratio between customer loans and customer deposits have been shrinking on average since the beginning of the crisis. However, all the coefficients of the interaction terms between the crisis and foreign affiliates are positive, and those for affiliates located in EU15-non-EMU countries and in the NMSs of Central and Eastern Europe, Malta and Cyprus (non-EU15) are statistically significant at the 1% level, showing that the impact of the crisis has been in these areas lower for foreign affiliates than for domestic banks.

Since, despite the trimming, our data might be affected by the presence of outliers, in column 2 we report the results obtained using a more robust quantile regression technique, evaluated at the median. The results substantially confirm the previous findings: the coefficient of the dummy for foreign affiliates located in EU15 is negative but statistically insignificant, while that of the dummies for the EU15-non-EMU countries and for the NMSs are positive and statistically significant, respectively at the 10% and at the 1% level. The only remarkable difference with respect to column 1 is that the dummy for affiliates located in EMU becomes negative, although it remains statistically insignificant. Finally, in column 3 we have estimated a model with fixed bank effects, which once again confirms the robustness of the previous findings.[29]

These results can be interpreted in light of Claims 6 and 7 above. Foreign banks had a stabilizing effect during the crisis in Eastern Europe's NMSs and in EU15-non-EMU countries, which is in line with Claim 7 that these banks can be effective providers of funds locally even during a systemic distress. This result is also probably driven by the fact that in the NMSs, MNBs are by far the dominant players, and domestic banking is extremely weak. However, in other areas these banks have essentially been behaving like national banks, showing that they had been equally affected by the pervasiveness of the crisis. This is in line with Claim 6.[30]

[29] Moreover, in the specifications of Panels 2 and 3, the average value of the coefficients of the year dummies before the crisis is significantly higher than that after the crisis.

[30] Indeed, an increase in the ratio of claims to deposits is not necessarily evidence of the functioning of ICMs. For a fixed level of loans, such a ratio would increase also in case customers withdraw their deposits and the bank matches such reduction in its aggregate liabilities by selling bonds. However, in an unreported regression we found no evidence of a reduction in customer deposits for the sample of banks analysed above. We thank Nicola Cetorelli for pointing this out to us.

Table 7. Loan-deposit ratio at the bank level: the effect of the crisis

	OLS	Median regression	Fixed effects
	(1)	(2)	(3)
Post crisis * EMU subsidiaries	0.008	−0.053	−0.007
	0.044	0.05	0.026
Post crisis * EU15-non-EMU subsidiaries	0.223***	0.264*	0.058
	0.037	0.114	0.049
Post crisis * non-EU15 subsidiaries	0.248***	0.308***	0.202***
	0.078	0.039	0.018
EMU subsidiaries (dummy)	0.191***	0.206***	
	0.061	0.032	
EU15-non-EMU subsidiaries (dummy)	0.081***	0.048	
	0.007	0.064	
Non-EU15 subsidiaries (dummy)	0.066	0.036	
	0.070	0.027	
Lagged leverage	0.055***	0.051***	0.167***
	0.006	0.001	0.006
Lagged total assets (ln)	0.399***	0.493***	−1.233***
	0.105	0.058	0.076
Year 2002	0.001	−0.004	0.007*
	0.009	0.008	0.003
Year 2003	−0.003	−0.013	−0.020***
	0.016	0.008	0.004
Year 2004	−0.018	−0.025***	−0.052***
	0.022	0.008	0.004
Year 2005	−0.015	−0.021**	−0.075***
	0.032	0.009	0.005
Year 2006	−0.002	−0.011	−0.075***
	0.039	0.008	0.005
Year 2007	−0.007	−0.024***	−0.097***
	0.050	0.008	0.005
Year 2008	−0.024	−0.039***	−0.131***
	0.057	0.009	0.006
Observations	23595	23595	23595
R^2 (Pseudo R^2 in column 2)	0.30	0.14	0.06

Notes: The dependent variable is the ratio between customer loans and deposits. EMU countries include: Austria, Belgium, Finland, France, Germany, Greece, Ireland, Italy, Luxembourg, the Netherlands, Portugal, Spain, Slovenia; EU15-non-EMU countries include Cyprus, Denmark, Malta, Sweden and United Kingdom; non-EU15 countries include Bulgaria, Czech Republic, Estonia, Hungary, Latvia, Lithuania, Poland, Romania and Slovakia. All regressions include time dummies; the regression in column 3 includes bank specific fixed effects. Column 1 reports estimates obtained using OLS; column 2 reports estimates obtained using quantile regression methods, evaluated at the median; column 3 is a fixed effect panel. In column 1, robust standard errors adjusted for clustering at the bank level are reported in parentheses; standard errors in columns 2 and 3 are unadjusted. The symbol *** indicates a significance level of 1% or less; ** between 1 and 5%; * between 5 and 10%.

Source: Bankscope.

In summary, these results based on bank specific data during the crisis show that foreign affiliates certainly did not have a destabilizing effect, since their loan-deposit ratio has either remained constant or increased. Contrary to a diffused misperception, we find no evidence that these banks have been funnelling resources away from any of their host countries. That the working of ICMs did not allow foreign affiliates to have a significant stabilizing effect within EMU is not entirely surprising, due to the systemic nature of the recent crisis, which has made it nearly impossible to smooth the shocks within a group of similar economies. If all banks are simultaneously hit by an identical shock, there is no benefit in transferring funds from one unit to the other. In fact, we find that ICMs indeed had a stabilizing effect precisely in the case of affiliates located in NMSs, where the impact of the shock was more diverse, because of the lower economic integration.[31]

5. CONCLUDING REMARKS: INSIGHTS FOR A BETTER REGULATORY DESIGN OF MNBs IN EUROPE

We conclude this paper by answering the following question: What are the policy implications that can be delivered by our results?

In Europe, multiple national authorities are involved in the supervision of a single MNB, often in an uncoordinated way and operating with often dissimilar regulatory frameworks. This current regime has several shortcomings. Supervisors tend to operate only in the interest of their own country, without taking into account the cross-border spill-over implications of their own decisions. Under several scenarios, this framework is unable to produce the relevant and timely information for prompt supervision and regulation. The shortfalls of the current regulatory and supervisory frameworks are already evident in ordinary times, but they become even more compelling in times of distress. As highlighted by the recent crisis, cooperation and coordination between national supervisors often proved ineffective, since the impact of the crisis was assessed mainly at the national level, and remedial actions were defined almost exclusively at the country level.

Given this suboptimal environment for regulation of MBNs in Europe, in this concluding section we illustrate a number of policy implications stemming from our findings, which may help fine-tuning regulatory reforms.

5.1. Multinational banks are not a source of instability

In the aftermath of the financial crisis, MNBs have been perceived as an important cause for systemic risk and a source of global volatility. However, we have shown that these conclusions are driven by an inadequate understanding of what these banks do and how they function, particularly concerning retail banking activities.

As shown by the econometric results of Section 3.1, affiliates of MNBs use extensively their ICMs, and this has a significant impact on the correlation between the rates of growth of customer loans and deposits. In normal times (before 2007), MNBs

[31] As pointed out by our discussant at the Panel Meeting in Madrid, Dalia Marin, this result for NMSs contrasts with the evidence that during the 1990s foreign affiliates in East European countries did not rely on parental liquidity to finance their activities. Indeed, we also showed in Section 3.1 that the correlation between customer deposits and loans for affiliates in NMSs have been particularly high even during the last decade. Taken together, these results suggest that MNBs might indeed have changed their behaviour during the recent financial crisis.

have been able to use the ICM to isolate local lending from the availability of local funds. In fact, the correlation of the rate of growth of local loans and deposits is lower for foreign subsidiaries of MNBs than for stand-alone domestic banks. Hence, MNBs through their ICMs can exert a stabilizing role in the presence of idiosyncratic shocks.

In times of systemic distress the evidence of Section 4 supports the view that MNBs did not weaken financial stability in local markets. During the crisis the ratio of local bank claims to liabilities did not decline, and it even increased in some groups of countries (for example the NMSs, where foreign banks account for the dominant share of total banking activities). This aggregate pattern is further confirmed by the micro-evidence based on the sample of the largest European banks, showing that, compared to self stand-alone domestic banks and domestic banking groups, subsidiaries of MNBs have been able to isolate their lending activities from fluctuations in funds, and that they have been better able to profit from positive upswings in lending conditions. The evidence also supports the view that this has been done through the ICM.

We can therefore conclude that our results do not provide support to the argument that a world with only small and domestic banks is safer. Rather, we show that the size and the global extensions of the activities of MNBs contributed positively to hedging the downturns of the crisis, even in transition economies like the NMSs.

5.2. ICMs are especially effective within integrated financial markets

We have also shown that the degree of market integration between the countries where foreign activities of MNBs are based influences the functioning of the ICM. In fact, ICMs appear to be especially at work within better integrated financial areas, like the EU, and less so across markets with severe regulatory and market barriers. In particular, our empirical findings of Section 3.1, based on bank level data, clearly illustrate that also in normal times the correlation between the rates of growth of loans and deposits of foreign affiliates is lower than that of domestic banks, especially for those affiliates that belong either to EMU or to the restricted set of countries that are more integrated in Europe (i.e., the EU15 group). To this extent, our evidence shows that ICMs and the external capital markets are by and large complementary. When the external capital markets are less integrated, due to regulatory constraints or because they involve different currencies, then MNBs' affiliates are *de facto* using the ICMs to a very limited extent, and therefore show no relevant differences with respect to domestic banks.[32]

[32] Although further scrutiny on the causes of this effect is needed, since the effect related to the euro seems to be stronger, a possible interpretation is that an ICM that operates across countries with different currencies incurs in the additional cost of exchange rate risk. Indeed, anecdotal evidence illustrates that activities of ICMs across countries almost always involve currency swaps. Furthermore, transfers of liquid assets within ICMs are often used in the country of destination as collaterals with the local central bank to obtain liquidity. Since the central banks tend to associate lower volatility to local treasury bills, limited integration (e.g. outside EU15) may involve significant impediments to ICMs.

At first sight this is not fully intuitive, as market integration imposes a trade-off on the ICM: easier movement of resources (due to more harmonized regulations and common currency), but highly correlated business cycles and returns, that reduce the scope for the global diversification of investments. The evidence supports the view that the first component of the trade-off prevails: ICMs function better if markets are more integrated. Indeed the fast rise of multinational banking in the last 10 years has taken place mostly within the EU, even though there are still considerable regulatory barriers between member countries.

5.3. Harmonizing the European regulatory framework

Since the ICM functions well especially within integrated markets, reducing the inconsistencies and differences in the regulatory framework across member states and coordinating bank supervision within the EU would provide better supervision on global activities of MNBs. This should be a priority, since it would be instrumental in fostering the efficiency of the ICM and market integration in retail and corporate banking.

5.4. Neutrality of rules with respect to the organizational mode

In Section 3 we illustrated that different types of foreign incorporation (branches and subsidiaries) give rise to different liability structures between the bank's units within the group, and hence different incentives to the functioning of ICMs. We have seen that an ICM works well and shows its 'bright side' if: (a) liquidity and capital are really free to flow among units, (b) the information is free to flow within the organization without impediments, and (c) the incentives within the organization and its units are well designed.

Although the 'single banking licence scheme' was introduced in Europe with the purpose of facilitating free access within the Single European Market and of ensuring a level playing field, the current regulatory framework in Europe shows a bias in favour of structuring MNBs with branches (with the single passport). In particular, regulatory approaches strongly differ if banks are organized with independently incorporated subsidiaries or with foreign branches.[33] However, branches may not be the best organization to address the internal incentive issues of point (c). In principle, with subsidiaries one could identify clear responsibilities of local managers and units and thus give them the right incentives.[34] Independent local managers

[33] The single licence applies to branches of an MNB that are subject to the regulation and supervision of the authority regulating the parent company. Subsidiaries instead are considered independent despite their being part of a group and each of them is under the regime of the authority of the country in which they are based. Thus, rules applied to affiliates of the same group often differ and conflict.

[34] It is also worth mentioning that a subsidiary structure may be preferred and rewarded by markets in time of distress since it naturally allows identifying units and cross-liabilities among them.

are in a better position to make use of 'soft information' that would instead be very difficult, if not impossible, to transmit for the functioning of a fully centralized ICM.[35] With an organization based on branches, instead, local managers in foreign countries may be exposed to and feel that the ICM actually expropriates the capital and liquidity that has been produced locally by their branches.

Clearly, one could argue that in the current environment branches are to be preferred since, to some extent, they allow a consolidated supervision of the MNB. However, it is also clear that this is simply the suboptimal consequence of the current state of affairs in regulation and supervision of MNBs. Along the same line of reasoning, reform proposals aimed at ring fencing subsidiaries in host countries and forcing systemically relevant branches to be transformed into subsidiaries, like those put forward within the FSB Standing Committee on Supervision and Regulatory Cooperation (Turner, 2009), may restrict considerably the optimal functioning of the ICM.

The reform of the European regulatory and supervisory framework should not ignore these organizational issues and introduce a neutral regime between branches and subsidiaries. Choosing the best organization for banks is the task of managers, and regulation should not impose a preference.

5.5. The 28th regime

Finally, we think that to achieve a coordinated and neutral regulatory framework, European countries should contemplate a new and specific framework for European MNBs, allowing these banks to set up a truly integrated organization with its well-functioning ICM, as illustrated in the previous pages. This framework would define the responsibilities and the powers of the parent company, the branches and independent subsidiaries, provided due protections to minorities and creditors are granted. In this respect, some commentators have referred to this proposal as a 28th regime for MNBs, in addition to those available to banks in the 27 Member States belonging to the EU. This regime should contemplate a specific treatment for MNBs in terms of regulation and supervision, along the line of the proposals that have already been discussed in Europe (i.e., enhancing coordination among countries through strengthened colleges of supervisors overseen by a newly created European Banking Authority, and possibly defining rules for the allocation of the costs of rescuing those banks in case of distress).[36] Banks should be then left free to

[35] Currently, national regulations on privacy limit the possibility for units to exchange information on their activities with their partners that are independent entities of the same group. This is another undesirable bias of regulation that affects the internal organization of MNBs.

[36] To some extent this new regime for truly European players is close to the dual system that is in place in the United States according to which banks active at the level of the entire nation are under the federal scrutiny (with a federal charter, associated federal laws and a federal supervisor).

choose whether to opt for this regime, which would guarantee the best functioning of ICMs.

Discussion

Gianmarco I.P. Ottaviano

Bocconi University and CEPR

The aim of this paper is to examine the behaviour of multinational banks (MNBs) during times of financial distress with a focus on Europe. In particular, it asks whether MNBs have a stabilizing or a destabilizing role in those times of trouble. The answer of the paper stresses their stabilizing role due to the support that the internal capital market (ICM) has given to foreign affiliates in distress, isolating their lending from the local availability of financial resources. This has happened notwithstanding the systemic nature of the recent crisis.

The paper argues that stabilization by MNBs has been particularly pronounced within the EU integrated financial market, and for the EMU countries. This finding is interpreted as showing complementarity between economic integration and the ICM of MNBs. Such complementarity naturally leads to a call for more integration of the European supervisory and regulatory frameworks overseeing multinational banks.

Overall, this is a timely well-written paper. Its contribution is accurately placed into context. It carefully builds on the existing literature while trying to systematize it. Several findings are interesting and convincing. Among them, two stand out. First, the ICM has a stabilizing role in the presence of idiosyncratic shocks across countries. Second, the ICM is neutral in the presence of systemic shocks in integrated areas where the impact of systemic shocks is symmetric.

At the same time, however, the discussion of the policy implications of these findings is sometimes confusing and blurs the actual results of the paper. Specifically, the paper provides a theoretical discussion of the possible pros and cons of the ICM, usefully highlighting a series of *ceteris paribus* and sometimes opposing effects (called 'claims' by the authors). The empirical analysis is then presented as a 'test' of the relative importance of these claims. Alternatively, it could also be seen as a rationalization of what the data show.

Since the empirical analysis is not structural, it would be important to better tie the policy implications to the empirical findings. In particular, the paper calls for two broad areas of policy intervention: the harmonization of regulation on MNBs; and the neutrality of regulation with respect to the organizational structures of MNBs. In the discussion, however, the distinction between harmonization and neutrality is blurred and sometimes confusing. The discussion of the policy implications could be improved by stressing the pros and cons of harmonization on the one hand, and those of neutrality on the other hand, linking both hands to specific findings, especially to the two key findings highlighted above.

Finally, multinational manufacturing firms are among the main actors in the world economy. It would be interesting to have some additional comment on whether the interests of those firms are better served by MNBs.

Dalia Marin

University of Munich

Why look at multinational banks?

Since 1990 most countries undertook financial integration by reducing impediments to cross-border financial transactions and an increased participation of foreign banks in the local banking system. This trend was particularly pronounced for Eastern Europe and the New Member States (NMS) where foreign multinational banks have become the dominant players in the local banking system in these markets. So the question arises whether the participation of multinational banks has been good or bad. This is a timely paper of high policy relevance.

In their paper the authors ask two questions: First, do foreign banks behave differently than domestic banks? Second, do multinational banks (MNBs) amplify or stabilize external financial shocks? What is their role in the financial crisis? I want to comment on these two questions and add some evidence on Austrian and German multinational banks in Eastern Europe. Let me start with the first question.

Do MNBs behave differently?

The authors argue yes. MNBs behave differently because they have an internal capital market (ICM). Why should the availability of an ICM make a difference? MNBs with an ICM can support affiliates in distress with liquidity or they may reallocate resources away from affiliates creating distress. This way ICMs may stabilize or destabilize local banking systems.

A Feldstein–Horioka approach

In their empirical analysis the authors do not provide direct evidence on ICMs. Rather they pursue an approach similar to that used by Feldstein and Horioka (1980) in their famous saving-investment puzzle. Feldstein and Horioka demonstrated that across OECD countries long period averages of national saving rates are highly correlated with similar averages of domestic investment rates. A cross-section regression of investment on saving covering 1960 through the mid-1970s yielded slope coefficients near unity. Later studies for the 1990s found similar but somewhat smaller coefficients. Surprisingly, in highly integrated financial markets domestic investment is predominantly financed out of national savings. Thus, the high correlation between investment and saving across countries suggests a small role for international capital flows.

Similar to Feldstein and Horioka, the authors test with a large panel of bank firm level data of 5,500 European banks whether or not the bank specific correlation between the rate of growth of bank lending and of local bank deposits is lower for multinational affiliate banks compared to stand-alone banks. A low correlation between bank lending and local deposits indicates that multinational affiliates are getting capital inflows from parent firms while stand-alone banks base their lending mainly on the availability of local deposits. The authors indeed find that the correlation between lending and deposits is lower in foreign affiliates of multinational banks in particular within the EMU and the EU15. In order to avoid endogeneity issues, the authors proceed to estimate whether the correlation between the growth rate of lending with the growth rate of deposits as the dependent variable is indeed lower for affiliates of banks in particular within the EU15 after controlling for a number of bank and country characteristics. They indeed find this. They also find that affiliates that are operating in geographically closer countries and in countries with less synchronized business cycles can count on more liquidity from parent firms enabling them to provide lending beyond available local deposits. The authors conclude from this evidence that affiliate banks have been a source of financial stability in host countries.

Direct evidence on internal capital markets

I want to turn now to some direct evidence on ICMs of Austrian and German multinational banks in Eastern Europe based on original firm level survey data of 2,200 direct investments in Eastern Europe of the Chair of International Economics of the University of Munich.[37] The data are a full population survey of Austrian and German foreign direct investment in Eastern Europe in the period 1990 to 2001. Austrian and German affiliate banks account for more than 50% of all banks in some of the NMSs. Does the direct evidence on ICM support the author's stability enhancing view of MNBs?

From Table 8 we can see that the internal capital market is by far the most important source of finance of Austrian and German multinational banks investing in Eastern Europe. On the side of parent banks in Austria and Germany, 87% of the parent banks said that they financed the investment of the affiliate bank in Eastern Europe internally rather than externally or in a mixed finance package. External financing is practically zero. Among the internal types of finance by far the most

[37] For more details on the data see Marin (2010).

Table 8. Internal versus external capital markets in investments to Eastern Europe[a]

Type of finance	Parent firm		Affiliate firm	
	Banks	Non-banks	Banks	Non-banks
	In % of total investment			
External financing	0.9	10.7	50.0	49.6
Internal financing	87.2	50.5	50.0	25.5
Internal and external financing	11.9	38.8	0	24.9
Total	*100*	*100*	*100*	*100*
External financing				
Credit raising in parent country	0	63.5	0	0.0
Credit raising in host country	0	15.8	33.3	47.3
Capital increase via issue of stocks in parent country	100	18.3	33.3	25.7
Capital increase via issue of stocks in host country	0	1.7	33.3	25.7
Supplier credit	0	0.8	0	1.2
Total	*100*	*100*	*100*	*100*
Internal financing				
Financing from profits and cashflows	72.2	68.6	100	93.0
Intracompany reallocation of funds	27.8	31.4	0	7.0
Total	*100*	*100*	*100*	*100*

[a] Eastern Europe includes the New Member States, South-East Europe, the former Yugoslavia as well as Russia and the Ukraine.

Source: Sample of 2,200 Austrian and German FDI projects in Eastern Europe, Chair of International Economics, University of Munich.

important source of finance is out of cash flow and profits (72%), while funds out of intra-firm reallocation from other units account for 28% of the bank investments in Eastern Europe. These numbers suggest that parent banks in Austria and Germany do from time to time reallocate funds away from some units in order to finance other (in this case Eastern European) units.

On the side of affiliate banks in Eastern Europe, the picture looks somewhat different: 50% of affiliate banks said that they finance their activity internally out of cash flow, while the other 50% come from external financing out of loans by other local banks, by raising capital through the issuing of stocks in either the parent or the host country. Surprisingly, however, the financing pattern of multinational non-banks does not appear to be that much different from that of multinational banks. Both bank as well as non-bank affiliates rely heavily on internal cash flow and loans raised from local banks.[38]

These numbers suggest that affiliate banks in Eastern Europe, once they are established, function autonomously and do not depend on parent banks to provide liquidity. Their activity is financed out of cash flow or by raising capital mostly locally. Taken together these data suggest that affiliate banks do not appear to be

[38] See also Marin *et al.* (2003), and Marin and Schnitzer (2006).

supported by an internal capital market of parent banks, while their original establishment is almost exclusively financed by internal funds of parent bank firms.[39]

Multinational banks and the financial crisis

I turn now to the second question raised by the authors on the role of MNBs in the recent financial crisis. Financial integration has been the subject of much debate following the emerging market crisis in the late 1990s with different opinions about capital account liberalization policies. The current global financial crisis poses similar questions in the face of international financial volatility. Therefore, it is important to understand whether foreign banks contribute or not to credit volatility in host countries. Foreign banks may play a stabilizing role by being better able to diversify risk and by being able to rely on parental liquidity when a host country shock hits. But at the same time foreign banks may act as a transmission mechanism of parent country shocks on host country lending.

Similar to de Haas and van Lelyveld (2006) this paper shows that the ICM has been used in the current financial crisis to stabilize financial markets in host countries. In order to test this, the authors do not look directly at how the ICM works in times of distress but rather they estimate a regression of the ratio of claims to liabilities in local currency of foreign affiliates in a panel of 49 developed and developing countries for the period between 1999 and 2009. They find that on average the ratio of local claims to local liabilities has increased since 1999 and has accelerated in the post-crisis period. They also show that this ratio has increased in all geographic regions in particular in the NMS. They also run a regression on the bank specific ratio of loans to deposits to investigate whether this ratio has changed significantly during the crisis and in particular for foreign affiliates in different European regions such as EU15 and the NMS. They find that foreign affiliates did not have a destabilizing role, since their loan-deposit ratio has remained constant. In sum, they find that foreign affiliate banks have been essentially behaving like national banks in all regions with the exception of the NMS in Eastern Europe where foreign banks had a stabilizing effect.

At a closer look at the direct evidence on ICM for Eastern Europe given in Table 8, I find the results of the authors for the NMS somewhat surprising. Clearly, affiliate banks in Eastern Europe do not rely on parental liquidity to finance their host activities. Therefore, the fall in cash flow in parent banks appears to have an effect only on new foreign investment activity in the banking sector rather than on already established affiliates in Eastern Europe. This way, the financial crisis in parent countries is less likely to have been translated to host countries. So far so good. But the financial crisis also led to a drop in profits in affiliate banks in Eastern

[39] The data are consistent with the findings of Goldberg (2005) who shows that international activities of foreign banks headquartered in the United States are not influenced by host country economic conditions.

Europe and this should have clearly shown up in the results of the empirical analysis. One caveat is that the data of Table 8 are from the pre-crisis period and the behaviour of parent and affiliate banks may have changed during the crisis. Another is that the Vienna Initiative, a forum which was created in early 2009 to coordinate the responses of major stakeholders to the financial crisis has already shown an effect in the empirical analysis.

Panel discussion

Athanasios Vamvakidis believed the questions raised in the paper were particularly relevant for the many emerging European countries where the share of foreign banks is very high. He noted the concentration of foreign-owned banks by origin varies across the region (e.g. Swedish banks are mainly located in the Baltics, southern Europe consists of a large share of Italian banks), and suggested this may partly explain the different behaviour of foreign-owned banks during the crisis especially when one takes into account policy coordination actions such as the Vienna initiative or IMF discussions held with particular parent banks and their subsidiaries.

Silvana Tenreyro remarked that during the Argentine crisis in 2001 affiliates received no support from their foreign partners despite demands to do so. The consequence of which was a greater decline in lending and in turn added to the perception that MNBs had a destabilizing effect on the economy. She suggested that this event also highlighted that greater integration of foreign banks may be crucial in reducing the potential destabilizing effects of MNEs. She also noted that although the recent crisis was a systemic one, countries experienced very different outcomes and suggested the authors could exploit this variation to further examine the role of ICMs.

Refet Gürkaynak found it difficult to accept the authors' assertion that MNBs limited fluctuations during the crisis and asked them to give a more detailed explanation in the paper as to how MNBs did so. He wondered how the capacity of MNBs to limit fluctuations differed between affiliates and subsidiaries. He commented it was unlikely that the British or the Dutch who were adversely affected by the branches of the Icelandic banks would accept the view that MNBs limited fluctuations.

Samuel Bentolila considered all the variables in the analysis to be endogenous and believed the authors should attempt to identify idiosyncratic country shocks to examine the role of ICM in a country's adjustment process. He noted an important avenue of research would be to investigate how MNBs differed in their dealings with households and business.

Rafael Repullo noted that although the paper focused on subsidiaries, he believed the results were likely to be stronger for branches because they are not incorporated in the host countries. Given that many affiliates were established only in the recent past, he worried that some of the estimates might be capturing a transition affect where new affiliates temporarily pursue an unbalanced strategy upon entry into a new market before adjusting over time. It is therefore important to distinguish between greenfield and buyout type entry of affiliates.

Georges de Ménil remarked the analysis is based solely on European data and it is important to highlight that multinational banking is relatively underdeveloped in Europe. Augustin Landier emphasized the importance of indentifying how MNBs and national banks serve the local market. He wondered was it the case that MNBs deal with large companies in hard information industries while national banks deal with small companies in soft information industries.

Richard Portes suggested there is likely to be a move towards subsidiaries away from branches in the future. He noted that many factors will contribute to this shift including gains in tax efficiency and also stronger macro prudential regulation which will be applied on a national basis.

In response to Gianmarco Ottaviano's comment on the importance of distinguishing between the impact of systemic and idiosyncratic shocks on MNB behaviour, Giorgio Barba Navaretti noted there is evidence to suggest that even during a systemic shock MNBs are better funded and able to support their branches. He agreed with the discussants that the lack of harmonization in the regulatory framework complicated the management of the banking crisis. Also from an MNB viewpoint, asymmetric national regulation probably inhibits the efficient functioning of these banks.

REFERENCES

Acharya, V. V. and M. Richardson (eds.) (2009). *Restoring Financial Stability: How to Repair a Failed System*, Wiley, Chichester.

Billett, M. and D. Mauer (2003). 'Cross subsidies, external financing constraints, and the contribution of the internal capital market to firm value', *Review of Financial Studies*, 16, 1167–201.

Boot, A. W. A. and A. Schmeits (2000). 'Market discipline and incentive problems in conglomerate firms with applications to banking', *Journal of Financial Intermediation*, 9, 240–73.

Brusco, S. and F. Panunzi (2005). 'Reallocation of corporate resources and managerial incentives in internal capital markets', CEPR Discussion Paper 2532.

Calzolari, G. and G. Loranth (2010). 'Regulation of multinational banks: a theoretical inquiry', European Central Bank Working Paper No. 431 and forthcoming in the *Journal of Financial Intermediation.*

Carletti, E., P. Hartmann and G. Spagnolo (2007). 'Bank mergers, competition, and liquidity', *Journal of Money, Credit and Banking*, 39, 1068–105.

Carlson, M. and K. J. Mitchener (2009). 'Branch banking as a device for discipline: competition and bank survivorship during the great depression', *Journal of Political Economy*, 117, 165–210.

Cetorelli, N. and L. Goldberg (2009). 'Global banks and international shock transmission: evidence from the crisis', Federal Reserve Bank of New York, December.

Chan-Lau, J. M., S. Mitra and L. L. Ong (2008). 'Identifying contagion risk in the international banking system: an extreme value theorem approach?', *mimeo.*

Chevalier, J. (2004). 'What do we know about cross-subsidization? Evidence from merging firms', *Advances in Economic Analysis and Policy*, 4, Article 3.
Clarke, G., R. Cull, M. S. Martinez Peria and S. M. Sánchez (2003). 'Foreign bank entry: experience, implications for developing economies, and agenda for further research', *The World Bank Research Observer*, 18, 25–59.
De Haas, R. and I. van Lelyveld (2006). 'Foreign banks and credit stability in Central and Eastern Europe: a panel data analysis', *Journal of Banking and Finance*, 30, 1927–52.
—— (2010). 'Internal capital markets and lending by multinational bank subsidiaries', *Journal of Financial Intermediation*, 19, 1–25.
Dermine, J. (2005). 'European banking integration: don't put the cart before the horse', Conference on *Cross-Border Banking, Regulatory Challenges*, 6–7 October, Federal Reserve Bank of Chicago.
Detragiache, E., P. Gupta and T. Tressel (2006). 'Foreign banks in poor countries: theory and evidence', IMF Working Paper No. 06-18 2006.
Eisenbeis, R. A. and G. G. Kaufman (2006). 'Cross-border banking: challenges for deposit insurance and financial stability in the European Union', Working Paper 15a, Federal Reserve Bank of Atlanta.
European Central Bank (2006). 'EU banking structures', Report of the European Central Bank.
Feldstein, M. and I. Horioka (1980). 'Domestic savings and international capital flows', *Economic Journal*, 90, 314–29.
Freixas, X. (2009). 'Systemic risk and prudential regulation in the global economy', in D. D. Evanoff, D. S. Hoelscher and G. G. Kaufman (eds.), *Globalization and Systemic Risk (World Scientific Studies in International Economics)*, World Scientific Publishing Co., Singapore.
Gertner, R. H., D. S. Scharfstein and J. C. Stein (1994). 'Internal versus external capital markets', *Quarterly Journal of Economics*.
Goldberg, L. (2005). 'The international exposure of US banks', NBER Working Paper 11365, May.
Hart, O. and B. R. Holmström (2010). 'A theory of firm scope', *Quarterly Journal of Economics*, 125, 483–513.
Havrylchyk, O. and E. Jurzyk (2006). 'Profitability of foreign banks in Central and Eastern Europe: does the entry mode matter?', BOFIT Discussion Paper.
Houston, J. F. and C. James (1998). 'Do bank internal capital markets promote lending?', *Journal of Banking and Finance*, 22, 899–918.
Houston, J. F., C. James and D. Marcus (1997). 'Capital market frictions and the role of internal capital markets in banking', *Journal of Financial Economics*, 46, 135–64.
Kahn, C. and A. Winton (2004). 'Moral hazard and optimal subsidiary structure for financial institutions', *Journal of Finance*, 59, 2531–75.
Khanna, N. and S. Tice (2001). 'The bright side of internal capital markets', *Journal of Finance*, 56, 1489–1528.
Kroszner, R. S. (2008). 'The effect of removing geographical restrictions on banking in the United States: lessons for Europe', *Financial Markets, Institutions & Instruments*, 17, 5–18.
Kroszner, R. S. and P. E. Strahan (2006). 'Regulation and deregulation of the U.S. banking industry: causes, consequences, and implications for the future', NBER Paper.
Laeven, L. and F. Valencia (2008). 'Systemic banking crises, a new database', IMF Working Paper 8.
Lamont, O. (1997). 'Cash flow and investment: evidence from internal capital markets', *Journal of Finance*, 52, 83–109.
Marin, D. (2010). 'The opening up of Eastern Europe at 20: jobs, skills, and "Reverse Maquilladoras" in Austria and Germany', in M. Jovanovic (ed.), *Handbook of Economic Integration*, Edward Elgar, forthcoming.
Marin, D., A. Lorentovich and A. Raubold (2003). 'Ownership, capital or outsourcing: what drives German investment to Eastern Europe', in H. Hermann and R. Lipsey (eds.), *Foreign Direct Investment in the Real and Financial Sector in Industrialized Countries*, Springer Verlag, Berlin.
Marin, D. and M. Schnitzer (2006). 'When is FDI a capital flow?', CEPR Discussion Paper No 6540.

McCauley, R., P. McGuire and G. von Peter (2010). 'The architecture of global banking: from international to multinational', *BIS Quarterly Review*, 25–37.
Morgan, D. P., B. Rime and P. E. Strahan (2004). 'Bank integration and state business cycles', *Quarterly Journal of Economics*, 119, 1555–84.
Ostry, J. D., A. R. Ghosh, K. Habermeier, M. Chamon, M. S. Qureshi and D. B. S. Reinhardt (2010). 'Capital inflows: the role of controls', IMF Staff Position Note, SPN/10/04.
Ozbas, O. and D. S. Scharfstein (2008). 'Evidence on the dark side of internal capital markets', *Review of Financial Studies*, 23, 581–89.
Peek, J. and E. S. Rosengren (1997). 'The international transmission of financial shocks: the case of Japan', *American Economic Review*, 87, 495–505.
Popov, A. and G. F. Udell (2010). 'Cross-border banking and the international transmission of financial distress during the crisis of 2007–2008', European Central Bank Working Paper No. 1203.
Rajan, R., H. Servaes and L. Zingales (2000). 'The cost of diversity: the diversification discount and inefficient investment', *Journal of Finance*, 55, 35–80.
Scharfstein, D. S. (1998). 'The dark side of internal capital markets II: evidence from diversified conglomerates', NBER Working Paper 6352.
Scharfstein, D. S. and J. C. Stein (2000). 'The dark side of internal capital markets: divisional rent-seeking and inefficient investment', *Journal of Finance*, 55, 2537–64.
Shah, S. and A. V. Thakor (1987). 'Optimal capital structure and project financing', *Journal of Economic Theory*, 42, 209–43.
Shin, H. and R. Stulz (1998). 'Are internal capital markets efficient?', *Quarterly Journal of Economics*, 113, 531–52.
Stein, J. C. (1997). 'Internal capital markets and the competition for corporate resources', *Journal of Finance*, 52, 111–33.
—— (2002). 'Information production and capital allocation: decentralized vs. hierarchical firms', *Journal of Finance*, 57, 1891–921.
Turner, A. (2009). 'The Turner Review: a regulatory response to the global banking crisis', Discussion Paper, Financial Services Authority.
Whited, T. (2001). 'Is it inefficient investment that causes the diversification discount?', *Journal of Finance*, 56, 1667–91.
Williamson, O. E. (1975). *Markets and Hierarchies: Analysis and Antitrust Implications: A Study in the Economics of Internal Organization*, Free Press, New York.

Inflation risk

SUMMARY

This article starts by discussing the concept of 'inflation hedging' and provides estimates of 'inflation betas' for standard bond and well-diversified equity indices for over 45 countries. We show that such standard securities are poor inflation hedges. Expanding the menu of assets to Treasury bills, foreign bonds, real estate and gold improves matters but inflation risk remains difficult to hedge. We then describe how state-of-the-art term structure research has tried to uncover estimates of the inflation risk premium, the compensation for bearing inflation risk. Most studies, including very recent ones that actually use inflation-linked bonds and information in surveys to gauge inflation expectations, find the inflation risk premium to be sizeable and to substantially vary through time. This implies that governments should normally lower their financing costs through the issuance of index-linked bonds, at least in an ex ante sense. Our findings thus indicate a potentially important role for inflation index linked bonds. We briefly discuss the pros and cons of such bonds, focusing the discussion mostly on the situation in the United States, which started to issue Treasury Inflation Protected Securities (TIPS) in 1997. We argue that it is hard to negate the benefits of such securities for all relevant parties, unless the market in which they trade is highly deficient, which was actually the case in its early years in the United States.

— *Geert Bekaert and Xiaozheng Wang*

Economic Policy October 2010 Printed in Great Britain

Inflation risk and the inflation risk premium

Geert Bekaert and Xiaozheng Wang

Columbia Business School; Criterion Economics

1. INTRODUCTION

In an imperfectly indexed monetary world, inflation risk is one of the most important economic risks, faced by consumers and investors alike. Individuals saving for retirement must make sure their wealth finances their expenses in retirement, whatever the inflation scenario. The liabilities of pension funds and endowments likely increase in nominal terms with inflation.[1] While the world has enjoyed relatively mild inflation during the last decade, the recent crisis has made market observers and economists wonder whether inflation will rear its ugly head again in years to come. Central banks across the world have injected substantial amounts of liquidity in the financial system and public debt has surged everywhere. It is not hard to imagine that inflationary pressures may resurface with a vengeance once the economy rebounds.

This article has benefited from the suggestions from participants at the 'Index Leningen' Conference, organized by Netspar and the Dutch Ministry of Finance in February 2009, and at the *Economic Policy* Panel Meeting in Madrid in April 2010. We also benefited from the comments of Frans de Roon, Roel Beetsma, Serge Vergouwe, Fabrizio Perri, and especially of two anonymous referees, the discussant, Cédric Tille, and the Editor, Philip Lane.
The Managing Editor in charge of this paper was Philip Lane.

[1] We ignore the important issue that official estimates of inflation are unlikely to represent an adequate representation of the relevant price changes for a particular investor. For example, endowments should focus on the cost inflation for items dominating their budgets, such as professors' salaries and real estate expenses.

Economic Policy October 2010 pp. 755–806 Printed in Great Britain

It is therefore quite important to ask whether inflation risk can be easily hedged in financial markets. In fact, in a number of countries, governments have issued securities, linked to an inflation index, which makes the hedging more or less perfect. The existence of a sizeable government inflation-linked bond market typically spurs the development of inflation derivative contracts, which could satisfy more complex inflation-linked hedging demands. This development in turn has instigated a debate on the benefits and costs, both for investors and for the government, of inflation-linked securities. A critical element in such a debate is the notion of the inflation risk premium, the compensation demanded by investors, for not being perfectly indexed against inflation or, put differently, the insurance premium investors pay governments to shoulder the inflation risk. There is apparently no consensus about the magnitude of this premium, with some recent articles even suggesting it to be negative (see, e.g., Grishchenko and Huang, 2010). The uncertainty surrounding the inflation risk premium also means that there is uncertainty about critical inputs to any strategic asset allocation, such as the real returns on cash and bonds.

This paper accomplishes three things. First, it discusses the concept of 'inflation hedging' and provides some estimates of 'inflation betas' for standard bond and well-diversified equity indices for over 45 countries. We show that such standard securities are poor inflation hedges. When we expand the menu of assets to Treasury bills, foreign bonds, real estate and gold, matters improve but mostly only marginally. Generally speaking, it appears easier to hedge inflation risk in emerging markets than it is in developed markets. Second, we describe how state-of-the-art term structure research has tried to uncover estimates of the inflation risk premium. While we focus primarily on the findings in one study (Ang *et al.*, 2008), we end the discussion with a survey of recent results that try to bring more data to the table, both in terms of inflation-linked bonds and survey data on inflation expectations. We provide some recent estimates of the inflation premium in the United States, the United Kingdom and the euro area, showing that historically inflation premiums have been mostly positive and often sizeable. Third, given the imperfect hedging capability of standard securities and a sizeable inflation risk premium, inflation index linked bonds can potentially play an important role in financial markets. We briefly discuss the pros and cons of such bonds, focusing the discussion mostly on the situation in the United States, which started to issue Treasury Inflation Protected Securities (TIPS) in 1997. We argue that it is hard to negate the benefits of such securities for all relevant parties, unless the market in which they trade is highly deficient, which was actually the case in its early years in the United States. The final section concludes.

2. INFLATION HEDGING

For existing securities to be good inflation hedges, their nominal returns must at the very least be positively correlated with inflation. Nevertheless, there are several ways to define the 'inflation hedging capability' of a security. Reilly *et al.* (1970) examine whether a security protects real purchasing power over time, by calculating the incidence of negative real returns. Clearly, higher yielding assets will almost surely do well on such measure, but may not prove good inflation hedges in the short run, if they fail to generate high returns at times when inflation is high, especially when it is unexpectedly high. Bodie (1976) measures how the variance of the real return of a nominal bond can be reduced using an equity portfolio as a gauge of the hedging capability of equities. In this article, we consider a very simple concept of inflation hedging, namely, the inflation beta, computed using a simple regression:

$$\text{Nominal return} = \alpha + \beta\ \text{inflation} + \varepsilon \qquad (1)$$

Here, ε is the part of the return not explained by inflation. If $\beta = 1$, the security is a perfect hedge against inflation. Note that it is conceivable that even a perfectly indexed security does not generate a perfect coefficient of 1 in the regression in (1). This is true because inflation may be correlated with value-relevant factors that are omitted from the regression. We discuss one such important factor, namely a measure of economic activity, in further detail below. Another reason why β may not be 1, even in a 'perfectly hedged' world, is the tax system. If investors in these securities are taxed on inflationary gains, shocks that cause a revision in expected inflation require more than proportional changes in nominal expected returns to keep after-tax expected real returns unchanged. The exact prediction is rather complex as it depends on the details of the tax system, whether inflation is expected or unexpected, and whether marginal investors in the security are taxable investors or not. Furthermore, an imperfect but stable and predictable relation between a security's return and inflation could suffice for hedging (see Schotman and Schweitzer, 2000), as it would be trivial to compute a hedge ratio. We examine the stability of the relationship explicitly below. Nevertheless, hedging may be difficult to accomplish in practice (especially if it involves short positions), and such hedge portfolios are not likely to be easily and cheaply accessible to retail investors. It remains interesting, therefore, to examine how strongly an asset's return comoves with inflation and whether it reacts one to one to inflation shocks, as measured by the inflation beta in (1).

2.1. Inflation betas of stocks and bonds

How do the main asset classes fare in terms of inflation hedging capability? We obtained nominal government bond returns, nominal stock returns and inflation data for over 45 countries. A data appendix contains more details, but the sample period for most series ends in January 2010, whereas the starting point varies from country to country, between January 1970 and January 2005. Generally, the data are more extensive for stocks than for bonds, and for developed markets than for emerging markets. We look at logarithmic annual returns, computed from monthly data. Using monthly data but a one-year horizon, results in the residuals of the regression analysis reflected in Equation (1) exhibiting positive serial correlation. We correct the standard errors for this using the standard approach advocated by Hansen and Hodrick (1980).

Figure 1 shows the betas from the regression in (1) for bond returns. Dark bars indicate that the beta is statistically significantly different from 1 (at the 10% level). We find that 19 out of 48 inflation betas are indeed significantly below 1, a further 5 countries exhibit negative betas, which are not statistically significantly different from 1. So in half the countries, bond returns react reliably negatively to inflation, earning negative returns in periods of high inflation. This should not be surprising. While expected inflation should be priced into the return on bonds, they will be particularly sensitive to shocks to unexpected inflation. We actually examine this further below. Note that in another eight countries the betas are below 0.5, meaning that real returns react quite negatively to inflation shocks.

But should stocks not fare better? After all, they are real securities, and whereas there are many ways in which inflation could be value relevant for equities it is difficult to argue in favour of a particular bias. There is already a rather voluminous literature on US data showing that equities are not particularly good inflation hedges; in fact the nominal returns of stocks in the United States and inflation are mostly negatively correlated.[2] In Figure 2, we extend this evidence to 48 countries. The inflation beta in the United States is indeed negative but it is not statistically significantly below 1. In fact, the coefficient became less negative by adding the recent crisis years, in which low stock returns and below average inflation went hand in hand. In any case, real returns on stocks and inflation are solidly negatively correlated in the United States for a sample extending from 1970 to the beginning of 2010. However, the United States is not the exception but rather the rule. The majority of the inflation betas are negative, and of the ones that are positive, most are way too low. In 15 countries, we observe inflation betas that are significantly below one, and in a further 16 countries the betas are negative but not significant. In only 12 countries is the inflation beta close to one in statistical and economic terms (say, higher than 0.5) or implausibly high as in Morocco or Hungary.

To get a more survey feel for the results, Table 1 presents the results for 'pooled regressions'. Here the inflation beta is estimated using all countries, allowing for a country specific intercept, but allowing only one beta per (regional) group.[3] Bonds exhibit inflation betas that are mostly positive but significantly below 1, at least in developed countries, meaning that their real returns are low when inflation is high. The inflation betas are higher in emerging countries, and the pooled beta is

[2] One classic paper is Fama (1981).

[3] We actually estimate two regressions, one for the developed/emerging split-up, and then another one for all the other groups.

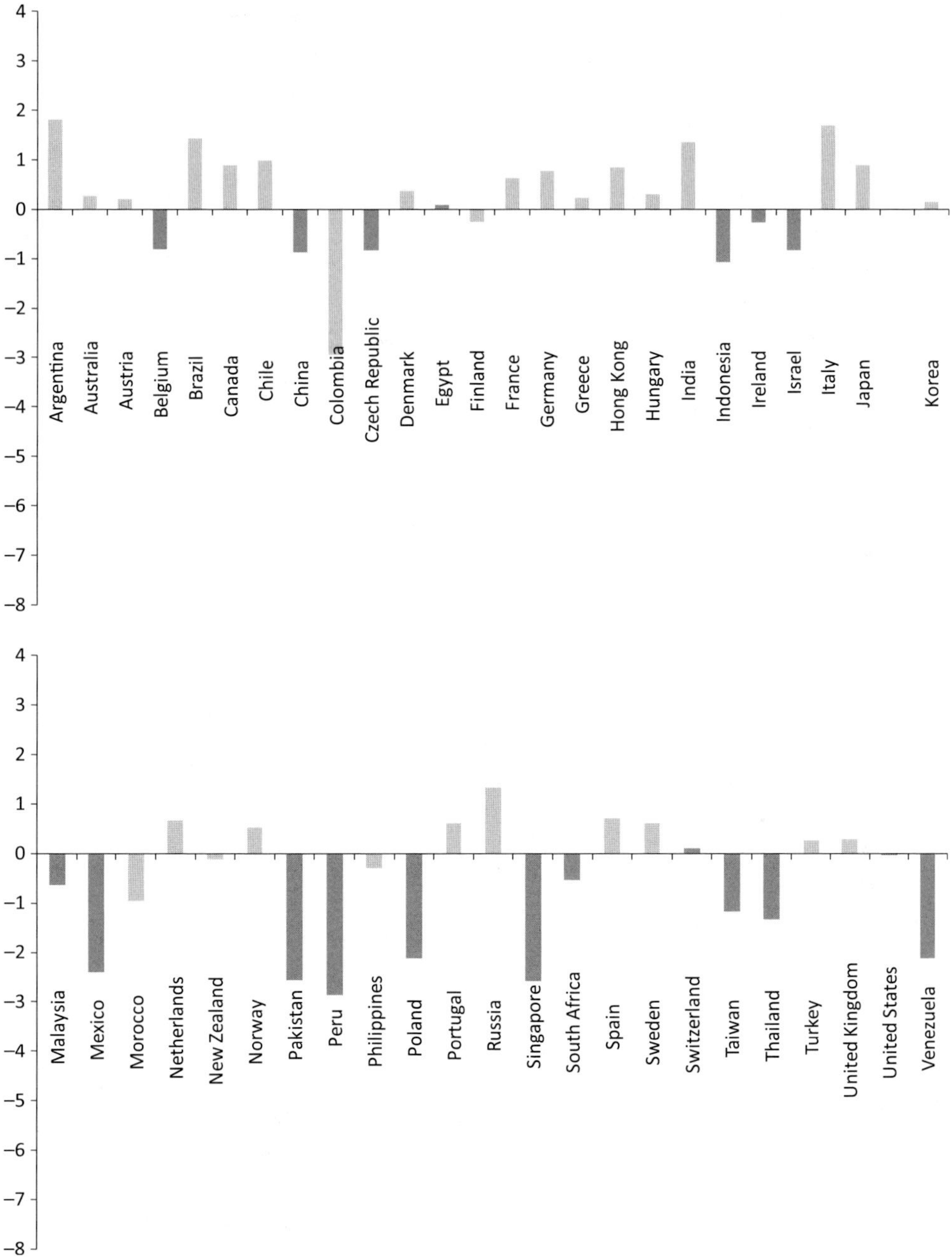

Figure 1. Inflation betas in international bond markets

Notes: The vertical bars indicate the inflation beta in Equation (1). Dark bars indicate that the beta is statistically significantly different from 1. Note that the data point for Jordan is missing.

indistinguishable from 1. The result is mostly driven by Latin America, as the inflation betas for bonds in Asia and Africa are negative. The picture is similar for stocks, in that here too the inflation betas are closer to one for emerging markets

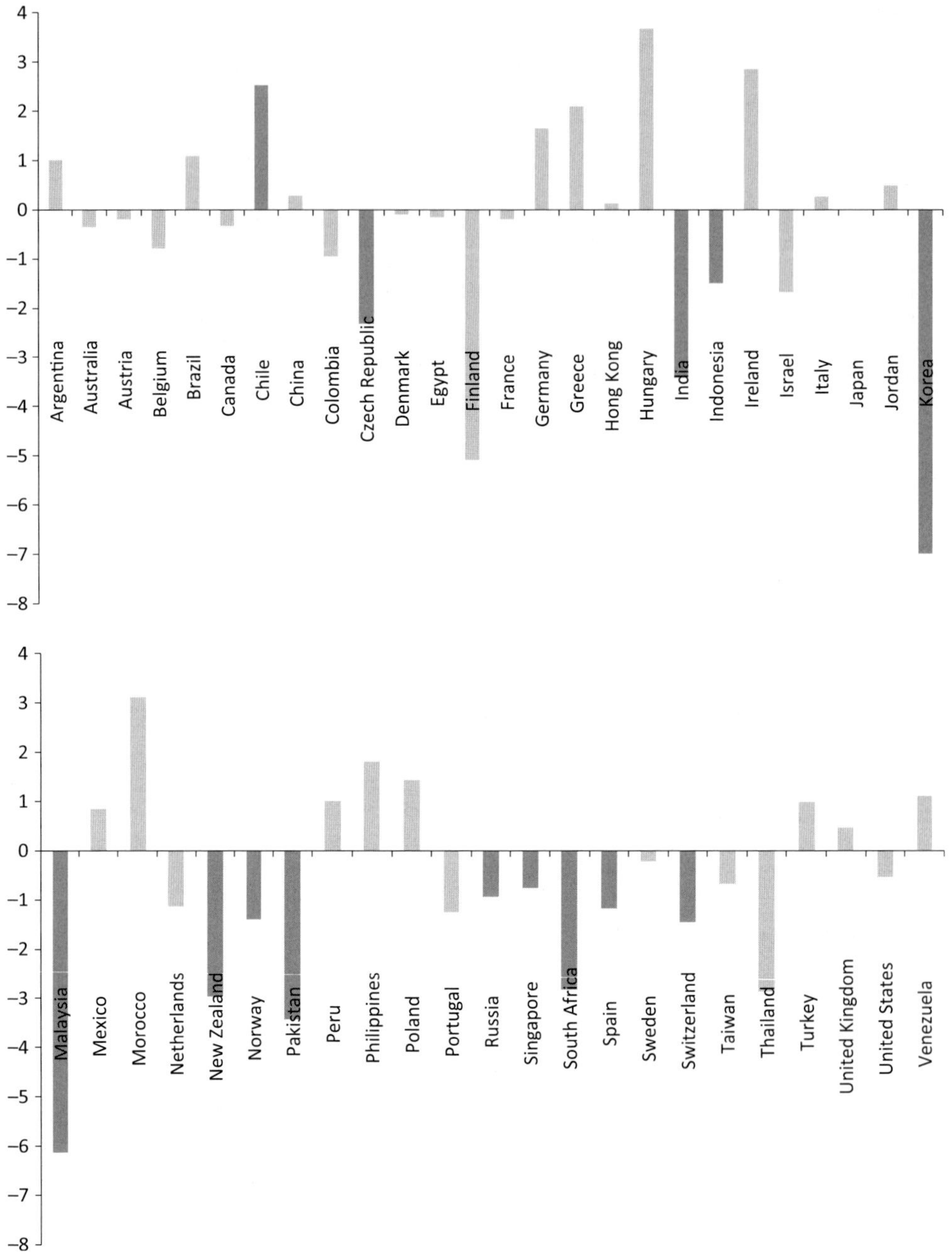

Figure 2. Inflation betas in international stock markets

Notes: The vertical bars indicate the inflation beta in Equation (1). Dark bars indicate that the beta is statistically significantly different from 1.

than for developed markets. The main difference is that stock returns are negatively correlated with inflation for all developed markets, a result largely driven by North America and Oceania. In the EU, the correlation is small, but not significantly different from 1. The positive coefficient for emerging markets is again driven by the

Table 1. Pooled results for inflation betas

	Inflation beta		Unexpected inflation beta	
	Bonds	Stocks	Bonds	Stocks
Developed	0.28 (0.13)	−0.25 (0.29)	−0.58 (0.19)	−0.44 (0.40)
Emerging	0.98 (0.34)	1.01 (0.07)	0.92 (0.33)	0.97 (0.09)
North America	0.27 (0.36)	−0.42 (0.81)	−0.44 (0.48)	−0.99 (1.26)
Latin America	1.10 (0.92)	1.05 (0.07)	1.20 (0.81)	1.07 (0.07)
Asia	−1.14 (0.42)	−0.83 (0.31)	−0.81 (0.39)	−0.86 (0.31)
Africa	−0.28 (0.22)	−0.78 (1.71)	−0.29 (0.23)	−0.83 (1.58)
Oceania	0.15 (0.40)	−0.56 (0.92)	−0.65 (0.46)	−0.81 (1.32)
EU	0.30 (0.15)	0.27 (0.43)	−0.53 (0.19)	−0.24 (0.63)
Non-EU Europe	1.29 (0.41)	0.32 (0.42)	1.15 (0.20)	−0.51 (0.41)

Notes: The estimates on the left-hand side are from a pooled regression of bond or stock returns on inflation. The regression is run twice, once allowing for different coefficients for developed and emerging markets; once allowing for different coefficients across the different regional groups listed in the table. The estimates on the right-hand side for unexpected inflation come from similar but multivariate regressions on expected and unexpected inflation, where only the second coefficient is reported. Hansen–Hodrick (1980) standard errors are between parentheses.

Latin American countries, as the correlation between inflation and stock returns is negative in both Asia and Africa.

The overwhelmingly positive coefficients on nominal bonds may give the impression that bonds are 'not so bad', but of course they likely reflect the effect of previously expected inflation being priced into bonds and inflation being persistent over time. The right-hand side of Table 1 reports results from a multivariate regression, regressing the returns onto two variables, expected inflation the year before and unexpected inflation (the difference between realized and expected). In Fama and Schwert (1977), a classic paper on inflation hedging, an asset is viewed as a complete hedge against inflation if it has coefficients equal to one on both variables in this regression.

Of course this regression requires an estimate of expected inflation. It is impossible to come up with accurate measures of expected inflation for all the countries in this sample, so we use a very simple procedure: we let expected inflation at time t be current year-on-year inflation at t. While this random walk model for inflation may appear inconsistent with the data, we suspect it is hard to beat by more complex models in out-of-sample forecasting. In fact, for the United States, Atkeson and Ohanian (2001) show as much.[4] The table simply reports the coefficient on the second component, unexpected inflation (which is really just the change in inflation). With only a few exceptions, we obtain what was to be expected: the unexpected inflation betas are further removed from 1 than were the 'total' inflation betas. This suggests that whatever link with inflation does exist comes

[4] The US inflation time series seems to exhibit ARMA(1,1) type behaviour at the monthly frequency. However, there is evidence of parameter instability in the coefficients, and there is strong seasonality in monthly inflation data. Both features of the data render the estimation of a monthly ARMA model on a set of international data, where many samples are quite short, rather useless. As we discuss later, for the United States, Ang *et al.* (2007) demonstrate that professional surveys provide the best forecasts. Such surveys are obviously not available for most countries in our sample.

through its expected part. For stock returns, all the betas are now negative except for Latin America (where the beta is still indistinguishable from one), but the Latin American region still drives the coefficient to 1 for emerging markets as a whole.

All of our results apply to one-year returns; this is a reasonable horizon to investigate, even when considering long-horizon investors, as portfolios are typically rebalanced at least once a year. However, it is conceivable that the inflation hedging capability of stock returns is more apparent at longer horizons, and, in fact, Boudoukh and Richardson (1993) claim that stocks constitute a better hedge for inflation at longer horizons. In Tables 2 and 3, we examine this issue for our extensive set of countries. We only consider pooled results for the larger groups here, as the longer horizons start exhausting the degrees of freedoms for many countries. Table 2 contains the inflation betas. For bond returns, the coefficients are nicely increasing with horizon and they are insignificantly different from 1 at the 5-year horizon for developed markets, and well over 1 for emerging markets. Perhaps this is not entirely surprising, as it may simply reflect the accuracy of longer-term inflation expectations and/or the existence of an inflation risk premium at longer horizons. The result may also reflect a strong cross-country relationship (bond yields in high inflation countries being reliably higher than bond yields in low inflation countries). For stock returns, the developed market betas increase with horizon but remain significantly below 1, even at the 5-year horizon. For emerging markets, they show little horizon dependence and are just about 1. The unexpected inflation betas, shown in Table 3, tell a different story, however. While the betas for bonds still increase with horizon, they remain significantly below 1 for developed markets, even at the 5-year horizon. For stocks, the betas remain significantly negative for all groups, except for emerging markets.

The negative relation between stock returns and inflation is the topic of a literature too vast to fully survey here. Suffice it to say that many recent articles rely on money illusion to explain this empirical relationship (see, e.g., Campbell and Vuolteenaho, 2004). However, the literature has also identified a number of rational channels, all of which have important consequences for the interpretation of the regression ran before. Fama's (1981) proxy hypothesis essentially argues that the stock market anticipates economic activity and if inflationary periods coincide with periods of low economic activity, a negative relationship between stock returns and inflation may result. Madsen (2005) makes a similar argument, focusing on 'supply shock' variables. Bekaert and Engstrom (2010) find some evidence in favour of the proxy hypothesis, but suggest that the bulk of the correlation between stock returns and inflation occurs through a discount rate channel. In recessions, risk premiums increase and hence, stagflationary periods may induce a negative inflation-stock return relationship. Lin's (2009) finding that inflation uncertainty has a negative effect on stocks in 16 developed countries is also suggestive of a discount rate channel. Finally, Doepke and Schneider (2009) focus on the redistributive effects of inflation. Episodes of unanticipated inflation reduce the real value of

Table 2. Inflation betas over longer horizons

	Bonds					Stocks				
	1-year horizon	2-year horizon	3-year horizon	4-year horizon	5-year horizon	1-year horizon	2-year horizon	3-year horizon	4-year horizon	5-year horizon
Developed countries	0.28 (0.13)	0.59 (0.15)	0.84 (0.17)	1.04 (0.18)	1.12 (0.19)	−0.25 (0.29)	−0.11 (0.27)	−0.05 (0.25)	0.01 (0.23)	0.12 (0.23)
Emerging countries	0.98 (0.34)	1.63 (0.34)	2.02 (0.52)	1.21 (0.57)	2.11 (0.65)	1.01 (0.07)	1.02 (0.03)	1.03 (0.03)	1.03 (0.03)	1.00 (0.03)
North America	0.27 (0.36)	0.67 (0.21)	1.04 (0.30)	1.13 (0.32)	1.39 (0.45)	−0.42 (0.81)	−0.40 (0.69)	−0.31 (0.59)	−0.25 (0.51)	−0.16 (0.45)
European Union	0.30 (0.15)	0.65 (0.19)	0.94 (0.23)	1.11 (0.23)	1.17 (0.23)	0.27 (0.43)	−0.09 (0.35)	−0.05 (0.32)	−0.10 (0.29)	−0.04 (0.28)

Notes: We repeat the pooled regressions from Table 1 but also perform them over longer multi-year horizons, up till 5 years. The standard errors correct for the overlap in the observations using Hansen–Hodrick (1980) standard errors.

Table 3. Unexpected inflation betas over longer horizons

	Bonds					Stocks				
	1-year horizon	2-year horizon	3-year horizon	4-year horizon	5-year horizon	1-year horizon	2-year horizon	3-year horizon	4-year horizon	5-year horizon
Developed countries	−0.58 (0.19)	−0.58 (0.15)	−0.22 (0.13)	0.19 (0.13)	0.36 (0.13)	−0.44 (0.40)	−0.59 (0.32)	−0.59 (0.33)	−0.66 (0.34)	−0.58 (0.31)
Emerging countries	0.92 (0.33)	1.57 (0.37)	1.93 (0.54)	1.08 (0.58)	2.09 (0.68)	0.97 (0.09)	0.98 (0.05)	1.03 (0.03)	1.04 (0.03)	1.03 (0.04)
North America	−0.44 (0.48)	−0.62 (0.33)	0.07 (0.19)	0.26 (0.31)	0.47 (0.34)	−0.99 (1.26)	−1.08 (0.90)	−0.74 (0.69)	−0.75 (0.55)	−0.84 (0.41)
European Union	−0.53 (0.19)	−0.43 (0.17)	−0.09 (0.17)	0.23 (0.17)	0.44 (0.16)	−0.24 (0.63)	−0.92 (0.54)	−1.26 (0.43)	−1.39 (0.36)	−1.21 (0.30)

Notes: We repeat the pooled regressions from Table 1 but also perform them over longer multi-year horizons, up till 5 years. The standard errors correct for the overlap in the observations using Hansen–Hodrick (1980) standard errors.

nominal claims and thus redistribute wealth from lenders to borrowers. Because borrowers are younger on average than lenders, an unanticipated inflation shock generates a decrease in labour supply as well as an increase in savings, hence reducing output. All these channels suggest that the relationship between inflation and stock returns may largely reflect a relationship between the stock market and a measure of economic activity. The stagflation stories of Fama (1981) and Bekaert and Engstrom (2010) suggest that how much the relationship between economic activity and stock markets affects the inflation-stock return comovement depends on the incidence of stagflations in a particular country.

To examine this effect in more detail, we obtained data on industrial production growth for most of our countries. We could not find adequate data for eight countries in our sample. Therefore, Table 4 displays both the original inflation beta from a univariate regression (which only differs from the estimate in Table 1 because the country set may be slightly different), and the beta on inflation in a bivariate regression, including industrial production growth as an additional independent variable. To help interpret the results, suppose such a multivariate regression yields the 'true' inflation and economic activity betas. Then, the univariate inflation beta we reported before, $\hat{\beta}_\pi$, can be decomposed as:

$$\hat{\beta}_\pi = \beta_\pi + \beta_{ip}\frac{\text{cov}(\text{inflation, ip})}{\text{var}(\text{inflation})}$$

where *ip* indicates industrial production growth and the βs on the right-hand side indicate the true inflation and industrial production betas from the multivariate regression. The ratio multiplying β_{ip} is the beta in a univariate regression of industrial production growth onto inflation and has the sign of the covariance between

Table 4. Effect of industrial production growth on inflation betas

	Inflation beta		Inflation beta accommodating industrial production growth	
	Bonds	Stocks	Bonds	Stocks
Developed	0.31 (0.14)	−0.12 (0.29)	0.30 (0.15)	−0.33 (0.29)
Emerging	0.97 (0.43)	1.02 (0.07)	−0.85 (0.29)	1.06 (0.04)
North America	0.27 (0.36)	−0.42 (0.81)	0.12 (0.40)	−0.04 (0.75)
Latin America	0.48 (0.62)	1.06 (0.07)	−2.89 (0.49)	1.08 (0.04)
Asia	−0.71 (0.45)	−0.50 (0.34)	−1.05 (0.38)	−0.62 (0.42)
Africa	0.25 (0.14)	1.85 (1.61)	−0.67 (0.36)	−2.73 (0.79)
Oceania	0.15 (0.40)	−0.56 (0.92)	0.21 (0.40)	0.38 (0.84)
EU	0.30 (0.15)	0.27 (0.43)	0.34 (0.17)	0.03 (0.43)
Non-EU Europe	1.38 (0.56)	0.44 (0.44)	0.36 (0.75)	0.93 (0.29)

Notes: The estimates on the left-hand side are from a pooled regression of bond or stock returns on inflation. We run the regression twice, once allowing for different coefficients for developed and emerging markets; once allowing for different coefficients across the different regional groups listed in the table. These estimates are very close to the ones reported in Table 1, but represent eight fewer countries. The estimates on the right-hand side come from similar but multivariate regressions on inflation (annualized), and industrial production growth, where only the inflation beta is reported. Hansen–Hodrick (1980) standard errors are between parentheses.

inflation and industrial production growth. For stock returns, the industrial production beta is likely positive, so that a preponderance of stagflations (a negative covariance between inflation and industrial production) would tend to make the univariate beta underestimate the true inflation beta. For bonds, the industrial production beta may actually be negative, as it is conceivable that real interest rates are pro-cyclical.

The table reveals that the inflation betas do increase for stock returns in North America, Oceania and non-EU Europe, once we control for industrial production, but we also observe some strong decreases, as in Africa for instance. Given that economic activity correlates positively with the stock market, a coefficient increase implies that on average the negative correlation between inflation and the stock market reflects a negative correlation between economic activity and inflation. It also explains why the recent crisis episode, with low inflation during bad economic times, has in fact increased the comovement of inflation and stock returns. That the coefficient decreases are concentrated in emerging markets may be related to the fact that we use nominal industrial production growth, and episodes of very high inflation may naturally induce a positive correlation between industrial production and inflation. We therefore put less emphasis on the emerging markets results. For bonds, we mostly observe decreases in betas. If the world is on average stagflationary, then this may reflect a negative industrial production beta for bond returns. An alternative possibility is that the shorter samples for bond returns reduce the incidence of stagflationary periods. Overall, once standard errors are taken into account, economic activity does not change our overall conditions. For developed markets, stocks and bonds remain poor inflation hedges.

2.2. Inflation betas for other asset classes

Many other assets have been suggested as potentially good inflation hedges. In this section, we expand the menu of assets to (short-term) Treasury bills, foreign bonds, real estate and gold. Treasury bills are riskless in nominal terms for the horizon equal to their maturity. The Treasury bills in our sample are either of the one-month or three-month maturity. For simplicity, we assume a flat term structure between one-month and three-month maturities, and create an annual return on Treasury bills by cumulating 12 end-of-month T-bill (gross) returns. The advantage of Treasury bill returns is that they can rapidly adjust to changes in (expected) inflation; however, they may therefore also not build in risk premiums for inflation risk, and may perform poorly when large, unexpected inflation shocks hit.

The return variation of foreign bonds is dominated by variation in currency values. Because long-term changes in currency values tend to reflect long-term relative inflation rates – that is, Purchasing Power Parity is a reasonable long-term model for exchange rates – foreign bonds may provide good insurance against inflation shocks, at least in the medium to long run. To avoid proliferation of potential assets to investigate, we create an equally weighted index of four major bond markets, representing the four major currency blocks: the dollar, the euro (deutsche mark), the pound and the yen. That is, we create an index of US, German, UK and Japanese government bonds. For the United States, Germany, the United Kingdom and Japan, only three foreign bonds are used in the portfolio.

For many households, a house represents the ultimate 'real' asset. However, the use of residential house prices would entail a host of data and interpretative problems that we want to avoid here. Therefore, we obtained data from EPRA, the European Public Real Estate Association, which maintains an extensive international data set on publicly traded real estate companies. Nevertheless, our data sample is reduced to 25 instead of 46 countries, and the earliest starting point for the return series is January 1990.

Finally, commodity investments have recently started to become a popular alternative asset class and may potentially serve as a natural hedge for inflation. If commodity prices are an important driver of inflation movements, it is conceivable that commodity price index changes may be highly correlated with general inflation. However, it is not that obvious that commodities really constitute a great inflation hedge. First, the relationship between commodity prices and actual inflation is complex, and varies through time. For example, in the past, oil price shocks typically passed through powerfully into general inflation, but more recently their effect has been more subdued, perhaps because of increased globalization, or because of competitive effects through 'cheap' Chinese exports abroad. Whatever it may be, the relationship does not appear stable over time. Second, and more importantly, exposure to commodities is typically accomplished through commodity futures. However, it is not clear at all that the returns to commodity futures, which are contracts in zero net supply, are highly correlated with inflation. Erb and Harvey (2006) show that while an index of commodity futures returns has a positive and significant unexpected inflation beta, its different components have betas that vary wildly across different commodities, and are often counterintuitive. They suspect that the inflation beta of the index is not stable at all over time. They also note that even a broad-based commodity futures index excludes many items measured in actual consumer price indices, used to compute inflation. Consequently, commodity futures are not likely effective inflation hedges. Nevertheless, gold has recently again received much popular attention as the safe asset that should protect against inflation shocks. We therefore obtained data on both spot gold prices (the GSCI index), and data on returns earned by going long gold in the futures market. For the latter, we actually use a total return index including the return on cash using T-bills.[5] We simply compute gold price changes to approximate the return on holding gold physically. Note that all gold returns and gold prices are in dollars and must be

[5] We thank Campbell Harvey for providing the gold price and futures data.

converted into local currency to assess their inflation hedging capability for each country. Hence, gold's hedging ability may also be due to currency movements, rather than to changes in gold prices *per se*.

The inflation betas for these four asset classes are contained in Tables 5 through 7. Table 5 considers inflation and unexpected inflation betas at the one year horizon, pooled over various country groups. The results for Treasury bills are as expected. The inflation betas are mostly between 0 and 1, but there is only one country group (non-EU Europe) for which the beta is not significantly different from 1. Treasury bills adjust to changes in inflation, but not sufficiently so. Not surprisingly, the Treasury bill betas with respect to unexpected inflation are lower still, and now go negative for about half the country groups, including North America. For foreign bonds, the coefficients are invariably positive and mostly not significantly different from 1. Hence, foreign bonds provide decent hedges for inflation shocks. This remains true for unexpected inflation shocks with the exception of North America, where the slope coefficient is –0.06, albeit very imprecisely estimated. The evidence for real estate is decidedly more mixed. The inflation beta is positive for North America, but negative for all other country groups for which we have data. For unexpected inflation betas, the coefficient also becomes positive for Asia. The inflation betas of gold investments are invariably positive and often quite large, especially for unexpected inflation betas. Of course, except for North America, these comovements may also partially reflect the hedging properties of foreign exchange exposure.

Tables 6 and 7 show the inflation and unexpected inflation betas, respectively, also for 3- and 5-year horizons. The inflation betas of Treasury bills with respect to both inflation and unexpected inflation mostly increase with horizon, but never become larger than 1. The inflation betas are now indistinguishable from 1 for five country groups, but the unexpected inflation betas are still significantly different from 1 for all groups. For foreign bonds, the betas either show little horizon variation (emerging markets), or they increase with the horizon. For example, the negative unexpected inflation beta for North America turns positive at the 5-year horizon, and becomes insignificantly different from 1. The real estate betas also increase with horizon. For gold the picture is more mixed, but in any case all betas are substantially positive at all horizons. A striking feature of all these results is that for emerging markets, inflation betas appear quite close to one, at all horizons. One possible interpretation is that inflation risk is relatively speaking a much more important risk in these economies that drives much of the variation in asset returns, whereas in developed markets, inflation shocks are of less importance. This potentially lowers the economic cost of the absence of an inflation-indexed security.

A contemporaneous article by Attié and Roache (2009), mostly focusing on the United States but containing some international results, mostly confirms our findings. Bonds, equities and real estate have negative unexpected inflation betas, but gold and commodities have positive betas. Using a vector autoregressive framework,

Table 5. Inflation betas for other asset classes

	Inflation beta					Unexpected inflation beta				
	Treasury bills	Foreign bonds	Real estate	Gold	Gold futures	Treasury bills	Foreign bonds	Real estate	Gold	Gold futures
Developed countries	0.54 (0.05)	1.65 (0.62)	−2.46 (0.91)	1.25 (0.40)	1.38 (0.49)	0.04 (0.06)	0.67 (0.34)	−0.43 (1.01)	2.30 (0.45)	2.36 (0.53)
Emerging countries	0.62 (0.09)	0.96 (0.03)		0.91 (0.03)	0.92 (0.03)	0.11 (0.06)	1.06 (0.03)		1.06 (0.03)	1.07 (0.03)
North America	0.53 (0.12)	0.11 (0.77)	2.04 (4.58)	1.45 (1.67)	1.24 (1.90)	−0.10 (0.16)	−0.06 (0.91)	2.19 (4.18)	3.96 (2.01)	2.92 (2.17)
Latin America	0.72 (0.11)	0.96 (0.03)		0.92 (0.03)	0.92 (0.03)	0.05 (0.10)	1.04 (0.03)		1.04 (0.03)	1.04 (0.03)
Asia	0.07 (0.07)	1.01 (0.05)	−0.20 (1.05)	0.94 (0.09)	0.93 (0.09)	−0.04 (0.06)	1.06 (0.09)	1.33 (1.54)	1.29 (0.17)	1.25 (0.17)
Africa	0.05 (0.15)	1.16 (0.38)		0.57 (0.43)	0.52 (0.45)	−0.05 (0.13)	0.98 (0.31)		0.81 (0.43)	0.78 (0.43)
Oceania	0.29 (0.11)	1.03 (0.48)	−2.18 (2.47)	1.10 (0.73)	1.29 (0.93)	−0.14 (0.16)	1.24 (0.52)	−1.93 (2.48)	2.19 (1.11)	2.52 (1.22)
EU	0.71 (0.06)	1.07 (0.10)	−4.33 (1.34)	0.99 (0.11)	1.01 (0.11)	0.01 (0.06)	1.12 (0.03)	−1.42 (1.36)	1.17 (0.07)	1.18 (0.07)
Non-EU Europe	0.70 (0.20)	0.86 (0.17)	−9.52 (3.27)	0.82 (0.16)	0.81 (0.16)	0.16 (0.14)	1.48 (0.21)	−8.50 (4.07)	1.46 (0.25)	1.43 (0.25)

Notes: The estimates here mimic the univariate regressions of Table 1, but use as the return series, Treasury bills, an equally weighted government bond return for four major markets, a local real estate return, and spot and futures gold returns.

Table 6. Inflation betas over longer horizons for other asset classes

	Treasury bills			Foreign bonds			Real estate			Gold			Gold futures		
	1-year horizon	3-year horizon	5-year horizon	1-year horizon	3-year horizon	5-year horizon	1-year horizon	3-year horizon	5-year horizon	1-year horizon	3-year horizon	5-year horizon	1-year horizon	3-year horizon	5-year horizon
Developed	0.54	0.70	0.79	1.65	2.01	2.30	−2.46	−1.44	−0.91	1.25	1.76	1.95	1.38	1.17	1.19
countries	(0.05)	(0.07)	(0.09)	(0.62)	(0.80)	(0.83)	(0.91)	(1.16)	(0.99)	(0.40)	(0.42)	(0.39)	(0.49)	(0.49)	(0.52)
Emerging	0.62	0.88	0.90	0.96	0.97	0.97				0.91	0.91	0.90	0.92	0.90	0.90
countries	(0.09)	(0.10)	(0.08)	(0.03)	(0.02)	(0.02)				(0.03)	(0.02)	(0.02)	(0.03)	(0.01)	(0.02)
North	0.53	0.64	0.72	0.11	0.81	2.10	2.04	4.19	8.03	1.45	2.13	2.07	1.24	0.27	−0.08
America	(0.12)	(0.16)	(0.17)	(0.77)	(1.09)	(1.07)	(4.58)	(4.93)	(4.36)	(1.67)	(0.95)	(0.58)	(1.90)	(0.60)	(0.55)
European	0.71	0.87	0.92	1.07	1.07	1.17	−4.33	−5.65	−5.73	0.99	1.01	1.13	1.01	0.91	0.92
Union	(0.06)	(0.08)	(0.09)	(0.10)	(0.13)	(0.21)	(1.34)	(2.12)	(1.94)	(0.11)	(0.16)	(0.25)	(0.11)	(0.12)	(0.17)

Notes: These regressions mimic the regressions in Table 2 but for different return series.

Table 7. Unexpected inflation betas over longer horizons for other asset classes

	Treasury bills			Foreign bonds			Real estate			Gold			Gold futures		
	1-year horizon	3-year horizon	5-year horizon	1-year horizon	3-year horizon	5-year horizon	1-year horizon	3-year horizon	5-year horizon	1-year horizon	3-year horizon	5-year horizon	1-year horizon	3-year horizon	5-year horizon
Developed	0.04	0.22	0.38	0.67	1.03	1.71	−0.43	−0.15	0.37	2.30	2.40	2.65	2.36	1.92	1.99
countries	(0.06)	(0.08)	(0.08)	(0.34)	(0.64)	(0.79)	(1.01)	(1.09)	(0.96)	(0.45)	(0.42)	(0.45)	(0.53)	(0.41)	(0.52)
Emerging	0.11	0.57	0.69	1.06	0.99	0.98				1.06	0.96	0.94	1.07	0.95	0.93
countries	(0.06)	(0.09)	(0.07)	(0.03)	(0.02)	(0.02)				(0.03)	(0.02)	(0.02)	(0.03)	(0.02)	(0.02)
North	−0.10	0.11	0.25	−0.06	−0.41	0.78	2.19	5.33	8.73	3.96	4.15	3.23	2.92	1.79	1.12
America	(0.16)	(0.10)	(0.06)	(0.91)	(1.02)	(1.12)	(4.18)	(4.27)	(3.80)	(2.01)	(1.13)	(0.70)	(2.17)	(1.03)	(0.97)
European	0.01	0.23	0.39	1.12	1.04	1.24	−1.42	−5.14	−5.15	1.17	1.09	1.35	1.18	0.97	1.07
Union	(0.06)	(0.08)	(0.10)	(0.03)	(0.13)	(0.26)	(1.36)	(1.65)	(1.48)	(0.07)	(0.22)	(0.35)	(0.07)	(0.16)	(0.25)

Notes: These regressions mimic the regressions in Table 3 but for different return series.

they find that it is difficult to protect a portfolio against unexpected inflation in the long term as well using traditional asset classes.

2.3. The stability of inflation betas

The large cross-sectional variation of inflation betas across country groups and horizons, given our varying sample sizes, may also reflect parameter instability. There are many reasons for the betas to change through time. We already discussed that an omitted variable such as economic activity may make the inflation beta hard to interpret and depend on the incidence of stagflations during the sample. An obvious and related cause for instability is the monetary policy regime. Recently, a great many countries have adopted explicit or implicit policies of inflation targeting, which may have caused inflation expectations to be more anchored and lower (see Mishkin and Schmidt-Hebbel, 2001), and more generally have changed its stochastic properties, including its correlation with asset returns. We would also expect that a proactive monetary policy would affect the hedging efficiency of index-linked bonds as it would lower inflation volatility and increase real interest rate volatility, potentially leading to higher correlations between nominal and index-linked bonds.

We conduct three different empirical exercises to examine parameter instability. First, using information in Mishkin and Schmidt-Hebbel (2001) and Mehrota and Sanchez-Fung (2009) we actually determine a date of the adoption of an inflation targeting monetary regime for 24 countries, 8 developed countries, and 16 emerging markets, which constitutes our first potential break date (see the data appendix for details). Because the number of countries is rather limited, Table 8 shows the results for only two groups, developed and emerging. Panel A contains the inflation betas, Panel B the unexpected inflation betas, in both cases for three different horizons. Pooling results across countries is absolutely necessary, as we find significant changes for only a few individual countries. The inflation betas of bond returns in developed markets are higher for inflation targeters, but the difference is only statistically significant at the 5-year horizon, where the coefficient is exactly 1 for inflation targeters. This result could indicate that inflation expectations are indeed better anchored in countries with inflation targeting regimes. For emerging markets, the bond inflation beta also is higher for targeters, and mostly significantly so, but there is not sufficient data to obtain results for the longer horizons. For stock returns in developed markets, there are no significant differences between the two groups. For emerging markets, it is striking that the betas decrease below 1, perhaps simply indicating that the magnitude of inflation shocks has decreased post inflation targeting.

Second, for the full country sample, we consider a break date in 1990, estimating different betas for the two periods. The inflation targeting adoption dates start in 1990 (New Zealand), with the last one being Venezuela in 2002. Generally, we expect the post-1990 sample to be more dominated by inflation targeting regimes and to have witnessed more active monetary policies. An appendix available on the web

Table 8. Stability of inflation betas across monetary policy regimes

	Bond pre-targeting			Bond post-targeting			Stock pre-targeting			Stock post-targeting		
	1-year horizon	3-year horizon	5-year horizon	1-year horizon	3-year horizon	5-year horizon	1-year horizon	3-year horizon	5-year horizon	1-year horizon	3-year horizon	5-year horizon
Panel A: Inflation betas												
Developed	−0.28	−0.31	−0.28	−0.38	0.38	0.96***	−1.31	−1.43	−1.40	−2.20	−2.64	−0.76
countries	(0.22)	(0.22)	(0.22)	(0.38)	(0.56)	(0.22)	(0.57)	(0.54)	(0.46)	(1.30)	(1.38)	(0.74)
Emerging	−1.76	N/A	N/A	−0.43*	N/A	N/A	1.12	1.10	1.11	−0.01*	0.22**	0.42**
countries	(0.69)			(0.42)			(0.05)	(0.02)	(0.01)	(0.58)	(0.38)	(0.29)
Panel B: Unexpected inflation betas												
Developed	−0.99	−0.78	−0.44	−0.41	−0.58	0.24**	−1.79	−1.93	−1.91	−1.81	−2.89	−2.04
countries	(0.35)	(0.12)	(0.16)	(0.37)	(0.38)	(0.21)	(0.71)	(0.52)	(0.46)	(1.23)	(1.67)	(1.02)
Emerging	−2.06	N/A	N/A	−0.35***	N/A	N/A	1.13	1.09	1.12	−0.64***	0.27	0.47**
countries	(0.47)			(0.41)			(0.06)	(0.01)	(0.01)	(0.54)	(0.53)	(0.30)

Notes: The estimates in Panel A are from a pooled regression of bond or stock returns on inflation. We run the regression allowing for different coefficients for developing and emerging markets. The estimates for Panel B come from a similar but multivariate regression on expected and unexpected inflation, where only the second coefficient is reported. Standard errors are between parentheses. The regressions are run for the countries which adopted inflation targeting during the sample period (see Appendix A). The coefficients are pre and post the monetary policy regime reported in Appendix A. The asterisk after the second column indicates whether a test for parameter stability rejects at the 10% (*), 5% (**) or 1% (***) level. N/A indicates that there were no data for that part of the sample and/or that country group.

reports the results, which we briefly summarize here. Note that results for the Emerging, Latin America and Africa pre-1990 groups are missing, because our data typically start after 1990. We do have an emerging category for stocks, but the number of data points before 1990 is relatively limited. Panel A reports the inflation betas for three different horizons. For bonds, the betas generally decrease, even turning negative from positive in a few cases (Asia and North America). One exception is non-EU Europe where the betas increase. The decrease in beta is significant at the 1% level for the developed markets group, for Asia and for the EU countries. For stocks we observe the same decreasing beta phenomenon, except for the EU countries. Here, the decrease in beta is significant for the emerging markets group, for Latin America, Asia and for Oceania. The longer horizon betas follow qualitatively a similar pattern. Panel B reports the unexpected inflation betas. In contrast to the inflation betas, the unexpected inflation betas for bonds are typically increasing post-1990. They mostly remain negative though, and the change is never significant at the 5% level. When viewed over different horizons, the pre-1990 betas increase strongly with horizon, but the post-1990 betas mostly increase only slowly with horizon. Consequently, at long horizons, several unexpected inflation betas are significantly below 1, and they are significantly lower than pre-1990 betas in several cases. For stock returns, there are no clear patterns in the betas across time, and for the longer horizon betas, only one test rejects stability at the 5% level (the Asia group). For the one-year horizon, however, there is a significant change in beta at the 5% level for five country groupings, the steep decreases in beta for North America and the EU being the most striking.

Third, for the United States, we can collect data going even further back than 1970. We collected bond and stock returns from 1960 onwards. A table appendix available on the web reports break tests for the United States, using four different break dates: the beginning of 1973, the start of a turbulent stagflationary period with two oil shocks; 1980, the date often mentioned by monetary economists as representing a break in monetary policy from accommodating to more active (see Boivin, 2006; Moreno, 2004); and finally 1990 and 2000. The results are perhaps surprising: there are almost no significant breaks in the coefficients. Where we do see some significance (at the 5% and 10% levels) is for the unexpected inflation beta of bonds and stocks with 1980 as the break point. The bond beta becomes more negative and the stock beta less negative. If the negative stock return inflation relationship reflects stagflationary periods, we would indeed expect it to be less prevalent after 1980. Moreover, the break we detect in 2000, where the coefficient goes from almost –4.0 to 2, is no surprise either, given the recent crisis. The bond result is somewhat hard to interpret, the more that the beta post-1990 and 2000 is again substantially less negative. In other words, the negative coefficient is really driven by the 1980s, and could perhaps be associated with the Volcker period, after which agents were positively surprised by inflation decreasing faster than expected.

2.4. Tracking inflation

While one security by itself may not prove a particularly good inflation hedge, it is possible that a portfolio of several securities hedges inflation quite well. To investigate this possibility, we create an inflation mimicking portfolio from our menu of our assets, a government bond index, local Treasury bills, a foreign bond index, the local stock market, gold returns, gold futures return, and a real estate index. Because gold spot and futures returns are substantially correlated, the gold futures series is eliminated from the portfolio. To find the inflation mimicking portfolio, we minimize the variance of the residuals of a regression of inflation on the asset returns, where the regression coefficients are constrained to add to one. This can be interpreted as a minimum variance portfolio problem, and we solve for the asset weights using simple covariance formulas. We explicitly do not constrain the weights to be positive, as the fact that the portfolio problem wants to short an asset is particularly informative. An Appendix provides more technical background.

We conduct this exercise for each country; and Table 9, Panel A averages the portfolio weights over various country groups. The results reveal that Treasury bills receive most of the portfolio weight. Only for non-EU Europe do other assets play a meaningful role. The numbers between parentheses represent the cross-sectional standard deviation of the weights across individual countries. Clearly, while there is substantial dispersion of the weights across countries, the weight on Treasury bills must be almost invariably high and the weights on the other assets rather small. While it is tempting to conclude that Treasury bills are the ideal asset to track inflation, it is important to realize that the portfolio problem minimizes a variance. The problem with the inflation mimicking exercise is that most asset returns are more variable than inflation, so that the positive weights may also reflect to a large extent the variance reducing properties of the assets, rather than their ability to hedge inflation risk. This explains why Treasury bills receive weights close to 1, as they simply are by far the lowest variability asset.

To see this more clearly, in Panel B we simply report the results from an unconstrained mimicking problem (which is equivalent to regressing inflation on the various asset returns and recording the coefficients). We also report the R^2, the variability of the 'portfolio return' divided by the variance of inflation. These R^2s tend to be larger for emerging markets than for developed markets, but this, unfortunately, does not necessarily reflect the existence of a better hedge portfolio. Most of the asset weights are actually negative. For emerging markets, foreign bonds receive positive weights here and there; for developed markets, T-bills have small positive weights.[6] For domestic bonds, the highest coefficient observed is barely 1%; for stocks all coefficients for all country groups are negative. In short, it is next to impossible to use an individual asset or a portfolio of assets to adequately hedge inflation risk.

[6] The large standard deviations for emerging markets reflect outlier estimates for Chile and Morocco.

Table 9. Tracking inflation

	Stocks	Bonds	Foreign bond	Real estate	Gold spot	T-bills	R^2
Panel A: Constrained weights							
All	−0.012	−0.060	0.024	0.009	0.059	1.005	
	(0.038)	(0.206)	(0.188)	(0.027)	(0.077)	(0.298)	
Developed	−0.004	−0.012	−0.037	0.009	0.064	0.981	
	(0.028)	(0.104)	(0.067)	(0.027)	(0.048)	(0.102)	
Emerging	−0.020	−0.104	0.078	n/a	0.054	1.028	
	(0.044)	(0.262)	(0.240)		(0.096)	(0.404)	
North America	0.003	−0.015	−0.006	0.027	0.075	0.917	
	(0.003)	(0.071)	(0.043)	(0.010)	(0.002)	(0.037)	
Latin America	−0.032	−0.071	0.114	n/a	0.007	0.982	
	(0.030)	(0.103)	(0.127)		(0.092)	(0.173)	
Asia	−0.018	−0.134	0.009	−0.018	0.065	1.156	
	(0.039)	(0.176)	(0.256)	(0.034)	(0.074)	(0.257)	
Africa	−0.044	−0.188	0.212	n/a	−0.003	1.024	
	(0.059)	(0.205)	(0.311)		(0.121)	(0.110)	
Oceania	−0.011	−0.161	−0.026	0.018	0.095	1.084	
	(0.035)	(0.020)	(0.002)	(0.007)	(0.057)	(0.102)	
EU	−0.008	−0.036	−0.054	0.011	0.062	1.028	
	(0.025)	(0.160)	(0.088)	(0.027)	(0.055)	(0.151)	
Non-EU Europe	0.038	0.222	0.150	0.006	0.133	0.455	
	(0.053)	(0.442)	(0.173)	(0.033)	(0.092)	(0.646)	
Panel B: Unconstrained weights							
All	−0.017	−0.064	0.036	−0.004	0.011	−0.159	0.484
	(0.033)	(0.165)	(0.170)	(0.017)	(0.055)	(2.888)	(0.250)
Developed	−0.004	−0.023	−0.007	−0.004	0.012	0.149	0.342
	(0.022)	(0.064)	(0.033)	(0.017)	(0.025)	(0.363)	(0.209)
Emerging	−0.028	−0.101	0.073	n/a	0.010	−0.442	0.609
	(0.037)	(0.215)	(0.227)		(0.072)	(4.004)	(0.216)
North America	−0.004	0.007	−0.020	0.009	0.011	0.231	0.248
	(0.005)	(0.055)	(0.047)	(0.014)	(0.018)	(0.054)	(0.013)
Latin America	−0.032	−0.079	0.093	n/a	0.006	−0.281	0.695
	(0.037)	(0.079)	(0.175)		(0.069)	(3.433)	(0.159)
Asia	−0.017	−0.068	0.017	−0.025	0.043	0.923	0.614
	(0.044)	(0.255)	(0.226)	(0.041)	(0.055)	(1.171)	(0.234)
Africa	−0.043	−0.272	0.190	n/a	−0.022	−6.355	0.470
	(0.072)	(0.305)	(0.235)		(0.064)	(9.259)	(0.238)
Oceania	−0.034	−0.068	−0.022	0.003	0.040	−0.274	0.457
	(0.005)	(0.129)	(0.018)	(0.015)	(0.010)	(0.342)	(0.413)
EU	−0.007	−0.043	−0.010	−0.001	−0.0004	0.079	0.311
	(0.012)	(0.048)	(0.030)	(0.004)	(0.021)	(0.254)	(0.156)
Non-EU Europe	−0.008	0.011	0.135	−0.015	−0.031	0.035	0.531
	(0.009)	(0.113)	(0.277)	(0.020)	(0.102)	(0.289)	(0.306)

Notes: For each country, we find the portfolio weights that minimize the squared tracking error with inflation and then aggregate these weights over various country groups. In Panel A, the weights sum to 1; in Panel B, they are unconstrained. For each weight, the number between parentheses indicates the cross-sectional standard deviation of the weights across countries.

A recent article by Bruno and Chincarini (2010) attempts a similar portfolio tracking exercise for a slightly different menu of assets, while also requiring a certain minimum real return. They also find a role for Treasury bills and no role at all for equities, but their results may also be driven by the variance reducing properties of Treasury bills.

3. THE INFLATION RISK PREMIUM

The inflation risk premium is the compensation investors demand to protect themselves against inflation risk. In this section, we decompose nominal bond yields into three economically important components including the inflation risk premium. We then discuss how the recent term structure literature has attempted to identify these components and summarize some concrete estimates of the inflation risk premium.

3.1. Definition and general identification

To understand how the inflation risk premium relates to bond yields, consider the following equation:

$$\begin{aligned} \underset{\text{Nominal rate}}{y_t^n} &= \underset{\text{Real rate}}{r_t^n} + \underset{\text{Expected inflation}}{E_t[\pi_{t+n,n}]} + \underset{\text{Inflation risk premium}}{\varphi_{t,n}} \\ &= r_t^n + \underset{\text{Inflation compensation/Break even inflation rate}}{\pi_{t,n}^e} \end{aligned} \tag{2}$$

Here, y_t^n is the yield on a nominal zero-coupon bond of maturity n; r_t^n is the yield on a perfectly indexed zero coupon bond of maturity n. The difference between the two is often called 'inflation compensation' or sometimes 'breakeven inflation rate', as it constitutes the inflation rate that *ex post* would make the nominal yields on both bonds equivalent. Inflation compensation economically consists of two components. The first is simply expected inflation; the second is the inflation risk premium.

A well-known theory of interest rate determination due to Fisher (1930), holds that the inflation risk premium ought to be zero. If true, there is no expected benefit to the government of issuing inflation protected securities. While actual inflation may differ from expected at any given time, unless systematic biases exist, the inflation surprises should cancel out over time, so that there is no expected benefit or cost to issuing TIPS over Treasuries. Most believe there is indeed an inflation risk premium. However, it need not be positive. It is tempting to conclude that the inflation risk premium is linked to the uncertainty or volatility of inflation, but its economic determinants are in most modern pricing models a bit more subtle. It is easy to show that the inflation risk premium should be positive if inflation is high in 'bad times'. If inflation would always occur when agents are exceedingly happy, they would not need an inflation risk premium.[7] Of course, this correlation between the wealth or consumption of agents and inflation may well vary through time, and

[7] In the parlance of modern finance, what is required is a positive correlation between the real 'pricing kernel' and inflation. The pricing kernel takes on high values in bad states of the world, because risk averse economic agents want to move consumption and wealth into these states, and they are therefore relatively expensive. In alternative models, pure uncertainty about future states of the world may generate risk premiums as well.

cause substantial correlation in the conditional inflation risk premium. Campbell *et al.* (2009) note that the current positive correlation between inflation and stock returns (as an indicator of 'wealth') may well mean that the inflation premium is now negative in the United States.

How can we identify the different components? At first blush, it looks like an easy task. Indexed bonds deliver r_t^n; inflation forecasts deliver the second term, and subtracting both of the obviously observable nominal yields gives us an estimate of the inflation risk premiums, for any horizon we fancy. Unfortunately, it is not that easy. TIPS have only existed for about 13 years, and, as we argue below, the first 7 years are likely not usable in any estimation. Inflation forecasting is at best an imprecise and difficult business. So, we are left with data on nominal yields and actual (not expected) inflation in most cases, although more recent studies have tried to expand the information used (see below). In other words, an econometrician would not view the task as easy but as impossible.

Over the years, a great many approaches have been used to identify the components in Equation (2). It is fair to say that in modern asset pricing, techniques have converged to the following approach:

- Formulate a no arbitrage term structure model that prices nominal and real bonds. The no arbitrage condition ensures that the pricing is consistent across the curve and across time. The modelling involves a stochastic process for a 'pricing kernel' that prices the bond's payoffs and is consistent with a number of economic principles and stochastic processes for a number of 'factors', that are deemed relevant for pricing the term structure (TS, henceforth). In some standard models, these factors could be the 'level', 'slope', and 'curvature' of the yield curve.
- Formulate an inflation model and link it to the TS model. This model should be consistent with data on inflation and hopefully, in conjunction with term structure data, yield accurate expected inflation numbers.
- Estimate the model using as much data as possible, but data on inflation and nominal bond yields are a must.

The estimated model then implies an inflation risk premium. This approach obviously suffers from an identification problem: The model has to be general enough so as to not impose restrictions on the findings, but some restrictions will be necessary so as to achieve identification of essentially three unobserved components with two sets of information (nominal yields and inflation). We revisit this identification problem later, and Box 1 provides some additional intuition.

Box 1. Identification in no-arbitrage term structure models

In most no-arbitrage term structure models, there are a number of exogenous factors or state variables driving the term structure, which are typically assumed to follow a particular stochastic process (say, a Gaussian vector autoregression), with a particular heteroskedasticity structure. In addition, there is a stochastic process for the 'pricing kernel', which prices all bonds. A strictly positive pricing kernel imposes no arbitrage, so that the pricing kernel is typically modelled in logs. In an economic model, the pricing kernel would correspond to the Intertemporal Marginal Rate of Substitution. The pricing kernel will contain the shocks to different factors multiplied by coefficients (these may be even time-varying processes) that capture how the shocks are 'priced', the so-called 'prices of risk'. Because the model contains latent variables, a first identification problem is simply to ensure that these variables are uniquely identified, requiring a number of parametric restrictions on the processes (see Dai and Singleton (2000) for a discussion of how to accomplish this for affine models). In addition, to identifying N prices of risk in linear models, at least $N + 1$ bonds are required. For example, with a short bond and a long bond, the term spread can identify one price of risk. Non-linearities, such as present in the ABW model (Ang *et al.*, 2008; see Section 3.2), may actually help identification.

The models discussed in the text differ from standard models, as the real and nominal side is differentiated. The nominal pricing kernel (in logs) equals the real pricing kernel minus (logarithmic) inflation, and an observable series, inflation, is typically added to the mix of data. The inflation time series by itself, and the assumption of rational expectations, often suffices to identify expected inflation. Without data on TIPS, however, nominal term spreads and their correlation with inflation must somehow identify both the inflation risk premium and real rates. Given a sufficient number of bonds, and a sufficiently parsimonious model, this is theoretically feasible, but often practically infeasible. It is often the case that the effect of key prices of risk parameters on real rates and on the inflation risk premium is similar and of opposite magnitude, making the average level of both indeterminate. To circumvent this problem, ABW imposed the inflation risk premium to be zero at the quarterly horizon. They then estimated a great many possible models and selected the best performing model to provide a decomposition of nominal yields into their three components. With another assumption on the one period inflation risk premium, the average level of real rates and the average level of the inflation risk premium would change accordingly. Models that bring information from TIPS and/or inflation forecasts to bear on the estimation problem obviously greatly reduce such identification problems.

3.2. Stylized facts regarding real rates and inflation risk premiums in the United States

A recent example of the just-described approach is Ang *et al.* (2008; hereafter, ABW). Their no-arbitrage term structure model is quite general. First, the model explicitly allows for the possibility that risk premiums vary through time, for example, with the business cycle. Second, the model accommodates 'regime switches' in interest rates. That is, certain parameters governing the behaviour of interest rates can abruptly change, potentially causing rapid changes in their mean or volatility, as has been observed in the data. Economically, regime switching behaviour can be generated by monetary policy changes or reflect business cycle variation, for example. Finally, the model allows arbitrary correlation between real rates and (expected) inflation. They use quarterly inflation and term structure data to estimate a large number of variants of the model over a fairly long period, 1952:Q1–2004:Q4. This long sample is important, as short samples may give a distorted view of long-term inflation risk premiums, especially if these premiums vary through time. ABW then select the model that best fits the data on the term structure, inflation, and their correlation and extract a set of stylized facts regarding real interest rates, expected inflation and the inflation risk premium, implied by the best model.

While not the focus of our discussion here, let us mention that ABW find that the term structure of real rates is, unconditionally, fairly flat around 1.24%, with a slight hump, peaking at a 1-year maturity. Real rates are quite variable at short maturities, consistent with an activist monetary policy buffeting short rates to affect inflation expectations, but smooth and persistent at long maturities. Campbell *et al.* (2009) argue that TIPS in the United States provide desirable insurance against future variation in real rates and therefore may carry a negative real term premium. Roll (2004) studies actual data on TIPS and finds the real curve to be flatter than the nominal curve. In the United Kingdom, recent evidence of declining real term premiums has been linked to demand pressures from institutional investors needing very long duration real exposure to hedge liabilities,[8] and perhaps similar factors may play a role in the United States as well. Nevertheless, formal estimates for the United Kingdom with data from 1983 to 1999 (see Risa, 2001) uncover solidly positive real term premiums.

Since the real rate curve is rather flat and the nominal yield curve in the United States is on average upward sloping, there must be, on average, a positive inflation risk premium that is increasing in maturity. Note that this is only true 'on average', because the expected inflation cannot have a maturity component, but at any given point of time, inflation expectations can also increase with maturity. Table 10 shows some properties of the inflation risk premium. The fact that the premium is about zero at the one quarter maturity is not a finding of the article, but rather an

[8] More specifically, the Pensions Act of 2004 requires UK pension funds to mark their liabilities to market, using discount rates derived from long-term (inflation-linked) government bonds (see Greenwood and Vayanos, 2010).

Table 10. Properties of the inflation risk premium in the United States

	Inflation regimes		
QTRS	1	2	Unconditional
1	−0.01 (0.01)	−0.01 (0.00)	−0.01 (0.01)
4	0.34 (0.11)	−0.14 (0.07)	0.31 (0.10)
12	0.98 (0.30)	0.12 (0.18)	0.91 (0.28)
20	1.19 (0.37)	0.48 (0.26)	1.14 (0.36)
	[normal]	[disinflation]	

Source: Ang *et al.* (2008).

imposed assumption to help overcome the identification problems imposed by Equation (2). It is clear that the inflation risk premium is generally positive and increases to over 1% at the 5-year horizon. ABW found two 'inflation regimes', a 'normal' regime where inflation is relatively high and the inflation risk premium substantial, and a regime in which inflation is decreasing (a disinflation regime) and inflation risk premiums are much smaller.

Figure 3 graphs the 5-year inflation risk premium over time. In general, the premium rose very gradually from about 75 basis points until the late 1970s, before entering a very volatile period during the monetary targeting period from 1979 to the early 1980s. It is then that the premium reached a peak of 2.04%. From then onwards, the trend appears downward, but with some rather big swings. During

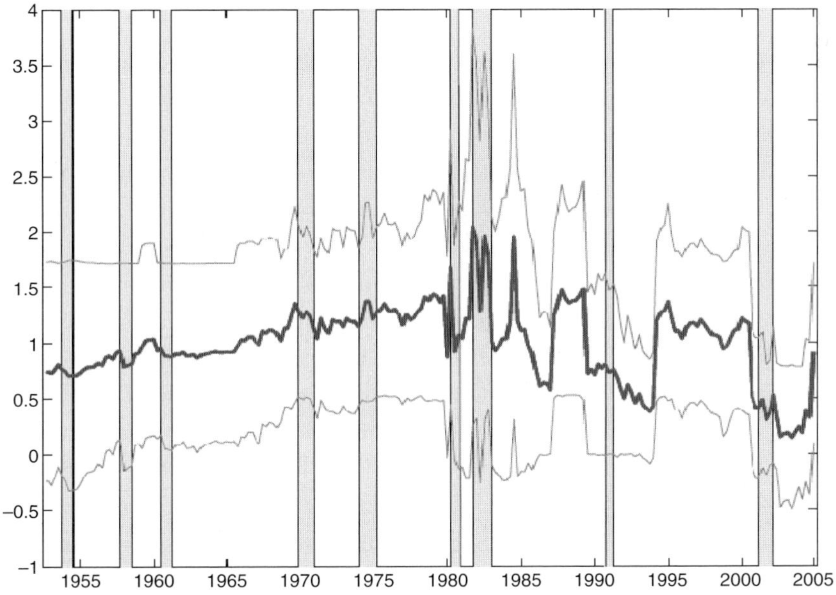

Figure 3. The inflation risk premium over time

Source: Ang *et al.* (2008). The dark line represents the inflation risk premium and the lighter lines a 90% confidence interval around the premium estimate.

the late 1990s equity bull market, the inflation premium remained relatively stable around 1%, then dropped to a low of 0.15% after the 2001 recession. Fears of deflation were apparent then. At the time of writing, the severe recession has significantly depressed the inflation risk premium. The long history in Figure 3 shows that the inflation risk premium has often decreased in recessions but it also shows that this situation may not last. It is surely conceivable that part of the variability we observe is due to estimation error (note the relatively wide confidence bands around the estimates), but alternative estimates for the United States (Buraschi and Jiltsov, 2005, for example), and for the United Kingdom (Risa, 2001) document similar variability in the inflation risk premium.

Because many investors have long investment horizons, it is of interest to compute inflation risk premiums for bonds with a longer duration. In the ABW model, zero coupon bonds of maturity 10 (20) years carry an inflation risk premium of 112 (84) basis points on average.[9]

3.3. Recent estimates of the inflation risk premium

The disadvantage of the ABW study is that it only uses nominal bond and inflation data. It would be obviously useful to test their findings with estimates that are informed by more data, in particular by data on inflation linked bonds. Recent research has tried to resolve the identification problem in Equation (2) by using data on index-linked bonds, and additional, exogenous information on inflation forecasts present in survey data.

3.3.1. The use of TIPS. With the exception of the United Kingdom, index-linked bonds in most developed countries have a fairly short history. This by itself limits their usefulness in extracting long-term inflation expectations and risk premiums. It is important, given the substantial time variation in inflation risk premiums discussed above, to use a fairly long history in assessing properties of the inflation risk premium. In the United States, we now have data on TIPS since 1997, which really does not represent sufficient data by itself, but the actual situation is worse, because of the poor liquidity of the TIPS market in its infancy years. Figure 4 shows the secondary market trading in TIPS over time. It increased tenfold, almost twice as much as the amount of TIPS outstanding. Bid-ask spreads in the TIPS market have decreased over time as well; market participation and turnover have generally increased. There is general agreement that the liquidity in the TIPS market has improved dramatically (see Roush *et al.*, 2008 for a detailed discussion). Moreover, the commitment made by the US government to the TIPS programme in 2002 helped resolve market uncertainty about the asset class. Today, the TIPS market is

[9] We thank Min Wei for computing these numbers. She also provided longer-duration numbers for the D'Amico *et al.* (2008) article, discussed in the next section.

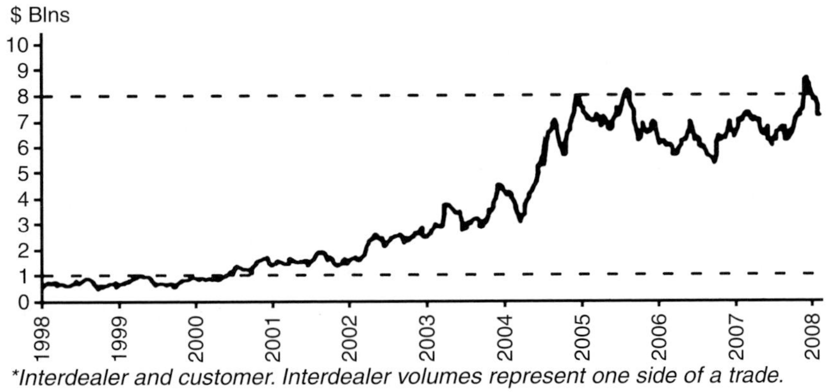

Figure 4. Treasury volume in the TIPS market

Source: Taken from Roush *et al.* (2008), Graph 2, Average Daily Secondary Market Trading Volume in TIPS. They used a 12-week moving average of the actual data.

liquid, but still not as liquid as the Treasury bond market. This seriously limits the usefulness of TIPS data in uncovering real yields. Denote zero coupon rates derived from TIPS, as $r_t^{n,\text{TIPS}}$. They can be thought of as consisting out of two components:

$$r_t^{n,\text{TIPS}} = r_t^n + LiQPR_t^n \tag{3}$$

where *LiQPR* represents a liquidity premium that may vary through time. The literature contains a number of liquidity premium estimates. Figure 5 presents a graph of the estimate by D'Amico *et al.* (2008). They compare a term structure model with and without TIPS to infer liquidity premiums. The liquidity premium is very large in the first 4 to 5 years (well over 1%), and then declines to hover below 50 basis points now. Gurkaynak *et al.* (2010) provide an alternative estimate, which

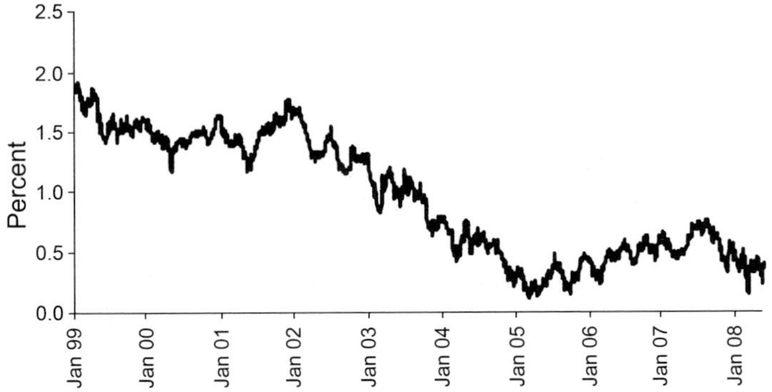

Figure 5. The illiquidity premium in the 10-year TIPS yield

Source: D'Amico *et al.* (2008).

shows the same secular decline, with again 2004 the critical year where liquidity premiums become relatively small.[10]

Nevertheless, the difference in liquidity between Treasuries and TIPS remains an issue even to date. When there is a flight to safety, as there was in the current crisis, investors flock to the most liquid security and liquidity premiums rise. This means that the most recent TIPS data may again reflect a sizeable liquidity premium. This liquidity problem is not limited to the United States, but applies to the euro area and even the United Kingdom as well: bid-ask spreads are invariably larger for the index-linked bonds, and time-varying liquidity premiums exist.

3.3.2. The use of survey forecasts. In many countries, there exist surveys of inflation forecasts by professionals and consumers. In the United States, there are a number of well-known surveys with a lengthy historical record, including the Livingston survey, the Michigan survey (consumers), and the SPF survey (Survey of Professional Forecasters). In a recent article, Ang *et al.* (2007) examine in much detail the quality of various forecasting methods for one-year-ahead annual inflation. In particular, they examine the out-of-sample forecasting performance of four different types of forecasting methods: time series models (which use past data on inflation to forecast future inflation); Phillips curve models (which link expected inflation to some measure of the 'output gap', a business cycle indicator); term structure models (which use nominal interest rates to forecast future inflation) and surveys, as mentioned above.

As already indicated, one of the most successful models is the random walk model, which simply uses the current inflation rate to forecast future inflation. However, ABW's main result is quite simple: Surveys consistently beat other models in terms of 'root mean squared error'; that is, the square root of the average squared forecasting errors. There are many potential reasons for the superior forecasting performance of the surveys: they may aggregate more information from more sources than is possible in most models, or may reflect information not present in any model (e.g. regarding policy decisions); they can also respond quickly to new information, whereas most models must assume some stability of existing relationships. ABW conjecture that the surveys perform well for all of these reasons: the pooling of large amounts of information, the efficient aggregation of this information and the ability to adapt quickly to major changes in the economic environment such as the drop in real volatility of the mid-1980s known as the Great Moderation, and now perhaps, the crisis conditions. This research suggests that the decomposition in (2) would benefit from using information in the surveys.

[10] The Federal Reserve Bank of Cleveland developed its own procedure to compute the liquidity risk premium but acknowledged it was no longer of practical use during the current crisis.

3.3.3. Recent estimates of the inflation risk premium. With this in mind, we searched the literature for recent studies that provide estimates of the inflation risk premium, using either information in inflation-linked bonds or surveys, or both. Table 11 mentions the studies and the various estimates for different maturities. Studies that use TIPS data *before* 2004 necessarily underestimate the inflation risk premium. That is because the high real interest rates observed then really reflected liquidity premiums, but not true real interest rates. When studies use TIPS data which likely embed significant liquidity premiums, we put an X in the line 'TIPS Problem'. The one US study that reports an average inflation risk premium that is negative (Grishchenko and Huang, 2010) suffers from this problem. In fact, they report negative inflation premiums before 2004 and slightly positive ones thereafter. The estimates in Christensen *et al.* (2008) are also likely downwardly biased, as they use TIPS from 2003 onwards. The picture emerging from the other three studies mentioned, however, is that the inflation risk premium is robustly positive. The magnitude differs, varying between 50 and over 200 basis points at the 10-year horizon. The larger estimates are more in line with previous studies, such as Buraschi and Jiltsov (2005), and Campbell and Viceira (2001).[11] We also report the sample period the various studies use. Taken together with the evidence in ABW, who use a very long sample period (1952–2004), it is striking that the inflation risk premium estimates are almost inversely related to the length of the sample period.

Table 11. Recent inflation risk premium estimates

Maturity in years	US					Euro		UK	
	HPR[a]	DKW	CM	GH	CLR	HT	GW	R	JLS
1	NA	35	19	NA	NA	NA	7	174	≈75
5	27	36	NA	−36 (−4)	0	25	25	184	≈100
10	51	64	216	6 (20)	0	0	NA	173	NA
20	82	NA	NA	NA	NA	NA	NA	NA	NA
30	101	NA	NA	NA	NA	NA	NA	NA	NA
TIPS		X		(X)	X		X	X	X
TIPS Problem				X		X			
Surveys	X	X	X	X			X		X
Start	1982	1990	1970	2000 (2004)	2003	1999	1999	1983	1992
End	2008	2007	2004	2008	2008	2006	2006	1999	2008

Notes: Full references for the studies mentioned here can be found in the reference list. The row 'TIPS' indicates that TIPS were used, but only in 'liquid' periods. The row 'TIPS Problem' refers to the fact that TIPS were used without accounting for (changes in) the liquidity premium. The row 'Surveys' indicates that survey forecasts were used to help identify expected inflation. The rows 'Start' and 'End' report the beginning and end of the sample period of the major data used in the study. For the GH study, we report estimates over a shorter 2004–2008 sample (which do not face a TIPS problem) in parentheses.

[a] They do not use TIPS data but use inflation swap rates from 2003 onwards.

[11] The estimate in Buraschi and Jiltsov (2005) is on average 70 basis points; in Campbell and Viceira (2001), albeit using a slightly different but related definition based on holding period returns, the estimate is 110 basis points.

Looking back at Figure 3, the estimates in ABW for the post 1999 period are also smaller and smoother than in the early part of the sample.

We also mention a few European studies. Both Hordahl and Tristani (2007) and Garcia and Werner (2010) find a very modest inflation premium of only 25 basis points at the 5-year horizon. However, it is likely that this low estimate reflects the short 1999–2006 sample period which was characterized by relatively subdued inflation. For the United Kingdom, where a long history of index-linked debt is available, we mention a recent study by Joyce *et al.* (2010), which does not report an average inflation risk premium, but does graph it over time. The graph confirms much of what was claimed in this study: the inflation risk premium is mostly positive, can be large, and varies considerably over time. Older studies, such as Evans (1998, 2003), stress the importance of time-varying inflation risk premiums in the United Kingdom, but surprisingly do not report estimates of their magnitude. There is one other unpublished study by Risa (2001), which fits an affine term structure model to UK nominal and index-linked gilts for data spanning 1983 to 1999. His inflation risk premium estimates exceed those reported for the United States by ABW (2008).

Ultimately, the variation in the estimates across the different studies reflects not only different methodologies, but also simply the use of different sample periods. Up until recently, the developed world witnessed a decade of relatively well-anchored inflation expectations and did not experience major shocks, which led to relatively low inflation risk premiums. Joyce *et al.* (2010) explicitly motivate starting the sample in 1992, because the United Kingdom adopted inflation targeting then, which they view as a structural break. D'Amico *et al.* (2009) restrict the sample period, because they fear that their model cannot handle the type of non-linear behaviour interest rates displayed during the 1980–82 period. However, the recent economic crisis and the clear signs that the Great Moderation has ended remind us of two problems all the studies reported in Table 11 face. First, unless we can convincingly argue that there has been a real permanent structural break, we should likely not rely on short samples to derive estimates of the unconditional properties of the inflation risk premium. Second, from the perspective of longer samples on interest rate and survey data, the affine (linear) structure all the models underlying Table 11 impose[12] is woefully inadequate. Term structure and survey data show significant non-linearities that these models cannot capture and which may well substantially affect our estimates of the inflation risk premium. For example, while survey inflation forecasts are currently moderate, the uncertainty about future inflation has certainly steeply increased over the last few years. Developing a tractable term structure model that accommodates both non-linearities and information from survey forecasts remains a considerable challenge for future research.

[12] The Haubrich *et al.* (2008) study does accommodate GARCH behaviour in volatility, but this will not suffice to capture the non-linearities present in interest rate and survey data.

4. TIPS TO THE RESCUE

Index-linked bonds protect investors against the risk of inflation by indexing the cash flows of the bonds to an inflation index. Consequently, such bonds potentially provide an important role in helping investors hedge an important economic risk. Here we provide a short summary of the potential benefits and costs of inflation protected bonds, ending the section with a brief survey of the experiences in the United States, the United Kingdom and the euro area. Lengthier discussions of the pros and cons of indexed debt with references to some of the quite old theoretical literature on the topic can be found in Campbell and Shiller (1996), Price (1997), Garcia and van Rixtel (2007) and Roush *et al.* (2008).

4.1. General benefits of inflation protected bonds

4.1.1. Market completeness, diversification and risk sharing. Because other securities are so imperfectly correlated with (unexpected) inflation, such bonds truly help financial markets become more complete, in the sense that financial markets should provide the possibility of getting payoffs under as many economic contingencies as possible. Given differences in risk aversion across investors, the co-existence of indexed bonds and of non-indexed bonds with inflation risk (and presumably higher returns), allows for overall better risk sharing (see Campbell and Shiller, 1996 for an elaborate discussion). This would make them almost surely overall welfare enhancing. It is also likely that the government is better able to shoulder inflation risk than individual investors (see van Ewijk, 2009), and it is even conceivable that indexed bonds would encourage people to save more, thereby potentially affecting the overall savings rate, and therefore economic growth.

Even if other securities could be used to (partially) hedge inflation risk, the existence of a long-term real safe asset would appear of great benefit to individual and institutional investors, especially if they have long-term liabilities. Institutional investors, such as pension funds and endowments, typically formulate a long-term ('strategic') asset allocation policy over broad asset classes. TIPS would constitute a perfect separate class: they represent a homogenous set of securities, and they likely display relatively low correlation with other assets, as there does not exist any other security that indexes away inflation risk. Moreover, at least in theory, we would expect the addition of TIPS to raise the 'utility' of the investor. For the aforementioned institutional investors, who typically use mean variance optimization to determine strategic asset allocations, TIPS should increase the optimal Sharpe ratio.

4.1.2. Market information on inflation expectations and real rates. As we discussed in Section 3, TIPS may potentially help provide market-based information on important economic variables, such as real interest rates and inflation expectations over different maturities. Such information is helpful for investors and policy-makers alike. Moreover, because this information is gleaned from market prices, it is available in real time, without any lag (as opposed to, for example, survey data on expected inflation).

4.1.3. Debt savings. If investors indeed fear inflation risk and demand compensation for incurring it when investing in nominal government bonds, the 'inflation risk premium' will be positive and an inflation index-linked bond will cost less to issue than a nominal bond of similar maturity, thereby reducing the debt costs of the government. As Campbell and Shiller (1996) point out, from a society's perspective, it is not at all clear that the government should try to minimize its financing costs. Nevertheless, it is quite likely that index-linked bonds may help to generate smooth, predictable financing costs in real terms, thereby averting distortionary taxation, which would be welfare enhancing (see also Roush *et al.*, 2008).

4.1.4. Inflation credibility. The existence of inflation-indexed bonds may even reduce the government's incentives to inflate (see Campbell and Shiller, 1996), although Fischer (1983) marshalls some evidence that indexed bonds increase an economy's sensitivity to price shocks. For the developed markets that have recently introduced TIPS, this would appear less important to begin with, as the central banks that set monetary policy should be independent of the Treasury (see Garcia and van Rixtel, 2007).

4.2. Costs to issuing inflation protected bonds

There is no doubt that TIPS markets have become increasingly important in many industrialized countries over the last decade, often experiencing rapid growth. Bloomberg now lists over 40 countries with index-linked debt, and major countries such as the United Kingdom, the United States, France, Australia, Canada and Japan all have important TIPS programmes. The existence of a government benchmark bond curve has spurred a thriving market in privately provided inflation derivatives in the United States and Europe. Yet, in all these markets, with the exception of the United Kingdom, the inflation-linked market still accounts for a minor, if rising, part of government debt. Given the distinct economic benefits of TIPS, why is that the case? Are governments reluctant to supply the bonds private agents are clamoring for, or are they simply sensing that the private demand does not warrant creating a new security? After all, the index-linked programmes started in a period of relatively low global inflation and inflation expectations.

It is likely impossible to even answer this question, but a critical examination of whether the *theoretical* benefits always hold *in practice* can provide a useful perspective.

4.2.1. Market completeness, diversification and risk sharing. If other financial assets were good inflation hedges, the case for indexed securities would be less compelling. We believe that our empirical evidence strongly suggests this is not the case, but opinions may differ and investors may mistakenly believe that their house, or gold investments will adequately protect them against inflation shocks. Briere and Signori (2009), for example, claim that inflation-linked bonds in the United States no longer provide meaningful diversification benefits relative to nominal bonds post 2003. From the government's perspective, there are, of course, real costs involved in setting up a new programme to issue bonds, indexed to inflation. Therefore, the benefits must be substantial enough to motivate expending the costs. Ensuring that the market is viable takes time, effort and commitment and it may not work. For example, in Japan, local institutional investors have proved very reluctant to invest in index-linked bonds (see Kitamura, 2009). If the welfare benefits are dramatic, you may wonder why not more private entities have issued index-linked bonds, and why the private market cannot create an inflation derivatives market by itself. Yet, the existence of a default-free benchmark is likely too important for this to happen. Finally, it is conceivable that certain governments feel they already shoulder too much inflation risk through other programmes, such as Social Security programmes.

4.2.2. Market information on inflation expectations and real rates. Most major central banks appear to make use of the information provided by TIPS markets; yet the interpretation of TIPS yields is far from simple. While they should represent a market reading on real interest rates, if the market has relatively poor liquidity, the TIPS rate may also reflect a liquidity premium, which may vary through time. Moreover, gleaning information about inflation expectations by comparing nominal and real rates is not only complicated by this liquidity premium, but also by the potential presence of an inflation risk premium, which also varies through time.

4.2.3. Debt savings. A reduction in debt costs is far from guaranteed. First, as mentioned before, the inflation risk premium theoretically need not be positive. Second, the new securities may lack liquidity, leading investors to demand a liquidity premium which drives up issuance costs. These liquidity premiums have been quite important in all major markets, and may make some governments doubt the usefulness of introducing TIPS, while TIPS-issuing countries refrain from increasing the relative supply.

4.2.4. Inflation credibility. The original argument against inflation-indexed bonds, especially in inflation prone countries, is that they would lead to less commitment to fight inflation, as indexed bonds made its effects less onerous. This argument seems of no consequence for the industrialized countries that introduced

TIPS recently, which all have independent central banks, keen on establishing anti-inflation credibility. Perhaps it does explain why TIPS were introduced in many major markets only when this inflation credibility was firmly established.

4.3. Concrete experiences with TIPS

Here we offer some quick comments on the experiences of three developed markets with inflation-protected bonds, the United Kingdom, France and the euro area, and finally, the United States, on which we focus most attention. This is warranted as the US TIPS market has become the largest index-linked market with over $500 billon outstanding at the end of 2008.

4.3.1. The United Kingdom. The UK programme is the oldest programme, with the UK government issuing indexed gilts since 1981. Importantly, the index-linked market is an important part of the total gilt market, representing close to 30% of the total market at the end of 2008, making it the largest index-linked programme in relative terms. Changes in UK financial regulation did prove critical in further boosting demand for indexed gilts. The Pension Act of 2004 requires pension funds to prove that they can meet their future liabilities, which has led to a strong demand for long-dated indexed gilts.

Deacon and Andrews (1996) estimate that, from the year of their introduction in 1982, to 1993, indexed gilts *ex post* reduced the cost of issuing government debt, and that, *ex ante*, the cost should be lower as the inflation risk premium is likely positive. Nevertheless, they also mention the presence of a positive liquidity premium making index-linked bonds more expensive than nominal bonds. Reschreiter (2008) still claims that nominal bonds embedded an *ex ante* risk premium for the 1984–2006 period, but indexed bonds did not, indicating there is indeed a positive inflation risk premium, which may lead to government savings in issuing indexed debt.

4.3.2. The euro area and France. France first introduced indexed Treasury bonds (the so-called OATis) in 1998. An issue of special interest in the euro area is to what inflation index these bonds should be indexed. France first used its local CPI, excluding tobacco. Later on, it started to issue bonds indexed to the HICP (the Harmonized Index of Consumer Prices), again excluding tobacco. The HICP is the euro-wide price index in terms of which the European Central Bank defines price stability, and it is regularly published by Eurostat. This index has now become the market benchmark in the euro area, with other countries issuing inflation-protected bonds (Italy, Greece and Germany) and financial products (swaps, futures) linked to it. The euro-area government linked bond market has now overtaken the UK market to become the second largest linker market in the world behind the United States, both in terms of outstanding amounts and turnover (see

Garcia and van Rixtel, 2007 for some relevant data). While the index linked market in the euro area may continue to experience rapid growth, initially there were teething problems, and the market was not very liquid. Yet, Bardong and Lehnert (2004) claim that even in its early days the market provided efficiency benefits in a mean-variance context.

A very important issue within the euro area is whether there should be bonds indexed to country-specific CPI indices, or whether any country issuing inflation-linked debt should use the euro-wide HICP. We believe that there are good reasons to use the euro-wide index. First, the experiences of various index-linked programmes teach us that it is not easy to build a liquid, credible bond market. Standardization should enhance liquidity, deepen the market, and further spur the development of derivative contracts. From this perspective, it may even make sense to institute a joint issuing programme across the euro member countries. Second, there is empirical evidence that inflation rates have substantially converged within the EU (see, e.g., Bekaert and Wang, 2009), although there is no guarantee that future events will not lead to occasional divergences.

4.3.3. The United States. The United States started issuing TIPS in 1997. While the TIPS programme in the United States initially met with some enthusiasm (see Sack and Elsasser, 2004), the programme grew rather slowly. Figure 6 shows the outstanding amount of TIPS, which grew from around \$150 billion at the end of the 1990s to close to \$500 billion at the end of 2008. The Treasury affirmed its commitment to the programme in 2002.

TIPS only gained very slow traction with individual investors. The left-hand side scale of Figure 6 shows the growth in assets under management in mutual funds focusing on TIPS, which was very gradual until about 2004, then

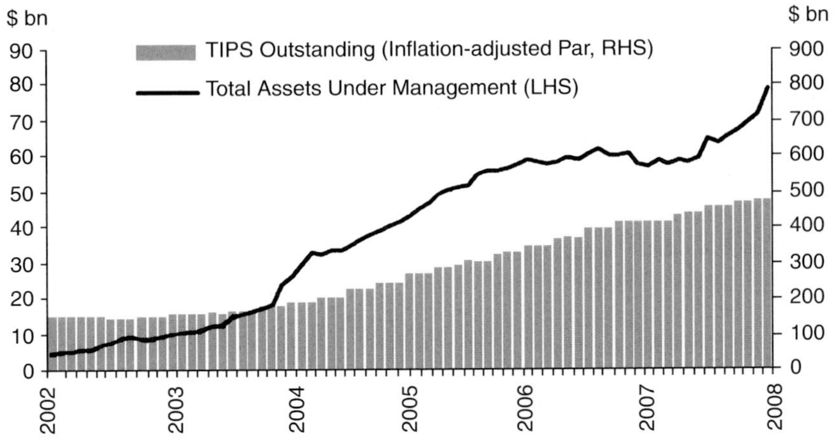

Figure 6. TIPS: Assets under management and outstanding amount

Source: Taken from Graph 3 in Roush *et al.* (2008).

accelerated to reach $80 billion at the end of 2008. TIPS were more of a success among institutional investors. In fact, many pension funds and endowments in the United States decided to create a new strategic asset class, comprising TIPS. For example, one of the largest endowments, Harvard Management Company (HMC) introduced TIPS as a new asset class with a 7% strategic asset allocation in 2000.[13]

As we argued before, it made perfect sense to introduce TIPS as a new asset class. The team at HMC concluded that TIPS increase the optimal Sharpe ratio, and formal research by Kothari and Shanken (2004) and Roll (2004) also suggest that TIPS would receive an important weight in an efficient portfolio.

But, not all was well with TIPS. An asset class should also have a sufficiently large market capitalization to absorb the demands of institutional and other investors and its market environment should show sufficient liquidity to allow active trading. Both conditions were not satisfied in the early years of the TIPS market. These problems potentially undermine some of the purported benefits of TIPS. For example, extracting information about real yields proved difficult. As a concrete example, when HMC, in 2000, introduced TIPS as a new asset class, it changed its long-run real interest rate from 2% to 3.5%. The primary reason was that its analysts observed real yields in the TIPS market substantially higher than 2%, and more of the order of 4%. This decision reflected two important errors in setting capital market assumptions. First, it is not a great idea to estimate a long-run return using only a few years of data. Not only is there much sampling error, but many returns show cyclical patterns, which call for a sample period that 'goes through a few cycles'. In addition, even in ideal circumstances, real yields will reflect market participants' expectations of future inflation which may not be borne out in actual data and inflation forecasting errors cannot be expected to average to zero over such a short period. Second, the TIPS market back then was in its infancy; TIPS represented a not very liquid and perhaps even a somewhat 'unknown, inefficiently priced' asset, as suggested by Sack and Elsasser (2004). As we argued before, in the beginning of the TIPS issuance period, likely up to 2004, real interest rates were much lower than suggested by TIPS data,[14] because of a liquidity premium. This rather substantial liquidity premium implies that *ex post* the US Treasury likely increased its debt costs relative to issuing nominal bonds (see Roush *et al.*, 2008; and Campbell *et al.*, 2009).

[13] See Viceira (2000) for an excellent Harvard case on the introduction of TIPS at HMC, which provided the source of some of the HMC material here.

[14] Of course, it is questionable that historical data should be used at all in setting capital market assumptions for expected returns. It may be better to 'reverse engineer' them from an equilibrium model such as the CAPM (see Sharpe, 1976). In that case, TIPS should be part of the optimal portfolio proportional to their relative market capitalization.

5. CONCLUSIONS

This article has made a number of relatively simple points about inflation risk. First, standard securities, such as nominal government bonds and equities, are very poor hedges of inflation risk, both in the short and in the long run. We estimated inflation betas for a very large cross-section of countries, showing that this is nearly universally true. When we expand the menu to include Treasury bills, real estate, foreign bonds and gold, the latter two fare a little better, often showing positive comovement with inflation. Treasury bills show positive comovement with inflation, but their substantial weight in tracker portfolios is mostly due to their variance-reducing properties. They fail to hedge unanticipated shocks to inflation. Tracking inflation with available securities remains quite difficult to accomplish. As a consequence, index-linked bonds are essential to really hedge inflation risk.

With index linked bonds, investors, policy-makers and economists can have a better sense of the magnitude of the inflation risk premium, the compensation investors demand to bear inflation risk in nominal bonds. Most studies, including very recent ones that actually use inflation-linked bonds and information in surveys to gauge inflation expectations, find the inflation risk premium to be sizeable and to substantially vary through time.

This implies that governments should normally lower their financing costs through the issuance of index-linked bonds, at least in an *ex ante* sense. However, some index-linked markets, and in particular the US market, have suffered from poor liquidity driving up real yields, and increasing the cost of issuance. While several measures can be taken to improve liquidity in the index-linked market, recent events demonstrate once again that in volatile market conditions, investors gravitate towards the most liquid securities (typically nominal Treasury bills and benchmark bonds) and liquidity premiums can become extremely large. Wright (2009) and Campbell *et al.* (2009) discuss in detail the anomalous behaviour of the TIPS markets following the Lehman Brothers collapse of September 2008, with yields on TIPS rising above yields on their nominal counterparts at one point. From the government's perspective such episodes undermine some of the purported benefits of index-linked debt. For central banks, the information content of the spread between real and nominal bonds becomes more difficult to interpret in economic terms; and the benefits in terms of debt costs are no longer ensured. The policy implication is that much effort must be expended to ensure that the TIPS market is credible, liquid, and trusted by important investors, but even then, occasional but hopefully short-lived flights to liquidity may occur.

From an economic perspective, such considerations seem less relevant. Having securities that allow the hedging of an important economic risk are almost surely welfare enhancing, and the investors in such securities (individuals, pension funds) tend to have long horizons, and are thus surely not unhappy with the presence of a potential liquidity premium. Without the government setting a default-free benchmark, it is unlikely that 'inflation-derivatives', which have grown rapidly, recently, would spring up in private markets. Therefore, the case for an index-linked market would appear easy to make, and we would not be surprised to see the relative importance of index-linked bonds increase across the world in years to come.

Discussion

Cédric Tille

Graduate Institute of International and Development Studies, Geneva and CEPR

Introduction

Inflation risk is a major component of investment decisions. For instance, a retirement savings plan designed for an inflation rate of 2% would prove quite inadequate should inflation turn out to be higher. Whether one should be concerned about inflation risk or not depends on whether investors can structure portfolios that offer a good hedge against this risk. The paper presents a thorough assessment of the ability to hedge against inflation risk, and proceeds in three stages. It first considers whether standard assets, such as nominal bonds and stocks, can hedge inflation, and argues that this is not the case. It then estimates the inflation risk premium in bond returns and finds it to be substantial. It then argues that indexed bonds are a useful asset to hedge against inflation risk, but their ability to deliver this benefit remains hindered by low liquidity.

Can standard assets hedge inflation?

The ability of an asset to hedge for inflation can be measured by regressing its return on inflation. A coefficient of one indicates a perfect hedge as every increment in inflation is then transmitted one-for-one in the nominal return of the asset, leaving its real return unchanged.

The paper presents an extensive assessment of the hedging ability of bonds and stocks. It finds that this ability is limited at the one-year horizon, except in the case of Latin American countries. While the hedging properties are better at longer horizons, or once we control for real activity, the authors argue that they remain limited.

Should we be concerned about this limited hedging ability of standard assets? The answer to this question hinges on what investors care about. For instance, do they consider inflation risk to be a major issue, or are they more concerned about other sources of risk? If they care about inflation risk, do they do so at a long horizon, for instance for retirement savings, or a shorter horizon?

Investors may not care much about inflation when it is low and stable, for instance thanks to a monetary policy squarely focused on price stability. If other sources of risk are more important, portfolios are structured to hedge against these other risks and not against inflation. If, for instance, stocks offer a good hedge against movements in labour income through the business cycle, their ability to hedge against inflation risk could be of relatively limited concern. If, however, inflation is high and volatile, the poor hedging properties of standard assets are a cause for concern.

The international evidence presented in the paper shows that the hedging properties are heterogeneous across countries. In particular, they are strongest in Latin America, a region that experienced sustained episodes of high and volatile inflation. Standard assets then offer a good hedge against inflation in the regions where it constitutes a major source of risk. The poor hedging properties in advanced economies could simply indicate that inflation has been brought under control and is not what worries investors the most.

Even if investors care about inflation risk, they may do so only at a specific horizon. A household saving for retirement will care about long-run inflation risk, and be less concerned about inflation movement at short horizons. The paper finds that the hedging properties of standard assets improve with the horizon, even though they remain incomplete.

The ability of bonds and stocks to hedge against inflation risk thus appears strongest in regions where this risk is substantial, and at the longer horizons about which investors are more likely to care. Still, this ability remains partial at best.

How big is the inflation risk premium?

Measuring the inflation risk premium is a complex task as we only have data on nominal returns and realized inflation, but little reliable data on expected inflation and real returns. Constructing a measure of the premium therefore requires some assumptions. The authors explain how the literature has converged to a method combining a term-structure model of interest rates and a model of inflation to estimate the risk premium.

They discuss such a framework that allows for regime switches and for the inflation risk premium to vary through time. They conclude that the premium has moved substantially, from about 150 basis points in the mid-1980s to 50 points in the early 2000s. The premium also shows substantial volatility, with large increases in 1994 and 2005 for instance.

The movements of the premium are to be taken with some care. They could simply reflect the limited precision of the estimates, which the authors fully acknowledge, as the standard errors amount to 100 basis points. In addition, the sharp movements are not accompanied by clear new information about the inflation prospects. The premium abruptly increases by 100 basis points in 1994, then falls by a similar amount in 2001, before increasing by 75 points in 2005. While there was a concern about deflation in the early 2000s, it is not the case that the inflation prospects at a 5-year horizon moved abruptly in these three episodes. One should therefore focus on the low frequency movements of the estimates. By that yardstick, the premium amounts to 50–75 basis points in recent years, which remains a sizeable number.

The authors provide a thorough review of other contributions on the topic. While the estimates of the risk premium cover quite a broad range, reflecting the challenges of the exercise, they are in line with the findings of the paper.

The experience with indexed securities

If inflation risk is substantial, inflation-indexed securities should represent a big improvement in the menu of assets. In addition to offering a benchmark real return, and thus a hedge against inflation, these securities allow one to measure inflation expectations from market returns, and could also lower the funding cost of government debt.

Despite these advantages, the markets for indexed securities have only gradually developed and remain much smaller than the markets for non-indexed government bonds. While the United States introduced TIPS securities in 1997, the volumes remained limited until the mid-2000s and are still relatively low. The limited volume of indexed securities results in a substantial liquidity premium relative to the standard non-indexed bonds. In addition to its average level, this premium can prove quite volatile, as happened during the 2008 crisis when the rush to the liquidity of non-indexed bonds led to a surge in the liquidity premium. This points to a possible threshold effect in the development of indexed markets. When volumes remain small and liquidity limited the hedging benefits of indexed bonds are marginal and investors do not find indexed securities attractive, thus keeping volumes small. If government issuance raises the volume of indexed securities, the liquidity premium can be expected to fall. These securities would then be more appealing to investors, leading to higher volumes that improve liquidity further. This higher liquidity would allow the securities to fully deliver their benefits in terms of inflation hedging.

The fact that UK indexed securities, for which the volume is substantial, still carry a liquidity premium suggests a note of caution, however. If non-indexed securities offer a good enough hedge against inflation, there is little reason for investors to prefer the indexed securities. As pointed out above, this could be the case if inflation is only a secondary source of risk for investors in developed economies. If inflation risk was a major worry, we would expect financial engineering to have developed private inflation-indexed securities, and the volumes of these assets to have surged. The rapid growth of credit default swaps, for instance, indicates that such developments are possible. Thus, indexed securities maybe remain in limited supply because the demand for them is not that strong.

Conclusion

The paper offers a thorough assessment of the ability of standard assets to hedge against inflation, and of the magnitude of the inflation risk premium. It argues that inflation is a sizeable risk and thus increasing the volumes of indexed securities would offer a strong benefit.

While stocks and bonds are a poor inflation hedge at short horizons in industrialized markets, their performance is better in economies with a history of high inflation and at longer horizons. If investors primarily care about long-run inflation, or about very volatile inflation, then standard assets offer a reasonable hedge. This would limit the attractiveness of indexed securities, possibly explaining why their volumes remain small.

Panel discussion

Romain Rancière believed the creation of an independent national statistical agency is crucial in the development of the market for inflation-indexed bonds as this removes the temptation for governments to understate their country's inflation rate and in turn fosters market confidence in inflation-indexed bonds.

Giuseppe Bertola agreed TIPS are useful in protecting incomes against inflation in professions where salaries are not indexed linked. He stated it is important to understand the conditions under which a government would be willing to supply inflation indexed bonds. He noted that since inflation is determined to some extent by government intervention, government incentives to inflate will depend on the extent to which they have issued inflation-linked bonds. Increased issuance of TIPS during periods of high inflation gives governments greater credibility against inflating. In the current climate, though, he wondered how significant a burden TIPS were for countries who would like to inflate some of their debt.

Refet Gürkaynak agreed that government involvement is necessary for the development of an inflation market as it is primarily governments who are willing to be on the paying side of inflation. He noted that there must be some optimal supply of indexed bonds which the governments would be willing to supply.

Micheal Manove pointed out that the need to hedge against inflation depends on the assets that one already holds. Georges de Ménil remarked that investment in stock markets is viewed as a poor inflation hedge due to inflation effects on corporate tax and the non-indexation of depreciation.

Richard Portes noted that the UK TIPS market has been very successful. Its growth and successful development is partly explained by the UK's experience of high and unstable inflation in the 1970s. He added that a large proportion of those who demand TIPS come from professions with inflation-protected pensions or own other hedged financial assets. The fact that agents with access to other means of hedging inflation still demand TIPS suggests that TIPS perform an important hedging function. He suggested one way to allay market fears that a country would inflate away their debt was to shift all bond issuances to TIPS.

It appeared to Cédric Tille that many issues of political economy were at the core of the discussion. He wondered if the existing literature examines the relation of inflation risk premia to measures of central bank independence. He also suggested that increased issuance of inflation-linked bonds could increase fiscal uncertainty during times of high inflation.

In response to Fabrizio Perri's discussion, Geert Bekaert noted that the inflation premium derived from his consumption model followed a very similar declining trend to that in the paper. On the difference in the magnitude of the inflation risk premiums, he stressed the model in the paper is more complex and that consumption based models always underestimate the inflation risk premium. He accepted that better modelling of the liquidity premium is an important issue as it has a significant bearing on the usefulness of TIPS and hedging against inflation. He agreed with Refet Gürkaynak that government's role as the main supplier of inflation linked bonds is important for the successful development of inflation-linked bond markets. He noted that derivative markets for hedging inflation only began to develop after the creation of government inflation-linked bonds. This suggests that the establishment of a default free benchmark is vital.

APPENDIX A: DATA APPENDIX

Our data are at the monthly level. The inflation data represent CPI data from IMF's International Financial Statistics; the stock return data are from MSCI and the bond return data from Datastream. The government bond indices of all the countries except India reflect all the maturities of the government bonds of that country. The average maturity differs across countries but for major markets it is likely around 7 years. For India, the index only reflects bonds with maturities between 1 and 10 years.

The industrial production data were downloaded from Datastream. When the overall index is not available for a certain country, we collect the manufacturing industry production index.

The real estate data were purchased from EPRA, the European Public Real Estate Association. The FTSE EPRA/NAREIT Real Estate Index Series only include real estate securities (defined as engaged in 'the ownership, trading and development of income-producing real assets') that are traded on an official stock exchange. A web appendix table lists the availability, per country, of the various series. All these series are converted to local currency.

For gold, we use the 'Bloomberg Generic Gold Price Index' as the spot price. We use the 'S&P GSCI Gold Total Return Index' as future prices; this series uses T-bills as collateral. For each country, the gold spot and futures returns are converted from dollars into local currency.

The short interest data represent Treasury bill rates from Datastream and International Financial Statistics, mostly with a 3-month maturity.

The foreign bond returns are derived from local government bond returns and currency values. For each country, we create the local currency return on an equally weighted index of US, German, UK and Japanese government bonds. For the United States, Germany, the United Kingdom and Japan, only three foreign bonds are used in the portfolio. Finally, for the United States, some results for stock and bond returns use a longer sample, starting in January 1960.

A table, available on the web, lists the start and end dates for bond and stock returns, real estate returns and the industrial production series.

APPENDIX B: TECHNICAL APPENDIX

For each country i, we compute the following variables:

- Monthly logarithmic returns (including dividends and coupons for bonds, stocks and real estate) in month t: $r_{i,t}$
- Returns aggregated over a horizon of h-months: $r_{i,t+h,h} = r_{i,t+h} + r_{i,t+h-1} + \cdots + r_{i,t+1}$. Ignoring dividends and coupons, this return represents the logarithm of the price at $t + h$ minus the logarithm of the price at time t.
- Year-on-year inflation in month $t : \pi_{i,t} = \ln(CPI_{i,t}/CPI_{i,t-12})$, where CPI is the consumer price index.
- Inflation over a 'k-year' horizon: $\pi_{i,t+k\times 12,k\times 12} = \pi_{i,t+k\times 12} + \pi_{i,t+(k-1)\times 12} + \cdots + \pi_{i,t+1\times 12}$
- Expected inflation for a horizon of k years: $\pi e_{i,t+k\times 12,k\times 12} = k\pi_{i,t}$
- Unexpected inflation for a horizon of 6 years: $\pi u_{i,t+k\times 12,k\times 12} = \pi_{i,t+k\times 12,k\times 12} - k\pi_{i,t}$

Using these variables, we run both univariate and bivariate regressions. The univariate country-by-country regressions take the following form:

$$r_{i,t+k\times 12,k\times 12} = \alpha_i + \beta_i \pi_{i,t+k\times 12,k\times 12} + \varepsilon_{i,t+k\times 12,k\times 12} \tag{A1}$$

Because we use monthly data, the 'overlap' in observations causes the errors to be serially correlated. We therefore adjust the standard errors using the Hansen–Hodrick (1980) method with lag $k \times 12$–1.

For the univariate pooled regressions, we run two regressions.

$$r_{i,t+k\times 12,k\times 12} = \alpha_i + \sum_j \beta_j \pi^j_{i,t+k\times 12,k\times 12} + \varepsilon_{i,t+k\times 12,k\times 12} \tag{A2}$$

where:

- $\{\beta_j, j = 1, 2, \ldots, J\} = \{\beta_{\text{developed}}, \beta_{\text{emerging}}, J = 2\}$, *or* $\{\beta_{\text{NorthAmerica}}, \beta_{\text{LatinAmerica}}, \beta_{\text{Asia}}, \beta_{\text{Africa}}, \beta_{\text{Oceania}}, \beta_{\text{EU}}, \beta_{\text{Non-EUEurope}}, J = 7\}$
- $\pi^j_{i,t+k\times 12,k\times 12} = \pi_{i,t+k\times 12,k\times 12}$ if country i in group j; 0 otherwise.

Standard errors are again adjusted using the Hansen–Hodrick (1980) method, as generalized to panel data by Devarajan *et al.* (1996).

Analogous standard errors are used for the bivariate regressions. The country-by-country regression is:

$$r_{i,t+k\times 12,k\times 12} = \alpha_i + \gamma_i \pi e_{i,t+k\times 12,k\times 12} + \beta_i \pi u_{i,t+k\times 12,k\times 12} + \varepsilon_{i,t+k\times 12,k\times 12} \tag{A3}$$

The bivariate pooled regression can be represented as:

$$r_{i,t+k\times 12,k\times 12} = \alpha_i + \sum_j \left(\gamma_j \pi e^j_{i,t+k\times 12,k\times 12} + \beta_j \pi u^j_{i,t+k\times 12,k\times 12}\right) + \varepsilon_{i,t+k\times 12,k\times 12} \tag{A4}$$

where

$\{\gamma_j, \beta_j, j = 1, 2, \ldots, J\} = \{\gamma_{\text{developed}}, \gamma_{\text{emerging}}, \beta_{\text{developed}}, \beta_{\text{emerging}}, J = 2\}$, or

- $\{\gamma_{\text{NorthAmerica}}, \gamma_{\text{LatinAmerica}}, \gamma_{\text{Asia}}, \gamma_{\text{Africa}}, \gamma_{\text{Oceania}}, \gamma_{\text{EU}}, \gamma_{\text{Non-EUEurope}}, \beta_{\text{NorthAmerica}}, \beta_{\text{LatinAmerica}}, \beta_{\text{Asia}}, \beta_{\text{Africa}}, \beta_{\text{Oceania}}, \beta_{\text{EU}}, \beta_{\text{Non-EUEurope}}, J = 7\}$
- $\pi e^j_{i,t+k\times 12,k\times 12} = \pi e_{i,t+k\times 12,k\times 12}$ if country i is in group j; 0 otherwise.
- $\pi u^j_{i,t+k\times 12,k\times 12} = \pi u_{i,t+k\times 12,k\times 12}$ if country i is in group j; 0 otherwise.

To describe our estimations more concretely, it is best to distinguish between the country-by-country regressions and the pooled regressions.

For the country-by-country regressions, let $y_{t,h} = r_{i,t+k\times 12,k\times 12}$; $x_t = [1 \ \pi_{i,t+k\times 12,k\times 12}]$ (univariate regression), or $x_t = [1 \ \pi e_{i,t+k\times 12,k\times 12} \ \pi u_{i,t+k\times 12,k\times 12}]$ (bivariate regression); $\varepsilon_{i,t+k\times 12,k\times 12} = u_{t,h}$, where we omit the country dimension. Then the regressions become

$$y_{t,h} = x_t \beta + u_{t,h} \text{ where } h = k \times 12 - 1 \tag{A5}$$

We estimate the regressions by ordinary least squares (OLS). It can be shown that $\sqrt{T}(\hat{\beta}_{OLS} - \beta)$ converges in distribution to N(0,θ), with:

$$\theta = \left(\frac{1}{T}\sum_{t=1}^{T} x_t' x_t\right)^{-1} \Theta \left(\frac{1}{T}\sum_{t=1}^{T} x_t' x_t\right)^{-1}; \quad \Theta = \sum_{j=-h+1}^{h-1} \hat{R}_u(j)\hat{R}_x(j);$$

$$\hat{R}_u(j) = \frac{1}{T}\sum_{t=j+1}^{T} \hat{u}_{t,h}\hat{u}_{t-j,h}; \quad \hat{R}_x(j) = \frac{1}{T}\sum_{t=j+1}^{T} x_t' x_{t-j}$$

where T is the sample size for each country i.

For the pooled regressions, let $y^i_{t,h} = r_{i,t+k\times 12,k\times 12}$; $x^i_t = [0 \ldots 0 \ 1 \ 0 \ldots 0 \ \pi^1_{i,t+k\times 12,k\times 12} \ \pi^2_{i,t+k\times 12,k\times 12} \cdots \pi^J_{i,t+k\times 12,k\times 12}]$ or $x^i_t = [0 \ldots 0 \ 1 \ 0 \ldots 0 \ \pi e^1_{i,t+k\times 12,k\times 12} \ \pi e^2_{i,t+k\times 12,k\times 12} \cdots \pi e^J_{i,t+k\times 12,k\times 12} \ \pi u^1_{i,t+k\times 12,k\times 12} \ \pi u^2_{i,t+k\times 12,k\times 12} \cdots \pi u^J_{i,t+k\times 12,k\times 12}]$ where the 1 is in the ith position; $\varepsilon_{i,t+k\times 12,k\times 12} = u^i_{t,h}$. Then the regressions become

$$y^i_{t,h} = x^i_t\beta + u^i_{t,h} \text{ where } h = k \times 12 - 1 \tag{A6}$$

The vector representation is $Y_{NT} = X_{NT}\beta + U_{NT}$ and it can be shown that $\sqrt{NT}(\hat{\beta}_{OLS} - \beta)$ converges in distribution to N(0,θ), with:

$$\hat{\theta}_{NT} = \left(X'_{NT}X_{NT}\right)^{-1} X'_{NT}\hat{\Omega}_{NT}X_{NT}\left(X'_{NT}X_{NT}\right)^{-1};$$

Ω_{NT} is symmetric, its lower triangular part can be written as:

$$a_{t+n,t} = \begin{cases} \hat{R}_u(0), & n = 0, t = 1, 2, \ldots, NT \\ \hat{R}_u(n), & n = 1, 2, \ldots, h-1, t \neq \lambda T - j + 1 \\ 0, & otherwise \end{cases}$$

where λ= 1,2,…, $N-1$, j = 1,2,…,n

$$\hat{R}_u(j) = \frac{1}{NT}\sum_{i=1}^{N}\sum_{t=j+1}^{T} \hat{u}^i_{t,h}\hat{u}^i_{t-j,h}$$

Note that in principle the country samples are unbalanced, and we use as much data as possible. We do require a minimum of 24 observations to include a country.

APPENDIX C: CREATING MIMICKING PORTFOLIOS

Let R_{t+1} represent a $k \times 1$ vector of returns on k available assets, and π_{t+1} indicate (annual) inflation. We want to create a portfolio, w, of the k assets, that 'tracks' inflation as well as possible. That is, with a vector of ones, we solve:

$$\min_w \text{var}(\pi_{t+1} - w'R_{t+1}) \text{ s.t. } w'e = 1 \tag{A7}$$

This problem is equivalent to running a constrained regression of inflation on the k returns (plus a constant) with the regression coefficients constrained to 1. We actually compute the solution from the covariance matrix of the data. First, note that the minimum variance portfolio of the assets is

$$w_{MV} = \left(\sum\nolimits^{-1} e\right)/\left(e'\sum\nolimits^{-1} e\right) \tag{A8}$$

where $\sum$ is the variance-covariance matrix of the returns.

Then, the solution to (A7) is given by:

$$w = \sum\nolimits^{-1}\text{cov}[\pi, R] + [1 - e'\sum\nolimits^{-1}\text{cov}[\pi, R]]w_{MV} \tag{A9}$$

where cov[π,R] is a vector containing the covariances between inflation and the set of asset returns. It is trivial to check that $e'w$ = 1. Also, the constraint implies that assets which are important in the minimum variance portfolio may also receive a lot of weight in the tracker portfolio. Finally, the first part of the equation would represent the result from an unconstrained regression.

REFERENCES

Ang, A., G. Bekaert and M. Wei (2007). 'Do macro variables, asset markets or surveys forecast inflation better?' *Journal of Monetary Economics*, 54, 1163–212.

—— (2008). 'The term structure of real rates and inflation expectations', *Journal of Finance*, 63(2), 797–849.

Atkeson, A. and L. Ohanian (2001). 'Are Phillips curves useful for forecasting inflation?' *Federal Reserve Bank of Minneapolis Quarterly Review*, Winter, 25(1).

Attié, A. P. and S. K. Roache (2009). 'Inflation hedging for long-term investors', IMF Working Paper.

Bardong, F. and T. Lehnert (2004). 'On the efficiency of European inflation-indexed government debt security markets', *Journal of Portfolio Management*, 30(4), 226–38.

Bekaert, G. and E. Engstrom (2010). 'Inflation and the stock market: understanding the "Fed Model"', *Journal of Monetary Economics*, 57(3), 278–94.

Bekaert, G. and X. Wang (2009). 'Globalization and asset prices', Columbia University Working Paper.

Bodie, Z. (1976). 'Common stocks as a hedge against inflation', *Journal of Finance*, 31, 459–70.

Boivin, J. (2006). 'Has US monetary policy changed? Evidence from drifting coefficients and real-time data', *Journal of Money, Credit and Banking*, 38(5), 1149–73.

Boudoukh, J. and M. Richardson (1993). 'Stock returns and inflation: a long-horizon perspective', *American Economic Review*, 83(5), 1346–55.

Briere, M. and O. Signori (2009). 'Do inflation-linked bonds still diversify?' *European Financial Management*, 15(2), March, 279–97.

Bruno, S. and L. B. Chincarini (2010). 'Hedging inflation internationally', Pomona College Working Paper.

Buraschi, A. and A. Jiltsov (2005). 'Inflation risk premia and the expectations hypothesis', *Journal of Financial Economics*, 75, 429–90.

Campbell, J. Y. and R. Shiller (1996). 'A scorecard for indexed government debt', in B. S. Bernanke and J. Rotemberg (eds.), *National Bureau of Economic Research Macroeconomics Annual 1996*, MIT Press, Cambridge, MA, pp. 155–97.

Campbell, J. Y., R. J. Shiller and L. Viceira (2009). 'Understanding inflation-indexed bond markets', *Brookings Papers on Economic Activity*, 1, 79–120.

Campbell, J. Y. and L. Viceira (2001). 'Who should buy long-term bonds?' *American Economic Review*, 91, 99–127.

Campbell, J. Y. and T. Vuolteenaho (2004). 'Inflation illusion and stock prices', *American Economic Review*, 94, 19–23.

Chen, R., B. Liu and X. Cheng (2005). 'Inflation, Fisher equation, and the term structure of inflation risk premia: theory and evidence from TIPS', Working Paper, Rutgers Business School.

Chernov, M. and P. Mueller (2008). 'The term structure of inflation expectations', CEPR Discussion Paper.

Christensen, J. H. E., J. A. Lopez and G. D. Rudebusch (2010). 'Inflation expectations and risk premiums in an arbitrage-free model of nominal and real bond yields', Federal Reserve Bank of San Francisco Working Paper 2008-23.

D'Amico, S., D. Kim and M. Wei (2009). 'Tips from TIPS: the information content of Treasury inflation-protected security prices', Finance and Economics Discussion Series Working Paper 2010-19, Federal Reserve Board.

Dai, Q. and K. Singleton (2000). 'Specification analysis of affine term structure models', *Journal of Finance*, 55(5), 1943–78.

Deacon, M. and P. Andrews (1996). 'The use and value of index-linked bonds', *The Financier*, 3(4-5), 13–25.

Devarajan, S., V. Swaroop and H. Zou (1996). The composition of public expenditure and economic growth. *Journal of Monetary Economics*, 37(2), 313–44.

Doepke, M. and M. Schneider (2009). 'Inflation as a redistribution shock: effects on aggregates and welfare', NBER Working Paper No. 12319.

Erb, C. and C. Harvey (2006). 'The strategic and tactical value of commodity futures', *Financial Analysts Journal*, 62(2), 69–97.

Evans, M. D. D. (1998). 'Real rates, expected inflation, and inflation risk premia', *Journal of Finance*, 53, 187–218.
—— (2003). 'Real risk, inflation risk, and the term structure', *Economic Journal*, 113, 345–389.
Fama, E. F. (1981). 'Stock returns, real activity, inflation, and money', *American Economic Review*, 74(4), 545–65.
Fama, E. F. and G. W. Schwert (1977). 'Asset returns and inflation', *Journal of Financial Economics*, 5, 115–46.
Fisher, I. (1930). *The Theory of Interest*, repr. 1965, Augustus M. Kelley, Clifton, NJ.
Fischer, S. (1983). 'Indexing and inflation', *Journal of Monetary Economics*, 12(4), 519–41.
Garcia, J. A. and A. van Rixtel (2007). 'Inflation-linked bonds from a central bank perspective', ECB Working Paper.
Garcia, J. A. and T. Werner (2010). 'Inflation risks and inflation risk premia', ECB Working Paper.
Greenwood, R. and D. Vayanos (2010). 'Price pressure in the government bond market", *American Economic Review*, 100(2), 585–90.
Grishchenko, O. and J. Huang (2010) 'Inflation risk premium: evidence from the TIPS market', Working Paper.
Gurkaynak, R., B. Sack and J. Wright (2010). 'The TIPS yield curve and inflation compensation', *American Economic Journal: Macroeconomics*, 2(1), 70–92.
Hansen, L. P. and R. J. Hodrick (1980). 'Forward exchange rates as optimal predictors of future spot rates: an econometric analysis', *Journal of Political Economy*, 88(5), 829–53.
Haubrich, J., G. Pennacchi and P. Ritchken (2008). 'Estimating real and nominal term structures using treasury yields, inflation, forecasts, and inflation swap rates', Federal Reserve Bank of Cleveland Working Paper No. 0810.
Hordahl, P. and O. Tristani (2007). 'Inflation risk premia in the term structure of interest rates', BIS Working Paper.
Joyce, M., P. Lildholdt and S. Sorensen (2010). 'Extracting inflation expectations and inflation risk premia from the term structure: a joint model of the UK nominal and real yield curves', *Journal of Banking and Finance*, 34(2), 281–94.
Kitamura, Y. (2009). 'Experiences in Japan: inflation indexed bond markets', Working Paper.
Kothari, S. and J. Shanken (2004). 'Asset allocation with inflation-protected bonds', *Financial Analysts Journal*, 60, 54–70.
Lin, S. C. (2009). 'Inflation and real stock returns revisited', *Economic Inquiry*, 47(4), 783–95.
Madsen, J. B. (2005). 'The Fisher Hypothesis and the interaction between share returns, inflation and supply shocks', *Journal of International Money and Finance*, 24(1), 103–20.
Mehrota, A. and J. R. Sanchez-Fung (2009). 'Assessing McCallum and Taylor rules in a cross-section of emerging market economies', BOFIT Discussion Paper.
Mishkin, F. S. and K. Schmidt-Hebbel (2001). 'One decade of inflation targeting in the world: what do we know and what do we need to know?' in N. Loayza and R. Soto (eds.), *Inflation Targeting: Design, Performance*, Challenges, Central Bank of Chile, Santiago, pp. 117–219.
Moreno, A. (2004). 'Reaching inflation stability', *Journal of Money, Credit and Banking*, 36(4), 801–25.
Price, R. (1997). 'The rationale and design of inflation-indexed bonds', IMF Working Paper.
Reilly, F. K., G. L. Johnson and R. E. Smith (1970). 'Inflation, inflation hedges, and common stocks', *Financial Analysts Journal*, 28, 104–10.
Reschreiter, A. (2008). 'Lower borrowing costs with inflation-indexed bonds: a trading rule based assessment', *Economic Letters*, 99(2), 272–74.
Risa, S. (2001). 'Nominal and inflation indexed yields: separating expected inflation and inflation risk premia', Working Paper.
Roll, R. (2004). 'Empirical TIPS', *Financial Analysts Journal*, 60(1), 31–53.
Roush, J., W. Dudley and M. Ezer (2008). 'The case for TIPS: an examination of the costs and benefits', Federal Reserve Bank of New York, Working Paper.
Sack, B. and R. Elsasser (2004). 'Treasury inflation-indexed debt: a review of the US experience', *Economic Policy Review*, 10(1), 47–63, Federal Reserve Bank of New York.

Schotman, P. and M. Schweitzer (2000). 'Horizon sensitivity of the inflation hedge of stocks', *Journal of Empirical Finance*, 7, 301–15.
Sharpe, W. (1976). 'Imputing expected returns from portfolio composition', *Journal of Financial and Quantitative Analysis*, 9(3), 463–72.
van Ewijk, C. (2009). 'Index linked bonds, pensions and government debt management', presentation at Netspar Conference, Den Haag.
Viceira, L. (2000). 'The Harvard Management Company and inflation-protected bonds', Harvard Business School Case 201-053.
Wright, J. H. (2009). Discussion of 'Understanding inflation-indexed bond markets', mimeo.